It's Your Life

Passport Series
Franklin G. Myers, Series Editor

Prentice-Hall, Inc., Englewood Cliffs, N.J.

It's Your Life

Autobiographical Writing

Franklin G. Myers
Lecturer in English Education
Manhattanville College
Purchase, New York

For Lois Waterman,
whose idea this was in the first place.

And with many thanks to Ben Mazza, Bill McCart, the late Paul Millane, and my many students who taught me much of this text while they learned to write.

Library of Congress Cataloging in Publication Data
MYERS, FRANKLIN G.
It's your life.

(Passport series)
Bibliography: p.
SUMMARY: A textbook containing instructions for writing an autobiography and basic language arts skills. Includes excerpts from several types of autobiography covering a range of ages and a variety of cultures.
1. Readers — Autobiography. 2. Readers — 1950- 3. English language — Composition and exercises. [1. English language — Composition and exercises] I. Title.
PE1127.A9M9 808'.0427 77-8653
ISBN 0-13-507665-X

It's Your Life
Franklin G. Myers

10 9 8 7 6 5 4 3

Designed by Madeline Bastis & Friends, Inc.

Prentice-Hall International, Inc., London
Prentice-Hall of Australia, Pty. Ltd., Sydney
Prentice-Hall of Canada, Ltd., Toronto
Prentice-Hall of India Private Ltd., New Delhi
Prentice-Hall of Japan, Inc., Tokyo
Prentice-Hall of Southeast Asia Pte. Ltd., Singapore
Whitehall Books Limited, Wellington, New Zealand

Acknowledgments

"Being A Baby" from *Fifty Poems* by Miriam Andrews. Reprinted by permission of the author and Branden Press.

"Phil George" from THE WHISPERING WIND, T. D. Allen, editor. Doubleday and Company, 1972. Used by permission of the author, Teacher of the young American Indian contributors to the anthology.

Chapter 1 from *Roots* by Alex Haley. Copyright © 1976 by Alex Haley. Reprinted by permission of Doubleday & Company, Inc.

Preface by Joseph P. Lash from ELEANOR AND FRANKLIN. This selection is reprinted from
(Continued on page 270.)

Preface

The *Passport* series consists of eight theme-centered books which integrate worthwhile literature with practical writing improvement lessons and which review the basics of Standard Written English. Each text contains literary selections revolving around the central theme, study questions and activities following each selection, structured lessons in composition based on the selections, vocabulary studies patterned after standardized college entrance test questions, and composition reminders followed by exercises in usage designed to improve writing skills.

The objectives of the series are

—to offer worthwhile literature from different times and cultures.

—to give pointers and practice in clear, concise writing.

—to provide practice for college entrance examinations.

—to strengthen command of English usage and vocabulary.

The eight texts in the *Passport* series may be used in the following order as a complete course, or individually in any sequence.

It's Your Life: Autobiographical Writing—an opportunity to discover and record your own personal history while reading autobiographical and related literature, and to practice the fundamentals of Standard Written English. The final chapter offers help in filling out college applications and preparation for college interviews.

That's Entertainment: Narrative Writing—a foray into the world of fantasy and satire. Composition lessons focus on narrating incidents and writing dialogue and description. The major work in the text is Paul Osborn's play, *On Borrowed Time.*

Worlds on Worlds: Journalistic Writing—a study of major themes in science fiction with related readings in science fact. Composition assignments involve writing leads, news articles, feature stories, interviews, and editorials. The text includes the award-winning novelette, *Time Considered as a Helix of Semi-Precious Stones,* by Samuel R. Delany.

The Heroic Spirit: Expository Writing—a survey of the heroic figure in fact and fiction. Selections from the literature of diverse cultures examine the qualities that make heroes and heroines. Writing skills needed for organizing an expository paragraph, defining terms, ordering details, and writing longer compositions are emphasized. The text includes Sophocles' *Antigone.*

Rebels and Exiles: Expository Writing—an investigation of individuals and groups who have chosen, or been forced into, rebellion or exile. Composition lessons center on writing topic sentences, thesis statements, opening and closing paragraphs, as well as organizing paragraphs according to chronology, space, reasons, and cause and effect. Bernard Shaw's *The Devil's Disciple* is included in the text.

The World's a Stage: Argument and Persuasion—a collection of five major dramas of Western culture. The plays included are Euripides' *Medea,* Shakespeare's *Twelfth Night,* Molière's *Tartuffe,* Ibsen's *A Doll's House,* and Anderson's *Joan of Lorraine.* The skills material stresses constructing clear, logical, and persuasive arguments.

Crimes and Clues: Logical Thinking and Writing—a journey through some of the masterpieces of detective fiction. The composition sections emphasize the importance of clarity of thought and expression in the writing of paragraphs of induction and deduction. The text includes *Rear Window,* by William Irish.

Magic Makers: Literary Analysis—a literary exploration of the supernatural with writing assignments that require analysis of plot, character, figurative language, point of view, and structure based on the literature selections. Shakespeare's *The Tempest* is the major work.

LITERATURE selections range from ancient to contemporary, from British and American literature to works from other lands. The books include a wide variety of genres—novel excerpts, plays, essays, poetry, short stories, reportage, myths and folk tales, biography and autobiography. The introduction to each selection explains how the piece is related to the theme of the book and offers suggestions for effective reading. Following each piece are study questions and activities designed to deepen understanding of the selections, suggest comparisons and contrasts with other selections, and offer research, writing, and discussion projects that delve further into the reading.

COMPOSITION lessons include models to examine before you attempt your own essays. The composition assignments are, for the most part, based on the literature selections. Some will require you to analyze one or several of the pieces; others will ask you to express your personal opinion about what you have read. The principal writing skills you will practice are outlining, constructing topic sentences and thesis statements, and achieving unity, coherence, and clarity. Most of the books concentrate on expository writing, the type you will use more than any other in your college courses. (Exceptions are *It's Your Life,* which teaches autobiographical writing; *Worlds on Worlds,* journalistic writing; and *That's Entertainment,* narrative writing.)

PREPARATION FOR COLLEGE ENTRANCE EXAMINATIONS is stressed in each text. Vocabulary exercises incorporating words drawn from the selections were created to familiarize you with the type of verbal test items you will encounter on college entrance tests, and with the terms used in the directions on these tests. You will practice recognizing synonyms and antonyms, solving verbal analogies, and choosing words to complete sentences. In addition, your teacher will give you practice tests that follow the form of actual college entrance examinations. When working with these exercises, keep in mind that familiarity and practice are two keys to giving you confidence and improving your performance on standardized tests.

COMPOSITION REMINDERS at the end of each chapter review the basics of Standard Written English, especially those related to clear, concise verbal expression.

The *Passport* series focuses on literature that is at once stimulating and enduring. You will find that serious consideration of the structure of the pieces you will read, as well as the timelessness of certain ideas and values, will heighten your reading enjoyment. You may also find that your understanding and appreciation of literature will deepen as you prepare carefully thought-out, well organized compositions based on the selections. Extending your reading and writing abilities by mastering the skills taught in these texts will strengthen your potential for college qualification and for success in your college courses.

Contents

2

Origins — Climbing the Family Tree

37

3

Arrivals — It Had to Be Me

50

4

Getting Personal — Preschool Childhood

5

School Days — How Influential Is Education?

8

What's Next — What Am I Good For?

9

Self-Appraisal — Who Am I?

10

Coming Events — Lessons for Later Reference

It's Your Life

Introduction

Who is the most important person you know? Given the humility which is instilled into us from early childhood, most of us would immediately begin to think of a person who has somehow "made it" in life—someone known for political, financial, or philanthropic achievements. However, this text will assume that the most important person you know, and the one you know best, is really yourself. It will further assume that some of what is now you is not now really known, has been forgotten, or has not yet been adequately seen as part of the you that now exists.

Discovering the parts of yourself should be adventurous. Part of the discovery will require that you do some research about your origins—about the significance of your name, about your ancestors, about what your parents can remember of you before you yourself began to store up memories; this is the part of you which you may yet never have known. Another part of the discovery will require that you search your memories for experiences which to this point have had some bearing upon the person you are today. You may need help in this part of your self-exploration; you may have to talk with long-time friends, certainly with your parents. And you may have old diaries, letters, camp journals, photograph albums, and similar mementos to aid you in your search. Finally, you will be asked to think of yourself today and to try to put together the important parts of your past that have significantly led to your present self and will lead to the future you.

"Every autobiography ever written is a lie," writes A. S. Neill, and thus casts some doubts about his own material. Yet in a sense Mr. Neill is right. Autobiographers use art to shape their material. Incidents needing to be highlighted may have details added to strengthen their impact; descriptions of others may omit details which we are ashamed to commit to print. The impact of all material is altered by the very words chosen, no matter how carefully, by the writer to convey a personal conception of truth.

In this book, you will find excerpts from several types of autobiography covering a range of ages and a variety of cultures. Two are from novels based at least loosely upon their authors' lives. One is from a frank autobiography in which the writer always speaks of himself in the third person. Some were related orally to a writer and then translated into print.

One was tape-recorded by a man who could scarcely read or write and then put to paper by a transcriber. Another is an actual letter asking for information. Most follow standard autobiographical style with the author speaking as "I."

The memories range from that of Eugene Gant, Thomas Wolfe's fictional self, who purports to recall his earliest days in the cradle, to that of the Renaissance goldsmith Benvenuto Cellini, who details a fight for his adult life. The subjects come from a variety of settings and cultures. With Cellini we are in a Roman prison of the sixteenth century; with the rest we are in the nineteenth or twentieth centuries but in a variety of places—with Mountain Wolf Woman on a Winnebago Indian reservation, with Toundi in the French Cameroun of Africa, with Y. A. Tittle in his freshman year, or with Roberto in a *vecindad* of Mexico City.

Selections are arranged so that they cover four stages of life—infancy, coming of age, higher education, and some adult adventures.

The first nine chapters of this text contain instructions for writing your own life's story up to the point where you now are. To help you set down your ideas with coherence and correctness, the text suggests an outline for you to follow. Each chapter is divided into three sections. The first section will give you instructions on how to do research for and write your chapter. It will be followed—in most instances—by several sample paragraphs from other student autobiographies and by one complete chapter, also written by a student.

The second section is called a check sheet. It contains correctly spelled words that have often been misspelled by students writing the particular chapter. In addition, it contains rules for punctuation, capitalization, and usage, as well as exercises to guide you in writing Standard Written English so that future readers of your first book may not only find that you were interesting but that you were not a nincompoop.

The third section contains a practice test so that you can test your recall of the rules the check sheet gave you. As the chapters continue, the practice tests grow more comprehensive. Each new test will require you to remember not only the check sheet for the current chapter but those from preceding chapters as well.

There is also a practical reason for you now to assess yourself—practical aside from the aid which writing your autobiography will give you in spelling, sentence construction, and problems in the usage of English. Within the easily foreseeable future you will be leaving high school—to go to college, to look for a job, to join the adult community which demands an increasing proliferation of personal sketches, résumés, and forms which must be filled out before you will even be considered for an interview. To prepare you for these less exciting bits of autobiography, the last section of the text suggests models and ways for you to make those tasks easier. And, always, if you keep a copy of the autobiography you are about to begin to write, you will have a factual account of your life up to now so that you can refer to it whenever necessary—all this in addition to a book which, when properly completed, should be a pleasure to you now, a happy embarrassment to you in your older years, and an absolute delight to your children and grandchildren.

1

Your Preface—What's in a Name?

Every book must have a beginning, and there is probably no better way for you to start writing your autobiography than with an investigation of what your name means.

Michael Alan Morrison. What's in that? Let's start with the last name, the surname. Morris, the root, is of Latin origin and means "Moorish," or "dark-skinned." The "-son" suffix indicates what we call a patronym, probably of North European origin; and the whole word means "son of Morris," or, more literally, "son of the Moor." The middle name, Alan, is of Celtic origin and means "comely, fair." The first name is of Hebrew origin and means "like unto the Lord."

Where can you find out about your own name? The quest may be hard or, for some, impossible. Given names—one's first and middle names—are fairly easy to trace. *Webster's New World Dictionary* gives the origin and meaning of many given names. And Winthrop Ames' *What Shall We Name the Baby?* has a comprehensive list of these names. Consulting either or both of these sources should tell you much about the meaning of your names. The bibliography at the end of this chapter will also list sources of information.

Surnames, or last names, are the real puzzle. Many of us bear names that began as part of another language. A Malena was a Russian raspberry; a Kohl, a German cabbage; a Stavros, a Greek cross; a Cavallo, an Italian horse. These in themselves would not be too difficult to trace except that in coming into English these names frequently changed their spelling. Thus, Malena can become Mallan; Kohl, Cole; Stavros, Staver; and Cavallo, Callum. Not infrequently, surnames meant something in the fifteenth century that they do not mean today because the word has changed its meaning or has been dropped entirely from living language. And a great many American families have changed their surnames upon coming to a new land, some, perhaps, feeling that an English-speaking land deserves an English-sounding name. Texts about names can give some help with your last name, especially if it happens to be a patronym. Parents can also help, and your family may be eager to tell you the derivation, meaning, and history of your family name. Librarians are also invaluable in your search. They may frequently guide you to a source that will help you discover the meaning of your surname.

Surnames are a relatively new thing in the history of civilization and did not begin until about the eleventh century. In fact, people were still being forced by law to take surnames in England as late as the fifteenth century. In general, surnames came from four sources, and a knowledge of these sources may help you to unravel the history of your own name.

Patronyms are names which incorporate the father's name as part of the surname. Johnson (son of John), McDonald (son of Donald), MacDougal (son of Dougal), Jones (son of Jon),

O'Brien (son of Brien), James (son of James), Jensen (son of John), and Fitzgerald (son of Gerald) are all patronyms.

Place names are those which derive from some place often symbolic of where the family lived when the name was taken. Deans are from a valley, Atwoods from a grove, Thorps from a village, Steins from a stony place, Becks from near a brook. Those of you with Anglo-Saxon surnames can generally find a meaning for your title by consulting a Middle English dictionary. Those of other origins can get some help by looking in a dictionary of the language their name stems from. Sometimes place names will be those of towns: Milano, Berliner, Paris.

Occupational names are those which come from the occupation of the person who was being named. A Clark was a scholar; a Webster, a weaver; a Baxter, a baker; a Smith, an ironworker. Many such names—Miller, Taylor, Shepherd, Carter, Mason, for example—are self-explanatory. Again, a dictionary of the language your name derives from will be of use if yours is an occupational name.

Kurt Vonnegut, Jr., self-portrait.

Nicknames were frequently taken as surnames. Browns, Blacks, Whites, Shorts, Longs, Strongs, Littles and many others are among those names that started out as an *eke-name* (an also-name). Again, foreign language dictionaries can aid you.

Many of you will not be completely satisfied that you have traced your name correctly. Don't despair; the experts won't agree either. Winthrop Ames claims that four expert glossographers have come to four entirely different conclusions about the origin and significance of his name. And some surnames mean absolutely nothing, though the history of that nothingness can be fascinating. The writer remembers from his childhood a family near him named Somebody. Their story was this. The grandfather emigrated, completely free from the evils of reading or writing, from central Europe shortly after the Civil War. His language, of course, was unknown to the immigration official at Ellis Island. Hearing the long name but unable to get from the grandfather any indication of how it might be spelled, the official renamed him on the spot. Michael Whatever-It-Was became Mike Somebody, an American who managed to go west, prosper, and fill his community with little Somebodies.

Once you have found out what you can about your name, write a short composition about it. In addition to supplying possible meanings to the words that compose it, you may wish to write about reasons the name was given you, the religious significance of the name, the arguments that preceded naming you, and other family history connected with your name and your subsequent nicknames. Those of you who like to think about the stars can add to your composition by talking of the zodiacal sign under which you came to light. Many books about astrology allege to describe the temperamental inclinations of Capricorns, Cancers, and the rest. Some even venture to make predictions about a certain star's son or daughter. And nearly all will list famous people born under your sign. How much truth there may be in horoscopes is a moot question, but reading the possibilities intrigues a great many people.

Planning for Research

Begin your work with a plan. Write down a number of questions you wish to have answered. Then seek the answers—from parents and grandparents, from the books in the library, from teachers, especially language teachers if your name is of foreign origin. And remember, if yours is an Anglo-Saxon name, that your English teacher may have some knowledge of that forbear of our own tongue.

A sample list of questions might look like this:

1. *Surname:* What language was it originally?
   Has it been changed since it came to this country?
   Do I want to write about my mother's surname before she married?
2. *Given names:* What do they mean?
   Why was I given the names I was?
   Did my parents agree upon my naming?
   Do I in any way live up to my names?
3. *Nicknames:* Who gave them to me?
   What occasioned the name?
   What were my reactions?
4. Is there any family history connected with my name? If I'm named after someone else in my family, do I measure up to my family's memory of that person?
5. What about my birthday and its significance? What is my sign of the zodiac? Flower? Birthstone? What temperament should I have by astrologers' predictions? Do I live up to it? What famous—or infamous—people share my birth date?

You probably will not find the answers to all the questions you put down, and you are not obliged to write about all the information you do gain. However, from your research, if it has been well done, you now have the raw material for the preface to your autobiography.

The Rough Outline

After you are satisfied that you have enough to write about, plan the way you will write it. To do this, you need to make a rough outline. Such an outline does not have to be fancy; no one but you is ever going to see it. But taking the time to make it will save you time in writing, and it will help you to use paragraphs instead of writing everything in one paragraph.

In making a rough outline, it is customary to use Roman numerals. Each numeral will represent one paragraph of your composition. It will be followed by a sentence that states roughly what your paragraph is going to talk about. In narrative writing, which this is, you will need to make a new paragraph whenever you change the subject. Generally, this will occur when you shift to a different time in your story, when you talk about a different person, or when you go to another place. Following is a rough outline for the short sample composition for Chapter 1, the Preface.

I. I never liked my initials, MAM.

II. My parents agreed on names for my sister and me.

III. Morrison, Scottish, means "son of Morris (a Moor)."

IV. My first name makes me a saint, ho ho!

V. My middle name from Mother's side means handsome.

VI. My horoscope is all wrong, almost.

VII. I'm no saint despite my name.

The following composition grew from that outline. It is shorter than many of yours will be and is not necessarily the best first chapter anyone of your age ever wrote. However, it indicates the writer's style and makes a satisfactory opening. The paper was written by a high school student, and nothing has been changed except the names.

Michael Alan Morrison

My parents apparently never realized, when naming me, that my initials would spell Mam. My schoolmates did, and in I.H.M., from the fourth grade on, I grew to detest being referred to as Michael-Mam. I seriously considered changing my last name to Norrison, but Dad persuaded me not to with the argument that the change would be immoral, illegal, and disrespectful.

Evidently there was no argument between my parents about my name. A boy was to be called Michael Alan; a girl, Gretchen Enid. She was, when she came along, but I never refer to her as the GEM.

I had always thought Morrison was a good Scotch name, and both my mother and father are Scotch right down to their pre-dinner drinks. However, the name is an English patronym meaning "son of Morris." Morris itself isn't even Scottish but Latin, and means "dark-skinned" or "the Moor." In Middle English and French, it was spelled "Moreys." How it ever got to Scotland I'll never know, but they do say that Frenchmen get around.

Michael is my saint's name. St. Michael the archangel is the captain of the angels. The word itself is from Hebrew and means "like unto the Lord." Michael is venerated not only by Christians but by Jews and Mohammedans.

Alan is the surname of my mother's side of the family. It comes closest to our Scottish ancestry because it is of Celtic origin and means "comely," which is just the opposite of "homely." It also means "fair" and doesn't really apply to my black hair and brown eyes. Ironically, all the Alans are dark, and I take after that side of the family.

I'd like to be able to believe what astrologers say the stars have in store for me. Born June 30, I've never been able to celebrate my birthday either in school or at camp. All those other little brats would have parties if they were born from September through early June. Not me; and I've always resented being an in-between. Maybe that's because my stars say I'm sensitive. I'm also supposed to be tenacious, like the crab that rules my house, but I certainly can't hold on to money. Henry VIII of England was also a Cancer, and I probably share his interest in girls. He probably never had a sister, though, so he could develop his interest more easily than I can.

That's just about it. Put the first letters of my names together, and you'll still get the wrong picture. I'm certainly no saint either, and I hope eventually to keep one wife for life. You'd better just call me what everyone else does now. I'm Mike.

The Rough Draft of Your Paper

What you have just read, of course, does not represent the first copy of what Mike wrote. He started with what we call a rough draft, one in which he scribbled to his own satisfaction and in a script that probably only he could read. Eventually what he wrote became the above composition. When he had finished, he went over what he had written, made corrections in spelling and sentence structure, crossed out what then seemed to him unnecessary, and changed words here and there so that each paragraph would be connected in some way with the next. The important thing to remember as you write your rough draft is to get yourself writing. There are few lonelier people than those people with an assignment to do as they sit mooning over a blank piece of paper. Get yourself going by writing some paragraph, the one you know most about. When you have started, you will find the task considerably more pleasant. But when you have finished the rough draft, check it carefully, put the paragraphs in order, and begin the task of revising for your first audience, your teacher.

Before sitting down to make your good copy, study the check sheet for each chapter. It will contain the correct spelling of many words you will find handy in the chapter. In addition, it will remind you of rules to be followed in your writing. Try not to violate any of these rules. Try also to remember the rules for all future writing. At various stages in your autobiography project, you will be tested on how well you have studied, used, and remembered the rules.

BIBLIOGRAPHY FOR NAME-HUNTING

Ames, Winthrop. *What Shall We Name the Baby?*

Arthur, William. *An Etymological Dictionary of Family and Christian Names.*

Attwater, Donald. *Names and Name-Days.*

Barnhart, Clarence and Others. *New Century Cyclopedia of Names.*

Funk, Wilfred. *Word Origins and Their Romantic Stories.*

Kolatch, Alfred J. *The Name Dictionary; Modern English and Hebrew Names.*

Lambert, Eloise and Mario Pei. *Our Names, Where They Came from and What They Mean.*

Matthew, Constance Mary. *English Surnames.*

Mencken, H. L. *The American Language.* (See Chapter X)

Pei, Mario. *The Story of Language.* (Refer to Part I)

________. *What's in a Word?*

Pine, Leslie G. *The Story of Surnames.*

Smith, Eldon C. *Dictionary of American Family Names.*

Southern New England Telephone Company. *The Book of Names.* (What this is, really, is a telephone book for the year beginning April 22, 1972, with the history of many surnames included in the number listings. Perhaps, by writing to the Company at 235 Main Street, Danbury, Connecticut 06810, you might be able to procure a copy for your school library.)

Wagner Leopold. *Names and Their Meaning.*

CHECK SHEET FOR CHAPTER 1

Analysis of Sample Preface

Read again the sample preface and try to answer the following questions based upon it. Doing so will help you as you begin your own organization.

1. How carefully does Mike in his preface follow his sentence outline?

2. Why did he not use in his teacher's copy the precise sentences of the sentence outline?

3. What evidences of a personal style can you find in the preface?

4. Do the separate paragraphs seem well connected to make a whole? Support your answer with proof from the text.

5. What reasons can you find for each comma used in the preface? Why does Mike use a semicolon in paragraph 2?

Standard Written English

The rules given for you to follow in this text are rules for what is called Standard Written English. It is a formal use of English, differing in some ways from that which we speak to one another and often differing widely from the ways in which we speak to our peers. It is the English language following rules learned by all literate speakers and writers today and used by them when they are writing or speaking to large audiences whom they consider to be as literate as they. Some of the rules may seem strange to you because of the section of the country in which you live. In the East, for example, many people would say, "I lost my wallet *somewheres* in this house." Yet, though they might say "somewheres," chances are that they would write the word without the final "s"; *somewheres* is dialectical, correct in its environment, amusing and considered incorrect outside its environment.

Some deviations from Standard Written English we call *colloquial.* "I'll get a plumber to *fix* the leak," nearly everyone of us would say. Yet, at this moment at least, we would amend the sentence in writing or speaking to someone with whom we're not on familiar terms. We would have our plumber *repair* the leak. The same is true of the word *got.* "I *got* lost," we say. "He *got* sicker. She *got* a good idea. We soon *got* tired." Yet we should not write as easily as we speak. We would prefer to see written: "I *was* lost. He *grew* sicker. She *had* a good idea. We soon tired." There is nothing wrong with talking colloquially or dialectically. In fact, there would be something grossly pretentious for you to speak differently from the way of your friends.

Today's Standard Written English will be that English which you are to write in your autobiography. There will be one major exception, of course. If you are quoting people, you will not have them speak as they might write. If your brother, say, in an anecdote you are writing about him, stated, "Get that there snake off of me," you would not pretty up his language to have him say, "Please remove that snake from my person" or, even, the more grammatical "Get that snake off me." Such a change would violate both the rules of reporting and the standards of spoken English.

Do remember that there are two major kinds of English, that which we speak—with variations depending upon the age and familiarity of our audience—and that which we write. The rules of this text are for that language we write to a formal audience, that which we use in doing most of our school writing, that which we will be using in college writing, and that which we will use when we want to assure someone that we are competent and learned, whether that someone be a person we wish to have as a friend or as a boss.

Spelling

Learn not only the spelling of the words but their meaning. For many of the words you will find questions. Answer the questions, and you will learn still more about how to solve the confusion we call English spelling.

1. Anglo-Saxon
2. astrology (Write its adjective and adverb forms)
3. emigrate (Write its noun form)
4. horoscope
5. immigrate (Write its noun form. What other part of speech can the noun form assume?)
6. librarians (Spell the place where they work)
7. origin (Write its adjective and adverb forms. Compare them with the same forms for *astrology*. What rule suggests itself?)
8. patronym (From what language is this word derived?)
9. persuade (Write its noun, adjective, and adverb forms)
10. prefix
11. suffix
12. surname (Look up its derivation to discover an interesting word story)
13. tenacious (Write its noun and adverb forms)
14. zodiac

Punctuation Review: the Comma

Look at the following sentences. They are all in need of commas. With a group of four or five other students determine where to punctuate the sentences so that they will make better sense. Be prepared to discuss with the class the reasons for the commas you put in.

1. I really can't tell whether my ancestry is English French Italian or American.

2. August 6 1974 will always be a significant date in American history.

3. We had studied and asked each other questions for hours the previous night but our test scores didn't really reward our efforts.

4. Let us know John when you will be able to meet us.

5. Moreover following this recipe calls for a steady hand and exact recall of the directions.

6. "Hold it a minute" I said "while I answer the telephone."

7. My grandfather started out as a plant policeman and he ended up owning the factory.

8. Bill ran for home plate slipped halfway to the bag fell on his head and had to be rushed to the hospital.

9. Call me at 914-5555002 or write me at Mt. Sinai Memorial Hospital 1850 Sixth Avenue Lump Gulch Colorado.

10. Lucille had not done her homework and the teacher was sarcastic "Come up to the board Lucille" she said "and write the sentence as you corrected it."

11. Everyone knows however that the earth is a sphere.

12. Jackie made the beds Deirdre did the cleaning Margot did the dishes and Dorothy watched the baby.

A Review of Some Comma Rules

You are already aware of the following uses of the comma. Quickly review them to be sure that you have remembered them and are following them.

1. Use commas to separate words, phrases, and clauses used in series. (Today's usage does not demand the comma before the conjunction in the series. Your teacher may wish to guide you by stating a preference.)

Words in Series: He likes to play basketball, football, soccer, golf, and hockey.

Phrases in Series: He made his money for college by selling magazines, by babysitting, by doing odd jobs, and by working in a grocery store after school.

Clauses in Series: He had teased, he had pleaded, he had wept, and he had cursed in order to get his way.

Question: What is the difference between a phrase and a clause?

2. Use commas to separate dates and addresses.

Dates: I started school September 7, 1965.

Addresses: I lived at 1710 Jackson Avenue, Ann Arbor, Michigan, until 1976.

3. Use commas to separate the independent clauses in compound sentences. These are always separated by only six conjunctions which you can remember as the FANBOY words: **f**or, **a**nd, **n**or, **b**ut, **o**r, **y**et.

Caution: Be sure to notice that you have a subject and predicate after the conjunction, for sometimes these words do NOT need commas before them.

Compound Sentences with Fanboy Words:

a. He worked for a long time, *for* he wanted to have a perfect painting.
b. He saw the dog in the road, *and* he swerved to avoid hitting it.
c. She has not failed so far, *nor* is she likely to.
d. She had eaten a lot of food, *but* she was hungry nonetheless.
e. Do your homework daily, *or* you will be liable to be left behind.
f. She has not succeeded so far, *yet* she still keeps on trying.

Fanboy Words Used Without Punctuation Preceding Them:

a. He sold the car *for* a good deal more money.
b. The engine sputtered *and* then stopped for good.
c. Neither his parents *nor* his friends encouraged him.
d. No one *but* us boys knew the secret. (Here *but* means *except*)
e. Either Clara *or* Irene can give you the correct answer.
f. He has not left *yet* for Detroit!

4. Use commas to set off words used in direct address,—that is, the person being talked to.

At the Beginning of the Sentence: Bill, come here.

In the Middle of the Sentence: Come here, Bill, and let me tie your shoe.

At the End of the Sentence: Come here, Bill.

5. Use commas to set off long transition words in the sentence.

At the Beginning: Moreover, we needed the material at once.

In the Middle: He arrived on time, however, despite his fears of being late.

At the End: It was a good movie, however.

6. Use commas to separate quoted material from the person being quoted.

At the Beginning: "Give it to me," said John.

In the Middle: "Give it to me," said John, "and I will polish it."

At the End: John said, "Give it to me, and I will polish it."

ASSIGNMENT 1

Write the preface to your autobiography. It will deal with the origins of your various names. You will find the task easier if you follow these steps:

1. Know your facts. Make a list in random order of what you have learned in researching your topic.

2. Selecting from these the facts you wish to use, make a rough outline.

3. Write your rough draft of the preface. Correcting it later will be easier if you leave a space between each line of writing.

4. Remembering the material you have studied in the check sheet, go over the rough draft and correct it. Reading it aloud as you revise it will be helpful. Be sure that each sentence is complete. Change words that seem inappropriate, add words, or delete them where necessary. Check your punctuation and spelling carefully.

5. Rewrite the preface and hand it in on the date set by your teacher.

PRACTICE TEST I

This test reviews only those rules noted on the Check Sheet for Chapter 1. Review the Check Sheet and then, without looking back, do the test. Each error will count as four points, if anybody's counting.

I. Number your paper. Beside the appropriate number, give the reason for the commas in each of the following sentences.

1. The Queen Mary has since been junked, but she was the best ship afloat when I was aboard her.

2. Nevertheless, there is still much work to be done on my project.

3. I have worked long hours, stayed up beyond my bedtime, gotten up earlier than the birds and still have not finished.

4. At ten in the morning January 2, 1975, we arrived at the Talahatchee Bridge, Talahatchee, Mississippi.

5. Hardly anyone else, I moreover, would be at the party on time.

6. The winds were soft and the sky clear, yet there was a stillness in the atmosphere that was ominous.

7. "Why," I said, "I just want to grow up to be an adult."

8. Skiing was not, however, a sport at which I became proficient.

9. Doreen had entered the room quietly and not slammed the door, yet there was about her attitude something decidedly impertinent.

10. Let me know, Sam, when you are ready.

II. Five of the following sentences need no punctuation, and five of them have need of punctuation. Number your paper. Beside the appropriate number, write OK if the sentence is correctly punctuated. Punctuate the five which need commas by writing the two words needing separation and placing the comma between them.

1. Six of my comrades were fishing for minnows in that shallow pond.

2. They were hoping to catch a lot of worms for they could sell them for bait.

3. He has not yet seen a flying saucer but he is still hoping to.

4. Everyone but Norma and her sister had arrived and begun to tune up.

5. The pro had set up a practice course and was busy instructing most of the young ladies in the club.

6. Suzanne was jealous of her sister's popularity and she had a hard time keeping her feelings to herself.

7. We did not go to the play after all because I had a cold and Mother was too tired.

8. Bill might grow up to become a famous doctor or he might just grow up to be another type of operator.

9. Father refused to umpire any more either for the American Legion or for the Little League.

10. Bobby said he would meet me by two o'clock yet he had not showed up by two-thirty.

III. Rewrite the following sentences, putting in the necessary commas.

1. "Come on over Phyllis and join the crowd" Ruth suggested.

2. Mother kept yapping at my brother to practice for she is a perfectionist and can't stand hearing errors.

3. Who lives at 10 Downing Street London England?

4. I believe furthermore that Jennifer hid the watch and then said she had lost it.

5. I had been told there was no Santa Claus and yet I found it hard to believe for some reason.

The Helpless Infant

The pieces that follow deal with the themes about which you will be writing in the first three chapters of the text. A poem gives advice that any baby instinctively knows. Two short narratives deal with the naming of children—one, an American Indian; the other, a native of Gambia. A biographer gives us the genealogical background of a famous American President and his wife. The selections end with an older man remembering what it was like to be a baby.

Bela Kalman, Stock Boston.

MIRIAM ANDREWS (1916–   ) is a practicing poet living in Westport, Connecticut, from which she helps publish the magazine *Poet Lore.* After you have read Thomas Wolfe's recall of infancy, page 27, compare his complaints with those mentioned in this poem.

Being a Baby

MIRIAM ANDREWS

Did you ever think
BEING A BABY?

Can't talk. Can't walk
away from stiff blankets,
mouldy kisses, staves
of arms on springs
tossing you in air.

Can't think straight,
things being pushed
in your mouth all hours.
bottom washed, powdered, patted
in full public.

Mushy toys. Mushy food.
Bars on your bed—
you feel as if
you're in a zoo.

Go ahead. Scream.
I would, too!

". . . his 'real' name, given him at birth by his great-grandmother, was officially bestowed with feasts and ceremonies."

PHIL GEORGE is not a helpless infant, nor was he when the following incident took place. It tells how he received his name when he was considerably older than most children. It also tells the reason for the name and its significance. Note, as you read, how the explorers Lewis and Clark, in naming a Western river, bestowed an English counterpart of its original Indian name.

The Naming of Phil George

TERRY ALLEN, editor

Phillip William George, after two years in Vietnam and a long year on the California desert as an Army dental technician, is now [in 1972] a freshman at Gonzaga University. He is a member of the Nez Percé Nation at Lapwai, Washington.

He spent much of his early life with his maternal great-grandmother, living and learning the ways of his ancestors. He arrived at the Institute of American Indian Arts in the fall of 1964, a graduate of Coulee Dam High School. He was a well-known traditional Indian dance champion of the Pacific Northwest. His art interests were in traditional costuming, music, dance, and writing.

Phil and the dance club of which he was president performed before national and international dignitaries in Washington. His poetry was read before Congress and translated into many languages for use on the Voice of America broadcasts. His poetry and prose have been widely published by educational and trade publishers.

Allan Mitchell, Black Star.

After Phil's eighth birthday, his "real" name, given him at birth by his great-grandmother, was officially bestowed with feasts and ceremonies. Relatives and friends attended from the Colville, Spokane, Yakima, Warm Springs, Umatilla, Flathead, and Rocky Boy reservations.

Lah-peh-ya-low-ett, the name of his great-grandfather, refers to two white swans gliding above still waters, symbolic of beauty, grace, purity, and peace. At the naming ceremony, Phil's Grandfather Seth explained the history of his father's sacred name.

"Lahpehyalowett lived across from the Palouse grasslands, east from the Kamiah valley. *Kamiah-pa* means 'the green valley with clear waters flowing through.' Lewis and Clark named the river Clearwater. The prairie adjoining pine forests allotted to Lahpehyalowett was perfect for horse raising. Because Lahpehyalowett owned hundreds of Appaloosa horses, the agent at Fort Lapwai named him Phillip, which means in Greek 'lover of horses.' "

Study Questions

1. Phillip was officially named late in his childhood. What part did he have in selecting the name? Was the name patronymic, occupational, a place name, or a nickname?

2. How was the origin of Phil's name considerably different from that of his great-grandfather?

3. Many of you have several names, only one of which you prefer to be called. Which of your names would you call your "real" name? Why?

4. If you were to have had a choice of naming yourself at the age of eight, what would you have chosen? Do you think your choice would have been a wise one?

". . . he walked to the edge of the village, lifted his baby up with his face to the heavens, and said softly, 'Fend kiling dorong leh warranta ka iteh tee.' (Behold—the only thing greater than yourself.)"

ALEX HALEY (1921–   ) spent twelve years investigating his ancestry. He had heard from his grandmother in Tennessee stories of an ancestor, Kunta Kinte, who had arrived a slave in Maryland before the American Revolution. He had also heard a very few of the words passed down from Kunta's African background through the generations to Grandmother Cynthia. With this sparse information, Haley eventually identified the language as Mandinka and the place as The Gambia. Finally, Haley made a trip to The Gambia and found stored in the memory of a *griot,* a village storyteller, the same story Grandmother Cynthia told him: Kunta, a proud young man of illustrious heritage, had been captured by slave traders one day when he had gone into the forest to cut wood for a new drum. Haley then reconstructed the story of Kunta Kinte and his "factional" life in Africa and as a slave in Maryland and Virginia. The story became *Roots* and was the publishing sensation of 1976 and the TV record-setting drama of 1977. The selection that follows is Chapter I of *Roots* and details the birth and naming of Kunta Kinte.

FROM

Roots

ALEX HALEY

Early in the spring of 1750, in the village of Juffure, four days upriver from the coast of The Gambia, West Africa, a man-child was born to Omoro and Binta Kinte. Forcing forth from Binta's strong young body, he was as black as she was, flecked and slippery with Binta's blood, and he was bawling. The two wrinkled midwives, old Nyo Boto and the baby's Grandmother Yaisa, saw that it was a boy and laughed with joy. According to the forefathers, a boy firstborn presaged the special blessings of Allah not only upon the parents but also upon the parents' families; and there was the prideful knowledge that the name of Kinte would thus be both distinguished and perpetuated.

It was the hour before the first crowing of the cocks, and along with Nyo Boto and Grandma Yaisa's chatterings, the first sound the child heard was the muted, rhythmic *bomp-a-bomp-a-bomp* of wooden pestles as the other women of the village pounded couscous grain in their mortars, preparing the traditional breakfast of porridge that was cooked in earthen pots over a fire built among three rocks.

The thin blue smoke went curling up, pungent and pleasant, over the small dusty village of round mud huts as the nasal wailing of Kajali Demba, the village alimamo, began, calling men to the first of the five daily prayers that had been offered up to Allah for as long as anyone living could remember. Hastening from their beds of bamboo cane and cured hides into their rough cotton tunics, the men of the village filed briskly to the praying place, where the alimamo led the worship: *"Allahu Akbar! Ashadu an lailahailala!"* (God is great! I bear witness that there is only one God!) It was after this, as the men were returning toward their home compounds for breakfast, that Omoro rushed among them, beaming and excited, to tell them of his firstborn son. Congratulating him, all of the men echoed the omens of good fortune.

Each man, back in his own hut, accepted a calabash of porridge from his wife. Returning to their kitchens in the rear of the compound, the wives fed next their children, and finally themselves. When they had finished eating, the men took up their short, bent-handled hoes, whose wooden blades had been sheathed with metal by the village blacksmith, and set off for their day's work of preparing the land for farming of the groundnuts and the couscous and cotton that were the primary men's crops, as rice was that of the women, in this hot, lush savanna country of The Gambia.

By ancient custom, for the next seven days, there was but a single task with which Omoro would seriously occupy himself: the selection of a name for his firstborn son. It would have to be a name rich with history and with promise, for the people of his tribe—the Mandinkas—believed that a child would develop seven of the characteristics of whomever or whatever he was named for.

On behalf of himself and Binta, during this week of thinking, Omoro visited every household in Juffure, and invited each family to the naming ceremony of the newborn child, traditionally on the eighth day of his life. On that day, like his father and his father's father, this new son would become a member of the tribe.

When the eighth day arrived, the villagers gathered in the early morning before the hut of Omoro and Binta. On their heads, the women of both families brought calabash containers of ceremonial sour milk and sweet munko cakes of pounded rice and honey. Karamo Silla, the jaliba of the village, was there with his tan-tang drums; and the alimamo, and the arafang, Brima Cesay, who would some day be the child's teacher; and also Omoro's two brothers, Janneh and Saloum, who had journeyed from far away to attend the ceremony when the drumtalk news of their nephew's birth had reached them.

As Binta proudly held her new infant, a small patch of his first hair was shaved off, as was always done on this day, and all of the women exclaimed at how well formed the baby was. Then they quieted as the jaliba began to beat his drums. The alimamo said a prayer over the calabashes of sour milk and munko cakes, and as he prayed, each guest touched a calabash brim with his or her right hand, as a gesture of respect for the food. Then the alimamo turned to pray over the infant, entreating Allah to grant him long life, success in bringing credit and pride and many children to his family, to his village, to his tribe—and, finally, the strength and the spirit to deserve and to bring honor to the name he was about to receive.

Omoro then walked out before all of the assembled people of the village. Moving to his wife's side, he lifted up the infant and, as all watched, whispered three times into his son's ear the name he had chosen for him. It was the first time the name had ever been spoken as this child's name, for Omoro's people felt that each human being should be the first to know who he was.

Then tan-tang drum resounded again; and now Omoro whispered the name into the ear of Binta, and Binta smiled with pride and pleasure. Then Omoro whispered the name to the arafang, who stood before the villagers.

"The first child of Omoro and Binta Kinte is named *Kunta!*" cried Brima Cesay.

As everyone knew, it was the middle name of the child's late grandfather, Kairaba Kunta Kinte, who had come from his native Mauretania into The Gambia, where he had saved the people of Juffure from a famine, married Grandma Yaisa, and then served Juffure honorably till his death as the village's holy man.

One by one, the arafang recited the names of the Mauretanian forefathers of whom the baby's grandfather, old Kairaba Kinte, had

James Foote, Photo Researchers, Inc.

often told. The names, which were great and many, went back more than two hundred rains. Then the jaliba pounded on his tan-tang and all of the people exclaimed their admiration and respect at such a distinguished lineage.

Out under the moon and the stars, alone with his son that eighth night, Omoro completed the naming ritual. Carrying little Kunta in his strong arms, he walked to the edge of the village, lifted his baby up with his face to the heavens, and said softly, "*Fend kiling dorong leh warrata ka iteh tee.*" (Behold—the only thing greater than yourself.)

Study Questions and Activities

1. How long did it take the baby's father to choose the name for his firstborn? What was the significance of this period of time?

2. Who is the first to hear the child's name? The second? The third? Who are the last to find out? How do the choice and announcement of name differ in our culture? To what of our customs might we compare the public announcement of Kunta's name?

3. After announcing the name, the arafang recites the baby's impressive lineage. Why do you suppose such a recital was considered important? How is it connected with the selection of the name? What customs that you know deal with a similar pride in lineage?

4. What was the father's final act on the naming day? How does it differ radically from most customs of the European and American tradition? Why do you suppose the father says his speech "softly"?

5. Which of the following correctly completes this analogy? Omoro: father :: (**a**) Kunta:Kinte (**b**) Brima Cesay: arafang (**c**) Allah:alimamo (**d**) mother:Binta

6. On a map of Africa find The Gambia. Why do you suppose so many slaves came from the West African coast?

7. The numbers seven and three are important to this African naming ritual. How have they been important to other cultures you have studied? Why do you suppose these numbers have held such significance for humanity for so long?

VOCABULARY: DEFINITIONS FROM CONTEXT

From the context of the following short sentences, find the meanings that can correctly be used to complete the sentences. Which of the words following each sentence comes closest to being a synonym of the underlined word in the sentence?

1. The arrival of a boy presaged special blessings.
(**a**) demanded (**b**) preserved (**c**) indicated (**d**) permitted

2. The name would thus be perpetuated.
(**a**) committed (**b**) continued (**c**) foretold (**d**) demonstrated

3. He accepted a calabash of porridge.
(**a**) container (**b**) helping (**c**) heap (**d**) symbol

4. The hoes had been sheathed with metal.
(**a**) consecrated (**b**) manufactured (**c**) pronged (**d**) covered

5. The alimamo entreated Allah.
(**a**) respected (**b**) revered (**c**) begged (**d**) sacrificed to

6. The smoke rose up, pungent and pleasant.
(**a**) musky (**b**) thick (**c**) odious (**d**) aromatic

7. It is ironic that the omens for Kunta were so good.
(**a**) auguries (**b**) ceremonies (**c**) blessings (**d**) ancestors

". . . the Roosevelts had a firm sense of their roots."

JOSEPH P. LASH (1909–) in 1971 wrote a biography that became a bestseller for months. In addition, it won the Pulitzer Prize and the National Book Award. The book, *Eleanor and Franklin,* was as much a biography of a marriage as that of the lives of its two principals, President and Mrs. Franklin Delano Roosevelt. The selection that follows is the preface. In it you will find the background of the Roosevelt family. It was a long-time American family that produced two Presidents, Theodore and Franklin D. Roosevelt. It produced as well Franklin's wife Eleanor, his distant cousin. Notice that it is written in the third person. You may want to try this technique of avoiding the "I" as you write Chapter 2 of your autobiography.

FROM

Eleanor and Franklin

JOSEPH P. LASH

The first Roosevelt, Claes Martenszen van Rosenvelt, arrived from Holland in the 1640s when New Amsterdam was a tiny settlement of 800 huddled in some eighty houses at the foot of Manhattan. Who Claes Martenszen was, whether solid Dutch burgher in search of larger opportunities or solemn rogue "two leaps ahead of the bailiff," as his witty descendant Alice Roosevelt Longworth has suggested, is not known. In either case, by the eve of the American Revolution when New York had become a bustling port of 25,000, there were fifty Roosevelt families, and Claes's descendants were already showing an "uncanny knack" of associating themselves with the forces of boom and expansion in American economic life.

In the Roosevelt third generation two of the brothers, Johannes and Jacobus, took the family into real estate with the purchase of the

Beekman Swamp, a venture that was to have "a lasting effect on the city and their own family fortunes." It was these two brothers, also, who started the branches that led ultimately to Oyster Bay (Johannes) and to Hyde Park (Jacobus). The pre-Revolutionary Roosevelts were prosperous burghers but not of the highest gentry, and in civic affairs they were aligned with the popular faction against the aristocrats.

The first Roosevelt to achieve gentility and distinction was Isaac, the great-great-great-grandfather of Franklin, who for his services to the American cause was called "Isaac the Patriot." Isaac was a trader in sugar and rum but ended his business career as president of New York's first bank. At his death Philip Hone, the diarist, spoke of him as "proud and aristocratical," part of the "only nobility" the country had ever had.

It took the Johannes-Oyster Bay branch of the Roosevelts a little longer to advance from trader to merchant prince. Isaac's cousin James, after service with the Revolutionary army, founded Roosevelt & Son, a hardware business on Maiden Lane that swiftly expanded into building supplies. When James's grandson, Cornelius Van Schaack Roosevelt, was head of the firm, it imported most of the plate glass that was used in the new homes being built in the prospering nation. Cornelius' chief distinction was his wealth; he was listed among the five richest men in New York. His son, on the other hand, the first Theodore, retired from business early in order to devote himself to civic activity and was one of the most esteemed men in the city.

By the beginning of the twentieth century the Roosevelt family was one of the oldest and most distinguished in the United States. Its men had married well—a Philadelphia Barnhill, one of whose ancestors arrived with William Penn; a Yankee Howland, whose family had arrived on the *Mayflower;* a Hoffman of Swedish-Finnish descent, one of the richest heiresses in Dutchess County; and one of the Bullochs of Georgia. The Hudson River Roosevelts led the leisurely life of country squires and Johannes' clan was building its country houses, stables, and tennis courts along the north shore of Long Island.

Conscious of having played their part in the transformation of New York from a frail Dutch outpost into a cosmopolitan city and of the country from a handful of seaboard colonies into a continent-spanning, imperial republic, the Roosevelts had a firm sense of their roots. While most of them had changed their church affiliation from Dutch Reform to Protestant Episcopal, they remained faithful church-goers and believers in the Protestant ethic, which sanctified a ruthless

Franklin and Eleanor Roosevelt and children. Culver Pictures.

competitive individualism on the one hand and, on the other, the love and charity that were the basis of the family's strong sense of social obligation. Standards of honor, conduct, and manners—the caste marks of the old-stock upper class—were further bred into the Roosevelt sons at Groton and Harvard. They went on to become bankers, sportsmen, financiers, and, in two cases, presidents of the United States. The Roosevelt women, however, were essentially private individuals concerned with supervising large households and launching their daughters into fashionable society. With a few notable exceptions, they led lives of genteel conformity and escaped public notice—until the advent of a girl who was to become known as First Lady of the World. ❦

Study Questions and Activities

1. How long has the Roosevelt family lived on this continent? Why do you suppose they came from Holland rather than England? What is today's name for New Amsterdam, where Claes Martenzen van Rosenvelt put down roots?

2. No doubt you noticed that Roosevelt later was anglicized to Roosevelt. What changes in spelling in your own surname were you able to find?

3. The author says that "pre-Revolutionary Roosevelts were . . . not of the highest gentry," but that Isaac was the "first to achieve gentility. . . ." What is meant by "gentry" and "gentility"? What other words come from the same root? From paragraphs 2 and 3 infer which side the Roosevelts supported during the American Revolution. Cite the text to support your inference.

4. How did the Roosevelt family make its money? What privileges and honors came along with their wealth?

5. Two brothers are credited with founding two famous Roosevelt families. These brothers, the author notes, moved "to Oyster Bay (Johannes) and to Hyde Park (Jacobus)." Consult a reference and find out which President was from Oyster Bay and which was from Hyde Park. Which family branch produced Anna Eleanor Roosevelt, Franklin's wife?

6. The underlined words in the following exercise appear in the preface you just read. Look at the words in context and then select, from the four choices that follow, the words or words most nearly alike in meaning.

- **a.** "whether solid Dutch burgher" (1) well-built – emigrant (2) obese – upstart (3) sound – dweller (4) stolid – bungler
- **b.** "aligned with the popular faction" (1) allied – side (2) estranged – percentage (3) spoken of – gossip (4) concealed – minority
- **c.** "a cosmopolitan city" (1) huge (2) world-renowned (3) urban (4) notorious
- **d.** "ruthless competitive individualism" (1) vital (2) merciless (3) altruistic (4) dignified
- **e.** "the advent of a girl" (1) announcement (2) survival (3) arrival (4) christening

"He understood that, . . . caught in that insoluble prison of being, we escape it never. . . ."

THOMAS CLAYTON WOLFE (1900–1938) lived a brief but distinguished life, leaving four major novels and many shorter pieces. Always autobiographical, his novels gave various names to their protagonists. In the following piece from his first novel, "the baby" is born, as was the author, in 1900 and is called Eugene Gant. His mother in the selection is Eliza; his father is referred to as Gant. The selection recounts memories that may seem impossible, for example, those the baby had while lying in his crib. It ends with an almost fatal misadventure. While your own memories do not have to go so far back in your Chapter 3, you may get some ideas from Eugene's. Like the previous selection, this one is written in the third person. You, too, might experiment with omitting the "I remember" or "I am told" as you work with material you remember mainly by having been told it.

FROM

Look Homeward, Angel

THOMAS WOLFE

"Well, what are you going to call it?" inquired Dr. Cardiac, referring thus, with shocking and medical coarseness, to this most royal imp.

Eliza was better tuned to cosmic vibrations. With a full, if inexact, sense of what portended, she gave to Luck's Lad the title of Eugene, a name which, beautifully, means "well born," but which, as any one will be able to testify, does not mean, has never meant, "well bred."

Lying darkly in his crib, washed, powdered, and fed, he thought quietly of many things before he dropped off to sleep—the interminable sleep that obliterated time for him, and that gave him a sense of having missed forever a day of sparkling life. At these moments, he was heartsick with weary horror as he thought of the discomfort, weakness, dumbness, the infinite misunderstanding he would have to endure before he gained physical freedom. He grew sick as he thought of the weary defeats before him, the lack of co-ordination of the centres of control, the undisciplined and rowdy bladder, the helpless exhibition he was forced to give in the company of his sniggering, pawing brothers and sisters, dried, cleaned, revolved before them.

He was in agony because he was poverty-stricken in symbols: his mind was caught in a net because he had no words to work with. He had not even names for the objects around him: he probably defined them for himself by some jargon, reinforced by some mangling of the speech that roared about him, to which he listened intently day after day, realizing that his first escape must come through language. He indicated as quickly as he could his ravenous hunger for pictures and print: sometimes they brought him great books profusely illustrated, and he bribed them desperately by cooing, shrieking with delight, making extravagant faces, and doing all the other things they understood in him. He wondered savagely how they would feel if they knew what he really thought: at other times he had to laugh at them and at their whole preposterous comedy of errors as they pranced around for his amusement, waggled their heads at him, tickled him roughly, making him squeal violently against his will. The situation was at once profoundly annoying and comic: as he sat in the middle of the floor and watched them enter, seeing the face of each transformed by a foolish leer, and hearing their voices become absurd and sentimental whenever they addressed him, speaking to him words which he did not yet understand, but which he saw they were mangling in the preposterous hope of rendering intelligible that which has been previously mutilated, he had to laugh at the fools, in spite of his vexation.

And left alone to sleep within a shuttered room, with the thick sunlight printed in bars upon the floor, unfathomable loneliness and sadness crept through him: he saw his life down the solemn vista of a forest aisle, and he knew he would always be the sad one: caged in that little round of skull, imprisoned in that beating and most secret heart, his life must always walk down lonely passages. Lost. He understood that men were forever strangers to one another, that no one ever comes really to know any one, that imprisoned in the dark womb of our mother, we come to life without having seen her face, that we are given to her arms a stranger, and that, caught in that insoluble prison of being, we escape it never, no matter what arms may clasp us, what mouth may kiss us, what heart may warm us. Never, never, never, never, never.

He saw that the great figures that came and went about him, the huge leering heads that bent hideously into his crib, the great voices that rolled incoherently above him, had for one another not much greater understanding than they had for him: that even their speech, their entire fluidity and ease of movement were but meagre communicants of their thought or feeling, and served often not to promote understanding, but to deepen and widen strife, bitterness, and prejudice.

His brain went black with terror. He saw himself an inarticulate stranger, an amusing little clown, to be dandled and nursed by these enormous and remote figures. He had been sent from one mystery into another: somewhere within or without his consciousness he heard a great bell ringing faintly, as if it sounded undersea, and as he listened, the ghost of memory walked through his mind, and for a moment he felt that he had almost recovered what he had lost.

Sometimes, pulling himself abreast the high walls of his crib, he glanced down dizzily at the patterns of the carpet far below; the world swam in and out of his mind like a tide, now printing its whole sharp picture for an instant, again ebbing out dimly and sleepily, while he pieced the puzzle of sensation together bit by bit, seeing only the dancing fire-sheen on the poker, hearing then the elfin clucking of the sun-warm hens, somewhere beyond in a distant and enchanted world. Again, he heard their morning-wakeful crowing clear and loud, suddenly becoming a substantial and alert citizen of life; or, going and coming in alternate waves of fantasy and fact, he heard the loud, faery thunder of Daisy's parlor music. Years later, he heard it again, a door opened in his brain: she told him it was Paderewski's "Minuet."

His crib was a great woven basket, well mattressed and pillowed within; as he grew stronger, he was able to perform extraordinary acrobatics in it, tumbling, making a hoop of his body, and drawing himself easily and strongly erect: with patient effort he could worm over the side on to the floor. There, he would crawl on the vast design of the carpet, his eyes intent upon great wooden blocks piled chaotically on the floor. They had belonged to his brother Luke: all the letters of the alphabet, in bright multi-colored carving, were engraved upon them.

Holding them clumsily in his tiny hands, he studied for hours the symbols of speech, knowing that he had here the stones of the temple of language, and striving desperately to find the key that would draw order and intelligence from this anarchy. Great voices soared far above him, vast shapes came and went, lifting him to dizzy heights, depositing him with exhaustless strength. The bell rang under the sea.

One day when the opulent Southern Spring had richly unfolded, when the spongy black earth of the yard was covered with sudden, tender grass, and wet blossoms, the great cherry tree seethed slowly with a massive gem of amber sap, and the cherries hung ripening in prodigal clusters, Gant took him from his basket in the sun on the high front porch, and went with him around the house by the lily beds, taking him back under trees singing with hidden birds, to the far end of the lot.

Here the earth was unshaded, dry, clotted by the plough. Eugene knew by the stillness that it was Sunday: against the high wire fence there was the heavy smell of hot dock-weed. On the other side, Swain's cow was wrenching the cool coarse grass, lifting her head from time to time, and singing in her strong deep voice her Sunday exuberance. In the warm washed air, Eugene heard with absolute clearness all the brisk backyard sounds of the neighborhood, he became acutely aware of the whole scene, and as Swain's cow sang out again, he felt the flooded gates in him swing open. He answered "Moo!" phrasing the sound timidly but perfectly, and repeating it confidently in a moment when the cow answered.

Gant's delight was boundless. He turned and raced back toward the house at the full stride of his legs. And as he went, he nuzzled his stiff mustache into Eugene's tender neck, mooing industriously and always getting an answer.

"Lord a' mercy!" cried Eliza, looking from the kitchen window as he raced down the yard with breakneck strides, "He'll kill that child yet."

And as he rushed up the kitchen steps—all the house, save the upper side was off the ground—she came out on the little latticed veranda, her hands floury, her nose stove-red.

"Why, what on earth are you doing, Mr. Gant?"

"Moo-o-o! He said 'Moo-o-o!' Yes he did!" Gant spoke to Eugene rather than to Eliza.

Eugene answered him immediately: he felt it was all rather silly, and he saw he would be kept busy imitating Swain's cow for several days, but he was tremendously excited, nevertheless, feeling now that the wall had been breached.

Eliza was likewise thrilled, but her way of showing it was to turn back to the stove, hiding her pleasure, and saying: "I'll vow, Mr. Gant. I never saw such an idiot with a child."

Later, Eugene lay wakefully in his basket on the sitting-room floor, watching the smoking dishes go by in the eager hands of the combined family, for Eliza at this time cooked magnificently, and a Sunday dinner was something to remember. For two hours since their

Thomas Wolfe in Berlin, Culver Pictures.

return from church, the little boys had been prowling hungrily around the kitchen: Ben, frowning proudly, kept his dignity outside the screen, making excursions frequently through the house to watch the progress of cookery; Grover came in and watched with frank interest until he was driven out; Luke, his broad humorous little face split by a wide exultant smile, rushed through the house, squealing exultantly:

"Weenie, weedie, weeky
Weenie, weedie, weeky,
Weenie, weedie, weeky,
Wee, Wee, Wee."

He had heard Daisy and Josephine Brown doing Caesar together, and his chant was his own interpretation of Caesar's brief boast: "Veni, Vidi, Vici."

As Eugene lay in his crib, he heard through the open door the dining-room clatter, the shrill excitement of the boys, the clangor of steel and knife as Gant prepared to carve the roast, the repetition of the morning's great event told over and over without variation, but with increasing zest.

"Soon," he thought, as the heavy food fragrance floated in to him, "I shall be in there with them." And he thought lusciously of mysterious and succulent food.

All through the afternoon upon the veranda Gant told the story, summoning the neighbors and calling upon Eugene to perform. Eugene heard clearly all that was said that day: he was not able to answer, but he saw now that speech was imminent.

Thus, later, he saw the first two years of his life in brilliant and isolated flashes. His second Christmas he remembered vaguely as a period of great festivity: it accustomed him to the third when it came. With the miraculous habitude children acquire, it seemed that he had known Christmas forever.

He was conscious of sunlight, rain, the leaping fire, his crib, the grim jail of winter: the second Spring, one warm day, he saw Daisy go off to school up the hill: it was the end of the noon recess, she had been home for lunch. She went to Miss Ford's School For Girls; it was a red brick residence on the corner at the top of the steep hill: he watched her join Eleanor Duncan just below. Her hair was braided in two long hanks down her back: she was demure, shy, maidenly, a timid and blushing girl; but he feared her attentions to him, for she bathed him furiously, wreaking whatever was explosive and violent beneath her placidity upon his hide. She really scrubbed him almost raw. He howled piteously. As she climbed the hill, he remembered her. He saw she was the same person.

He passed his second birthday with the light growing. Early in the following Spring he became conscious of a period of neglect: the house was deadly quiet; Gant's voice no longer roared around him, the boys came and went on stealthy feet. Luke, the fourth to be attacked by the pestilence, was desperately ill with typhoid: Eugene was intrusted almost completely to a young . . . negress. . . . One day she took him out on the side porch to play: it was a young Spring morning, bursting moistly from the thaw of the earth. The negress sat upon the side-steps and yawned while he grubbed in his dirty little dress along the path, and upon the lily bed. Presently, she went to sleep against the post. Craftily, he wormed his body through the wide wires of the fence, into the cindered alley that wound back to the Swains', and up to the ornate wooden palace of the Hilliards.

They were among the highest aristocracy of the town: they had come from South Carolina, "near Charleston," which in itself gave them at that time a commanding prestige. The house, a huge gabled structure of walnut-brown, which gave the effect of many angles and no plan, was built upon the top of the hill which sloped down to Gant's; the level ground on top before the house was tenanted by lordly towering oaks. Below, along the cindered alley, flanking Gant's orchard, there were high singing pines.

Mr. Hilliard's house was considered one of the finest residences in the town. The neighborhood was middle-class, but the situation was magnificent, and the Hilliards carried on in the grand manner, lords of the castle who descended into the village, but did not mix with its people. All of their friends arrived by carriage from afar; every day punctually at two o'clock, an old liveried negro drove briskly up the winding alley behind two sleek brown mares, waiting under the carriage entrance at the side until his master and mistress should come out. Five minutes later they drove out, and were gone for two hours.

This ritual, followed closely from his father's sitting-room window, fascinated Eugene for years after: the people and the life next door were crudely and symbolically above him.

He felt a great satisfaction that morning in being at length in Hilliard's alley: it was his first escape, and it had been made into a forbidden and enhaloed region. He grubbed about in the middle of the road, disappointed in the quality of the cinders. The booming courthouse bell struck eleven times.

Now, exactly at three minutes after eleven every morning, so unfailing and perfect was the order of his great establishment, a huge gray horse trotted slowly up the hill, drawing behind him a heavy grocery wagon, musty, spicy, odorous with the fine smells of grocery-stores and occupied exclusively by the Hilliard victuals, and the driver, a young negro man who, at three minutes past eleven every morning, according to ritual, was comfortably asleep. Nothing could possibly go wrong: the horse could not have been tempted even by a pavement of oats to betray his sacred mission.

Accordingly he trotted heavily up the hill, turned ponderously into the alley ruts, and advanced heavily until, feeling the great circle of his right forefoot obstructed by some foreign particle, he looked down and slowly removed his hoof from what had recently been the face of a little boy.

Then, with his legs carefully straddled, he moved on, drawing the wagon beyond Eugene's body, and stopping. Both negroes awoke simultaneously; there were cries within the house, and Eliza and Gant rushed out of doors. The frightened negro lifted Eugene, who was quite unconscious of his sudden return to the stage, into the burly arms of Doctor McGuire, who cursed the driver eloquently. His thick sensitive fingers moved swiftly around the bloody little face and found no fracture.

He nodded briefly at their desperate faces: "He's being saved for Congress," said he. "You have bad luck and hard heads, W. O."

"You . . . scoundrel," yelled the master, turning with violent relief upon the driver. "I'll put you behind the bars for this." He thrust his great length of hands through the fence and choked the negro, who mumbled prayers, and had no idea what was happening to him, save that he was the centre of a wild commotion.

The negro girl, blubbering, had fled inward.

"This looks worse than it is," observed Dr. McGuire, laying the hero upon the lounge. "Some hot water, please." Nevertheless, it took two hours to bring him round. Every one spoke highly of the horse. . . .

But all this, as Eliza knew in her heart, was part of the plan of the Dark Sisters. The entrails had been woven and read long since: the frail shell of skull which guarded life, and which might have been crushed as easily as a man breaks an egg, was kept intact. But Eugene carried the mark of the centaur for many years, though the light had to fall properly to reveal it.

When he was older, he wondered sometimes if the Hilliards had issued from their high place when he had so impiously disturbed the order of the manor. He never asked, but he thought not: he imagined them, at the most, as standing superbly by a drawn curtain, not quite certain what had happened, but feeling that it was something unpleasant, with blood in it.

Shortly after this, Mr. Hilliard had a "No-Trespassing" sign staked up in the lot.

Vocabulary

Eliza was better tuned to cosmic vibrations. With a full, if inexact, sense of what *portended,* she gave to Luck's Lad the title of Eugene . . . . (27:5); he thought quietly of many things before he dropped off to sleep—the *interminable* sleep that *obliterated* time for him . . . . (27:9); The situation was at once profoundly annoying and comic: . . . he had to laugh at the fools, in spite of his *vexation.* . . . . (28:30); He saw himself an *inarticulate* stranger . . (29: 9); striving desperately to find the key that would draw order and intelligence from this *anarchy* . . . . (29:41); the cherries hung ripening in *prodigal* clusters . . (30: 5); Swain's cow was . . . singing in her deep voice her Sunday *exuberance* . . (30: 14); he saw now that speech was *imminent* . . . . (32:26); Luke, the fourth to be attacked by the *pestilence,* was desperately ill with typhoid . . . . (33:5); But all this, as Eliza knew in her heart, was part of the plan of the Dark Sisters. The *entrails* had been woven and read long since . . . . (34:31)

Study Questions and Activities

1. Gant and Eliza are the parents of Eugene. Which of the two is the more completely characterized? For the one you choose, make a list of character traits, being sure that you have evidence from the passage to prove each trait.

2. After recalling the event of his birth, Eugene spends eight paragraphs detailing his thoughts during his first two years. He begins the passage with "Lying darkly in his crib . . . ." Discover how many of the infant's thoughts justify the author's use of the adverb "darkly."

3. Several times the infant Eugene recalls a bell. What do you think the bell symbolizes? Give reasons for your answer.

4. The infant, Wolfe writes, "was poverty-stricken in symbols." What sort of symbols did he lack? How did he make his craving for symbols known to his family? What symbol did he first make his own?

5. After rereading the infant's thoughts, make a prediction as to the kind of man he might grow up to be. Be sure to have a textual basis for your predictions.

6. Find the paragraph describing the Hilliards' house; it begins with "They were among the highest aristocracy of the town . . . ." On a sheet of unlined paper make a sketch of the house and its grounds, using the author's words as your guide. Exchange sketches with other members of your class to see how well the author has guided you.

7. The incident in which Eugene barely escapes with his life uses two blacks as villains. Do you think Wolfe is displaying racial prejudice here? Argue your case.

8. As a result of the accident, Wolfe writes, "Eugene carried the mark of the centaur for many years . . . ." Explain the allusion.

9. What is the irony in the last sentence of the piece?

10. The selection mentions that the brother Luke was seriously ill with typhoid fever, once a common and often fatal illness. Today the disease is fairly rare, though just as lethal. What reasons can you advance for today's control of typhoid?

11. After reading Mrs. Andrews' poem, discuss the difference in tone between the poem and the thoughts of the infant Eugene.

VOCABULARY

At the end of many of the literary selections you will find a list of words that have appeared in the writing. The vocabulary words which will be your responsibility to know will be italicized and accompanied by their immediate context. Some of these words may already be familiar to you; others will be new. Those that are unfamiliar or puzzling you should put in your notebook. Before going to the dictionary, though, try to guess the meaning of the word from its context, or find the word in the selection and see if you can guess its meaning from the way it is used in the complete sentence. (The numbers in parentheses will help you locate the word in the selection; they indicate page and line.

Thus (43:17) indicates page 43, line 17.) If you are taking a foreign language, search your mind for a similar word in that language. Above all, make a guess.

Then consult a dictionary, remembering to scan the various meanings the word might have. Find which meaning fits best in the context of the sentence in which the word was used. Then write that meaning and any others of modern usage in your notebook after the word. Look also for other forms of the word and the parts of speech they function as. Enter these as separate words so that, in learning the one word, you may in actuality be learning several.

Now begin to use them. Startle your family at the dinner table by using an especially high-powered word—correctly, of course. Use one or two when you write to your friends and relatives. Amaze your teachers by using some of your new vocabulary in your discussions and compositions. Before long these words will be yours for keeps.

Should you find other words in the selection that you have to look up, add these to your list. Be careful, though, that you do not make your task too large.

Some selections will have quite a few words listed after them; others will have many fewer. Authors choose their words partly because of the particular audience for which they are writing. Those writing for a literate adult audience will expect that group to have a reasonably large vocabulary; those appealing to the young or to popular taste will choose their words accordingly. And some writers of the selections lacked the education that you now have; these will scarcely baffle you with the words they use.

At the end of the book you will be given a vocabulary test. Most of the words in that test will be taken from the words, or their other forms, in the lists. As you take this test, you will be following the form currently used by many standardized tests given for scholarships and college entrance requirements. You can thus familiarize yourself with the logic of these tests while at the same time trying your growing word power.

Exercise

Now that you have studied the words on page 35, test your memory with the following questions. Each capitalized word is followed by four other words. One is an **antonym,** a word opposite in meaning to the capitalized word. Find the antonym and write its letter next to the appropriate number on your paper.

1. INARTICULATE (**a**) coherent (**b**) verbose (**c**) logical (**d**) tedious

2. ANARCHY (**a**) chaos (**b**) monarchy (**c**) order (**d**) celerity

3. INTERMINABLE (**a**) endless (**b**) fatal (**c**) oblique (**d**) finite

4. PRODIGAL (**a**) thrifty (**b**) salubrious (**c**) devious (**d**) maladroit

5. IMMINENT (**a**) adjacent (**b**) delayed (**c**) unnecessary (**d**) opposite

6. VEX (**a**) castigate (**b**) inspire (**c**) pacify (**d**) rescue

The first successful fountain pen. New York Public Library Picture Collection.

2

Origins— Climbing the Family Tree

Everyone has an interesting ancestry. Some can trace theirs back to the *Mayflower*, but most of us have to settle for less talked-about passages from Europe, Africa, or other continents. What can you find out about your ancestors, and how far back can you trace them?

By interviewing your parents or other relatives, discover what you can about your family tree. The result may convince you that you should write about a lot of different people and where they came from. Or you may hear about one or two especially interesting ancestors who you think will deserve the most space. Some may even find that, without consulting a distant cousin in some faraway outpost, they can find nothing about any ancestor more distant than their parents.

Lillian Hellman, self-portrait.

To discover what you can about your ancestors, try to answer such questions as these:

1. What about the ancestors on both my mother's and father's sides of the family? What were their names? What state or country did they live in?

2. Do I have an especially colorful ancestor? Did anyone fight in a war long past? Go searching for gold? Run for an important office?

3. If my ancestors migrated from another country, do they have stories about the trip over? If they came in great poverty, as many of our forbears did, what hardships did they suffer both on ship and after they arrived?

4. Are there any family traditions that stem from my ancestors' beliefs or experiences? What association do various heirlooms in my house have with the people who once owned them?

5. Does my family have a coat of arms? A motto? A slogan of any kind? If so, what is its significance?

Getting Started: Planning the Interview and Some Illustrations

Now is a good time to pick one another's brains. Get a group together and, collectively, make out an interview form. To do this, try a technique we call **brainstorming**. To brainstorm requires, first of all, having all members of the group suggest as many questions for an interview as they can think of. Start by having each member of the group scribble as many questions as he or she can. Then listen as the questions are read aloud. In the listening process, you will probably hear some ideas that are wonderfully relevant to your quest. No doubt you will also hear others that seem trivial. Discard those but add the questions that seem useful so that, by the end of your planning session, you will have a list of questions that you can put to members of your family. If there is time, each group can, toward the end of the class period, report its findings to the entire class so that everyone can profit from the planning period.

Your paper which contains all the questions you want to use is your interview form. As you research your second chapter, you will try to find answers to the questions. You may even have to write to or visit an older relative noted for her or his information about family background. Don't worry if you cannot find answers to everything. Few if any people will be able to. As you conduct your interviews, it may be helpful to utilize a miracle of science, the tape recorder. Carry it with you and tape the entire conversation. Then, as you play it back, note those items which you can make use of as you write.

Your brainstorming session for this chapter ought, also, to concern itself with illustrative material for the chapter. Besides those funny pictures of Grandpa in the family album, how else can you add life to your words? Your brainstorming group might try to come up with answers to these questions. How could you utilize a map in this chapter? How could you introduce color into the map and, therefore, the book? How does one go about drawing a family tree? How can you add color if you use a family tree? How can you make a genealogical chart? Will color work with such charts? If you cannot find answers to these questions, appoint a member to find examples in the library. Make notes on the material brought back so that, if the right times comes, you too can make such illustrations.

Writing the Anecdote

Almost surely, as you interview, you will come upon little stories about your ancestors. Don't neglect them. We call such little stories *anecdotes*, and they make splendid illustrative material in a composition. Anecdotes do not have to be long, but they should make a point. They may point out a person's characteristic, they may be just a joke, or they may illustrate a serious point. What follows is the raw material for an anecdote. Study the material and then write it into no more than five sentences. Listen to one another's ways of utilizing the material. You will then be better prepared to deal with the anecdotal material you come upon as you interview.

1. Grandma Smith saved her money.

2. She made her first solo trip to Sunday School when she was three.

3. Her mother gave her a penny for the collection.

4. She came home with two pennies.

As you study the sample writings, notice how their authors have utilized anecdote. Develop your own techniques and use anecdotes from now on to spice your manuscript.

More About Writing the Rough Draft

Remember to write your first copy rapidly and in pencil so that you can easily erase mistakes. Many people prefer to write on alternate lines so that they can better correct mistakes they see when reading over what they have written.

After you have written your rough draft, read it aloud slowly and carefully. Change sentences you do not like the sound of. Check the spelling of words you think may be misspelled. Be sure that your paragraphs are in the proper place and that you have more than one paragraph. Be sure also that you do not have a lot of small paragraphs consisting of only a sentence or two.

Spend some time making your first paragraph of each chapter interesting and appropriate. This is the one which most affects the reader, and it should be the best writing you produce. If you are following a theme throughout your autobiography, introduce it here. Three sample first paragraphs follow. Read them for ideas they may suggest to you. All of them are reproduced as they were written, with the exception of changed names. The titles before each paragraph are those given the chapters by their authors.

The Warp and the Woof

After looking over our family records, I have begun to feel like one inconsequential design on an elaborate Oriental rug. I tried hard to pick out with my eye all the threads that contributed to this small variegated design. Why does anybody get excited about being a descendant of any one person? Aren't we just about as much kin to one person as the river is to the ocean? One week's research and I feel like a true son of Adam and first cousin to anybody.

My Movie—Scene I—Paternal Ancestors

As I have heard of my ancestors, I have tried to picture them in the places and against the background and times in which they lived. Let me introduce you to my family in the summertime of 1881. Rutherford B. Hayes was President. The Civil War had been over for sixteen years, but was still present in the memories of the men and women of the time.

At Home with Grandma

In a tiny village near Teheran, Iran, stood a farmhouse built of stone. Surrounding the houses were acres of hilly land covered with many trees. Leading from the rear of the house was a long grape arbor which covered the outdoor dining room. Here, every morning, the Aram family gathered for breakfast. Anne, the youngest of the family of eight, loved eating under the arbor because she enjoyed reaching up and picking the grapes. Anne was eight years old and had few friends. The houses were far apart, and travel by donkey was difficult. Thus, Anne spent most of her time alone, roaming the hills, climbing the trees, and riding her donkey. When she was nine, she went to live with her eldest brother in Baku, a Russian city on the Caspian Sea. Here she was sent to school, where she made friends. She still enjoyed playing alone, however, and every day went out to the beach where she spent many hours lazying in the sea. This behavior was not considered very ladylike. It was the year 1881, and girls were not supposed to be running about like boys. Girls belonged in the kitchen. The adults worried about Anne and would shake their heads and say, "Whatever will you grow up to be, running around like that?" "Oh," she would answer, tossing her head, "a lady, I guess."

A Short Sample Composition

What follows is a sentence outline and a Chapter 2 prepared from that outline. As you can easily see, the writer was not able to find out too much information. Neither was he as specific as he might have been. However, as it stands, the composition rates a better than average score.

The Sentence Outline

I. Am I a descendant of Charlemagne?

II. My ancestors are from four different countries.

III. One ancestor, a Scot, was at Valley Forge.

IV. My Irish ancestress played a trick on her husband.

V. One great-grandfather went to the Klondike.

VI. My mother did not meet my father at a Yale prom.

The Composition:

Before My Time

According to a nutty relative who spends most of her time in the Genealogy Room of the New York Public Library, I am a direct descendant of Charlemagne. So, probably, are about eight million other people.

I suppose nobody cares about the many relatives in between, so I'll climb a little way up the family tree and say that the ancestors whom my mother remembers came from Scotland, Ireland, England, and Switzerland. The earliest arrivals came in colonial times from Scotland. The most recent came from Switzerland during this century.

One of the Scots was a soldier at Valley Forge. In his spare time he taught the soldiers how to read and write. We have letters written during his later years. In one of them, like a true Smith, he was grousing about not getting his soldier's bonus. I remind myself of him every time my allowance is overdue.

The past is full of stories. One of them is about my Irish great-great-grandmother. She got mad at her husband, packed the cow off to the fair and never came back. She had sold the cow and bought a sailing passage from Ireland to America. Here she moved to upstate New York and sent for her children, one of whom was my great-grandfather.

My other great-grandfather started out from Michigan for the Klondike. Before he reached Seattle, he had lost his galoshes. Two years later he came back from the North without a nickel.

That side of my family eventually moved to Spokane, where my mother was raised. As a student at Smith College, she went to Yale as often as she was invited; but she never met my father, who was a student there. He was always in New York City visiting his family. They later met at a house party in Idaho. At twenty-two they were married and settled in a New York City apartment.

CHECK SHEET FOR CHAPTER 2

Analysis of Samples

1. What anecdotes can you find in the four samples?

2. Which of the four opening paragraphs do you prefer? State your reasons.

3. Which of the sample paragraphs lead the reader to suspect the writer has a theme for the entire book?

4. What examples of personal style do you find in the samples?

5. How could the writer of "Before My Time" have been more specific?

6. How would a family tree or a genealogical table have helped him be more specific?

7. What illustration has the writer of "Before My Time" prepared for in his text?

8. What examples of colloquial language can you find in the samples? Does this usage help or hinder the writer's style?

Spelling

1. ancestors
2. ancestry (Write the adjective form)
3. autobiographies (How does this plural illustrate a general spelling rule?)
4. descent, descendant
5. eventually
6. feud
7. genealogy (Write the adjective and adverb forms. Have you seen similar changes previously?)
8. grandmother, grandfather (Note that each is a single, nonhyphenated word)
9. inter, interring, interred (Where does the accent fall on the first word?)
10. maternal, paternal (Write the adverb form of each word)
11. pogrom
12. quarrel, quarreling, quarreled (Where does the accent fall on the first word?)
13. refer, referring, referred (Where does the accent fall on the first word?)
14. travel, traveling, traveled (Now compare the accents on Words 9, 12, 13, and 14 and come up with a generalization about two-syllable words ending in -el or -er)

What's Wrong with These Sentences?

Form a group to play the game of spot the error. Be aware that the game grows progressively difficult. The twelve sentences that follow contain not only lapses in punctuation but in other things. What's wrong in each sentence? How should it be corrected?

1. "Yes Tommy may come in and play" Mother said.

2. Tommy came in happily his shoes were muddy, though, and Mother was soon sorry she had invited him.

3. Just as suddenly as she had invited him in, she told him to get out, which didn't please Tommy at all.

4. In those long lazy days we had time to read to think and to grow.

5. Summer, the best time of the year, a time to forget about cares and to have fun.

6. I came into the room at nine o'clock, I sit down, and I waited a half hour before Mrs. Burbank showed up.

7. My parents tried to think of reasons for their move. Reasons that would convince us kids we'd like it in Detroit.

8. I decided to take a short nap, three hours later I woke up and we were in San Juan.

9. He was the sort of person which I instantly dislike.

10. I wrote a note saying I had had a toothache. Which my mother said was the poorest excuse she'd ever seen.

11. Riding on that 747 was a gruesome experience. One that I'll never forget.

12. Early in my life I began to disagree with my elders, however, until now I had sense enough to keep my thoughts to myself.

More About Commas, Rules 7 and 8

7. Use a comma to separate "yes" and "no" from the rest of the sentence when you begin with those words.

Yes, I'll join you at noon.
No, he refuses to come.

8. When using adjectives in a series, we generally separate them by a comma.

His rough, tough manner disconcerted me.

Jill was lonely, frustrated, angry, and prepared for a fight.

Avoiding Major Sentence Errors

1. The incomplete sentence (IS)—*Which he believed in anyway.* Unless it is used to begin a question, the word WHICH is used only to begin a *Dependent Clause,* never a sentence. The same applies to the words *who, whom, what,* and, although not a question-opener, *that.* The incomplete sentence is one that does not make sense. It may have a subject and predicate and still not make sense.

2. The Run on Sentence (RS)—*Dogs were the main household pet they were more or less used as vacuum cleaners and napkins.* This should have been made into two sentences. A run on sentence is the running of two or more ideas into one cluttered sentence with incorrect or no dividing punctuation.

3. The Comma Splice (CS)—*Grandma Eakins says she is only thirty-nine, we know this is not true because my mother had her fortieth birthday last August.* Two complete sentences may not be joined by a comma. You may:

a. Make two separate sentences, using periods and capital letters.

b. Use a semicolon instead of the comma if the two sentences are closely related. This is often the best solution.

c. Subordinate one of the two ideas. "Though Grandma Eakins says . . .," or "We know Grandma Eakins is not really thirty-nine because . . ."

Misuses of "Which"

In clauses, the word WHICH should refer to the word it follows (It was the sunsets which he liked). Do not use it to refer to an idea or to a group of words which precede it.

Wrong Usage:

a. The king expelled the Huguenots, which sent my ancestors abroad.

b. The winters were cold, which bothered my Italian grandmother.

c. He liked skiing, swimming, and skating, which developed his leg muscles and overcame his limp.

In clauses, do not use WHICH to refer to persons; it refers to animals and things. The words WHO, WHOM, and THAT may refer to people.

The All-Important Verb

The single most important part of speech in our language is the verb. It is so important that we also use it, in changes of form, as an adjective, an adverb, and a noun. In addition, it is the major way we have of denoting time. The way we use verb tenses, which are time signals, is of paramount importance to any clear writer.

To begin with, think of nearly all verbs as having four important parts:

Present tense: talk(s), show(s), hit(s), go(es)

Present participle (and gerund form): talking, showing, hitting, going

Past tense: talked, showed, hit, went

Past participle: talked, showed, hit, gone

The **simple present** is easy enough: Today I *talk*. John *shows* improvement. He *hits* well. We *go* to the movies often.

We form another kind of present tense by adding the conjugation of "to be" (I
he
am, you are, she is, we are, you are, they
it
are) to the present participle: I *am talking* now. She *is showing* us the movie. They *are hitting* us with snowballs. We *are going* to the theater.

We form the **simple future** by adding "will" to the present tense of the verb: I *will talk* tomorrow. You *will show* me someday, I know. He *will hit* better next week. We *will go* along with you.

The **simple past** is also easy, as it is used to express completed action: Yesterday she *talked* to us about France. We *showed* the class our project earlier. Bill *hit* the ball over the fence. I *went* to town this morning.

By adding the past tense conjugation
he
of "to be" (I was, you were, she was, we
it
were, you were, they were), we can form another useful tense: I *was talking* to Susie until the teacher stopped me. She *was showing* me how to do my lesson. He *was hitting* better last week. We *were going* to visit you, but we had company.

The **present participle** (or gerund form) has two important uses. First, it can function as a noun and thus make an important word that simultaneously expresses action and becomes a name of something: *Talking* (gerund-subject) is Louise's and Tim's favorite pastime. There will be a *showing* (gerund-predicate noun) of the movie again tomorrow. Jack does a lot of fancy *hitting* (gerund-object of preposition). Second, it can function as an adjective and become an important element in making different types of sentences: *Going* to town, we saw two deer. (Notice how this form simplifies the wordier "We were going to town, and we saw two deer.") A *talking bird* is not a rarity in my home. Mr. Butts made a slide *showing* the splitting of a cell.

The **past participle** form poses two problems. Most verbs form their past and past participial forms by adding *-ed: talked, showed, furnished.* Some, however, as a result of our peculiar linguistic heritage, vary in these forms: *go-went-gone, do-did-done, hit-hit-hit, lie-lay-lain.* It becomes important, therefore, that we remember these irregular forms.

Learning the correct past form of an irregular verb keeps us from making errors of ignorance in formal writing and speaking: He *done* it. We *seen* a snake. He *snuck* into the room. While we may, among our friends, use these expressions with impunity, they are not yet part of the canon of Standard Written English.

We also need the past participial forms for making three important tenses: the present perfect, the past perfect, and the future perfect. The **present perfect** is formed by adding the present tense "have"
he
(I have, you have, she has, we have, you
it
have, they have) to the past participle of the verb: I *have talked* too much. We *have gone* to London often.

The **past perfect** is formed by using the past tense of have (*had* with first, second, and third persons) with the past participle: I *had* finally *showed* my last slide. He *had hit* his fourth home run of the season.

The **future perfect** is formed by placing "will have" in front of the past participle: I *will have talked* for an hour before I finish. We *will have gone* to Paris by the time you arrive.

In later lessons we will come back to these vexing but important changes of verb. For the moment, keep in mind the following:

1. Nearly every verb has four forms; be prepared to give them. Exception: *Must* and *ought* are strange verbs. Learn their past forms: Today I *must;* yesterday I *had to.* Today I *ought;* yesterday I *should have.*

2. If you start in one tense—say, the present—stay with that tense throughout your sentence. We can use the present tense to express things going on now and for things that have gone on and are still going on. Thus, "I *like* peanut butter" indicates a current taste. However, "Oliver Twist *becomes* a prisoner of Fagin," although it describes an action in the nineteenth century, may be used in the present tense because Oliver lives today in Dickens' novel. If you are working in the present tense and have to use a past tense, the correct sequence is the present perfect. "We *live* in Denver, but we *have lived* in four other cities."

3. If you start in the past tense, stay with that tense or its variations. "I *liked* peanut butter" indicates that the taste for that delicacy has left you. "Oliver Twist *became* Fagin's prisoner" is also correct because we are now thinking of him as a character who is part of our past experience. If we are using the past tense and wish to indicate another action completed still earlier, our shift is to the past perfect tense, although we can sometimes just as easily continue with the simple past. "We *lived* in Dubuque in 1970, but we *had lived* in St. Louis before our move."

The Irregular Verbs

Should you be in doubt about the changes of some of the common irregular verbs, a list follows of such verbs that frequently cause trouble. You can also look up the principal parts of any verb in the dictionary. If you find no parts listed, the verb will be regular. That is, it will add "-d" or "-ed" to its past and past participial changes. If only three parts are listed, the past and past participial forms will be the same. If there is a *dial.* (*dialectal*) notation, remember that the form is not a standard usage.

Present	Present Participle and Gerund	Simple Past	Past Participle
beat	beating	beat	beaten
begin	beginning	began	begun
bite	biting	bit	bitten
blow	blowing	blew	blown
break	breaking	broke	broken
bring	bringing	brought	brought
burst*	bursting	burst	burst
choose	choosing	chose	chosen
come	coming	came	come
dig	digging	dug	dug
dive	diving	dove or dived	dived
do	doing	did	done
draw	drawing	drew	drawn
drink	drinking	drank	drunk
drive	driving	drove	driven
eat	eating	ate	eaten

* *bust – busted* as a verb is used only colloquially

Present	Present Participle and Gerund	Simple Past	Past Participle
fall	falling	fell	fallen
fly	flying	flew	flown
forget	forgetting	forgot	forgotten
freeze	freezing	froze	frozen
give	giving	gave	given
go	going	went	gone
grow	growing	grew	grown
know	knowing	knew	known
lay (to place)	laying	laid	laid
lie (to rest)	lying	lay	lain
ride	riding	rode	ridden
rise	rising	rose	risen
run	running	ran	run
see	seeing	saw	seen
shake	shaking	shook	shaken
sing	singing	sang	sung
sink	sinking	sank	sunk
sit	sitting	sat	sat
speak	speaking	spoke	spoken
spring	springing	sprang	sprung
steal	stealing	stole	stolen
swear	swearing	swore	sworn
swim	swimming	swam	swum
take	taking	took	taken
throw	throwing	threw	thrown
wear	wearing	wore	worn
write	writing	wrote	written

Some regular verbs give trouble because we analogize them with words having similar changes. Review this list of frequently misused regular verbs.

Present	Past and Past Participle	Present	Past and Past Participle
climb	climbed	pass	passed ("past" is a different word)
deal	dealt		
drag	dragged	pay	paid (Note the spelling)
drown	drowned	prove	proved
flow	flowed	raise	raised
have*	had	say	said
lie (prevaricate)	lied	sweep	swept
lose	lost	swing	swung
mean	meant	weep	wept

* Many forget and incorrectly write this "of": He must *of known* it.

Exercise

Ten of the following sentences contain verbs that do not conform to the rules of Standard Written English; five sentences are correct. Number your paper to correspond with the exercise and write OK if the verb is correct. If it is incorrect, write its correct form.

1. The Wyoming team hasn't been beat in the last two seasons.

2. The bread had risen until it overflowed the tins while Dad was mowing the lawn.

3. We haven't discovered yet who broke the vase, but we think the baby done it.

4. We had past the crossroads before Mother took out the map.

5. The play had only began when fire broke out in the dressing rooms.

6. The leaves would have fallen off if the plant had been given too little water.

7. Two pieces of the best set of china were broken when the dishwasher went sick last night.

8. When Felipe sunk the tying shot, the crowd went wild.

9. The drama club has not yet chose the girl to play Titania.

10. If Carl has seen the lake, you can be sure he has swum in it.

11. The unemployed should have something better to do than just setting around.

12. Costa hadn't ever rode a roller coaster before he came to Atlanta.

13. The earthquake did little damage to the house, but the family was somewhat shaken up.

14. In previous winters the family has always went to Arizona for a few weeks.

15. Anna Marie let out a yelp when the Siamese sprang onto her shoulder.

A Matter of Style: Numbers and Abbreviations

Each periodical and large publishing house has a **style sheet.** This contains consistent uses of elements in our language which are simply not agreed upon by everybody. Your style sheet, which will follow that of a great many publications, should include the following consistencies.

1. Use Arabic numbers for dates: April 7. In 1942.

right: Japan sneak-attacked on December 7, 1941.

wrong: Father was born in nineteen-sixteen.

2. Except as part of a title (Dr. E. A. Dobbs), **don't abbreviate.**

right: We live in Scarsdale, New York; and we came from Michigan.

wrong: He lives in R. I., but he prefers Mass.

3. Write out numbers that can be written in one or two words. Use figures for numbers taking more than two words.

right: Father was one of 150 conscripts from his canton.

wrong: It took 2 days to go to church, which was located 15 miles over the mountain.

ASSIGNMENT 2

Write Chapter 1 of your autobiography. It will deal with as many branches of your family tree as you can scale. Do the necessary research, making notes as you learn your facts. From your notes cull those ideas that seem essential to your purpose. After a rough outline, compose your rough draft. Revise it carefully, being sure to put into practice the material studied in the first two chapters of the text.

PRACTICE TEST II

This test covers errors noted on the Check Sheet for Chapters 1 and 2. Review the Check Sheets and then, without looking back, do the test. The teacher may want to check your work or to give you another test of the same type. Each error will count as three points, if anybody's counting.

I. Seven of the following sentences are incomplete, run on, or comma spliced. Rewrite each flawed sentence correctly.

1. An incident in my father's life that I still hear too much about.

2. He sailed from Hamburg when he was ten, the voyage took over a month.

3. As children, Mother and Father lived next door to each other; Mother used to beat him up at least once a week, he says.

4. Which is nothing to brag about, believe me.

5. In those days a man could get land free all he had to do was farm it for five years.

6. Father chose to do his homesteading in the Dakota territory, therefore, he had a long journey ahead of him.

7. By his time there were railroads as far west as Sioux City. But a long journey by horseback from there on.

8. Almost as soon as he had reached his land, he contracted malaria.

9. He had to write a letter to the nearest doctor who lived forty miles to the south in the letter he had to describe his symptoms.

10. Then the doctor would diagnose the symptoms, think of a prescription and send it to him by the next person going north.

II. Make the suggested changes in the following words, being sure that your result is spelled correctly. Place only the word on your paper.

1. Remove a letter from DESCENT and make the word an adverb that will fit correctly into the following sentence:

Yesterday she wore faded jeans, but for the interview today she is more ________ dressed.

2. Write the plural of ANCESTRY.

3. Make TRAVEL into its present perfect form to fit the following sentence:

I ________ ________ much since I was two years old.

4. Make an adjective or verb from QUARREL to fit the following sentence:

I was often ________ until I learned to respect the rights of others.

5. Consult the guide at the front of your dictionary and read about etymologies. Then look up the word MATERNAL and write the language from which it originates.

6. Do the same for AUTOBIOGRAPHY. How many words of that language make up the one English word?

III. Each of the following sentences has *one* error. Write the error and its correction on your paper.

1. For 21 days, my mother says, she lived on nothing but oysters and shrimp.

2. Dad is always giving up smoking, which amuses us because he never gets around to giving it up.

3. In New Orleans, La., I saw my first destructive flood.

4. My brother was born in Denmark, but he comes to this country two weeks later.

5. Our house in Conn. was larger than the one we had previously.

6. For four years he lived in Arkansas, then he moved to Alabama.

7. He saw that he has made the same mistake he made the previous day.

8. The brother who was in Vietnam, phoned Carla on her birthday.

9. Yes you are welcome to use our phone.

10. Mother lived an easygoing indolent life in the South before her marriage.

IV. For the following sentences choose the verb or verbs which make the most satisfactory tenses for the sentence. Write the verb on your paper.

1. We saw many new sights on this trip west, many that we never (saw, have seen, had seen) previously.

2. I do my homework between four and six every afternoon, a practice that I (follow, have followed, am following) since my seventh-grade experience.

3. I (have always been, am, had been) welcome at their house since my rescue of their pussycat.

4. Wilma (has traveled, traveled, had traveled) extensively before she went to Moscow.

5. Jack, in *Lord of the Flies,* cannot accept defeat; he (cried, cries, has cried) when he (lost, loses, has lost) the election.

6. My next-door neighbor is my model; he (had gone, has gone, goes) skiing every winter since he was ten.

7. Poetry was a subject I never enjoyed until I (had, have, have had) Miss Jacobsen in ninth grade.

A REINFORCEMENT TEST ON VERBS

Use this test as an open-book exercise, using a dictionary or English handbook to help you wherever necessary. On your paper, write the other three parts of the following verbs.

Present	Present Participle	Past	Past Participle
1. see	________	________	________
2. ________	crashing	________	________
3. ________	________	laid	________
4. ________	________	________	swung
5. do	________	________	________
6. ________	sitting	________	________
7. ________	________	implied	________
8. ________	________	________	felt
9. swim	________	________	________
10. ________	bidding	________	________
11. ________	________	referred	________
12. ________	________	________	written
13. run	________	________	________
14. ________	drinking	________	________
15. ________	________	spoke	________
16. ________	________	________	taken
17. begin	________	________	________
18. ________	coming	________	________
19. ________	________	rang	________
20. ________	________	________	thrown

3

Arrivals–It Had to Be Me

Naturally, the most interesting person in your family is you. In the third chapter of your autobiography it is time to think about your arrival. If you haven't yet had your parents meet, your first paragraph of this chapter is all but foreordained. Once you appear, the main subject of your opus shifts to you—the hero or heroine of your book.

Your research for this chapter should take you first to your parents. Cajole them into bringing out your baby books, photograph albums, tapes, and home movies if they have them. Ask them about times you frightened them, made them laugh, brought them to tears, astonished them with your precocity. Get all the information you can find about yourself before your own memories began to form.

This chapter also gives you the chance to bring your family tree up to date. Here is the place to record the arrival of brothers and sisters and to talk a little about your relations with them. Here also you can record the family pets, often an integral part of a family. Record the happiness they have brought you, of course; but remember also that they have probably been some trouble and that their departures have caused you sadness.

Finally, this chapter gives you a chance to bring your family from the place where you arrived to the place you live now. If yours has been a roving family, you will be able to make comparisons about your opinions of the places you have lived, the fun or sadness you had while there, your reactions to leaving for a new location.

Use this chapter as a kind of bridge in your autobiography. From now on what you will write will be primarily concerned with you and your development. Here is the place to end those writings which have been largely dependent upon your research and interviews and to begin those that concern your own recollections.

Getting Started

Get together with a group of classmates again to prepare interview sheets. This time these sheets will be concerned not only with questions you will ask others but with questions you ask yourselves. Begin by sharing your reading experiences. What has each of you found in your outside reading that has given you ideas for your own work? Continue as you did for the previous chapter. Put down as many ideas as you can. Then discuss the ideas among yourselves. The questions listed below are only starters; enlarge upon them.

James Baldwin, self-portrait.

1. Where was I born and when? Were there any unusual circumstances associated with my birth? What sort of a baby was I? How did I behave at parties? At family get-togethers? When meeting strangers? When did I first creep, walk, talk, cut my teeth?

2. Who are the other members of my family? How did I react to them? How did they react to me? What pets do I consider almost like brothers or sisters?

3. Where are the various places I have lived? How much time did I spend in each? What are my fondest memories or greatest loathings as I recall them?

4. What about my present home? What do I like most about it? How does it compare with others I remember? How do the neighbors compare with others I have known? What is my favorite part of this home?

5. How did my parents meet? Was it love at first sight? Have I listed adequately their names, history, and background? What did they think when they learned they were going to have a "me"?

6. What illustrations can I use for this chapter? Can I add color by putting in a map of family moves? What drawings, caricatures, or montages can I do? Of my present room? Of an early much-loved hiding place? What photographs are available at home? Do I need to make copies of some of them?

All the sample writings that follow were actually written by students. The only changes made are those of names.

From "**Freehand Sketch**": A First Paragraph

The person in question, Ralph Simons Donald, was born in the Orange Memorial Hospital, East Orange, New Jersey. The memorable date was March 5, 1963. It was Sunday, and all Sunday babies are supposed to lead a charmed life, or something to that effect. Unfortunately, I have not reaped the reward of this superstition. In some ways I have been very fortunate, however.

From "**Horace Was Right**": A Paragraph on Reaction to Places

When we lived in Providence, my family used to spend its summer vacations at the beach, usually in Cape Cod. As Kansas City had practically no lakes or ponds, our swimming there was confined to pools. As a result, the entire family took up golf in a big way, and we all continue to enjoy it. Since returning east, we are getting our share of the ocean again. Another thing I noticed that was different was the climate. In Kansas City it becomes a lot hotter in the summer, and a little colder in winter than it does here. If I could take the ocean and climate back to Kansas City, I would like it; but it would be still better to bring Kansas City to the East. I like Kansas City so much that I think Horace Greeley was right when he said, "Go West, young man, go West!"

From "**Anything Can Happen**": A Paragraph Combining Parental Recall

Because I was born on a Sunday, my brother nicknamed me "Tiny Tim." Don't get the wrong impression, though; the name made fun of my weight. I tipped the scales at eight pounds and one ounce at birth. I'm afraid my brother gave me the wrong nickname because all I did was lie there and whine until I would hear someone say, "Oh, what a cute baby!" Then I'd sit and admire myself. Mother says there was little to admire. She claims she kept a mosquito netting over my carriage. Why? I was so homely that, whenever anyone wanted to see me, she would make up an excuse and say I was sleeping or something. Furthermore, it wasn't until I was a month old that I started to wear blue clothes instead of pink. You see, after that obnoxious thing born before me, my brother, Mother hoped that a girl would be different and just knew that God would not be so mean as to give her another boy, especially one like me. Therefore, pink clothes were made for the expected girl, and when I came I had to suffer.

From "**Born Yesterday**": A Paragraph About Sibling Relationships

The first addition was that of my brother, John Stewart Fosdick II, who was born August 26, 1965, in New York City. Johnny has teased, tormented, plagued, bothered, and bewildered—but not bewitched—me ever since I was old enough to know what it was all about. He played a game with me called "got you last" that thoroughly annoyed me. Sometimes I tried to ignore him when he started hitting me; but if he persisted, I'd blow up and there would be consequences for us both. Mother kept telling me that he would grow out of it, but I'm afraid she was wrong.

From "**First Glimpse**": A Paragraph About a Favorite Home

Red Pine was a poultry farm with endless chicken houses, store rooms, ranges, and garages. There were men coming from the buildings and men going into buildings, men loading grain onto trucks, men going to the egg room with a basket of eggs under each arm, and men loading chickens onto trucks. But, best of all, was our house. Although there were cottages where the hired men lived, our house stood out. It was huge and rambling with four chimneys and three porches. There were eighteen rooms, but somehow the house never seemed empty or lonely. The bedrooms were off the library while the guest rooms were upstairs over the kitchen and the living room. The rooms over the kitchen were pine-paneled, and the rooms above the living room were done in different shades. Mom papered them as a hobby, and they always looked bright and cheerful. Our living room was large and inviting. Chairs of every description stood in all parts of the room—Dad's easy chair by the radio and Mom's rocker by the piano. Over the couch were hung my great-great-grandparents, staring coldly from their massive gold frames and watching our every move.

From "**Little Scatterbrain**": An Anecdote

I have no recollection of Eastchester, but I'm afraid my family does. One evening in the middle of dinner, an unexpected visitor arrived. The guest was my aunt's skiing instructor, a tall, proud German. The only polite thing to do was to invite him to stay to dinner. With horror my grandmother remembered the lone turkey leg left on the platter. She rushed into the dining room, and there I sat happily contemplating the drumstick in my hand. My grandmother rushed to its rescue; and while we wrestled for the leg, the rest of the family tried to keep the instructor's attention in the living room. I pulled myself up to the full stature of my one and one-half years and fought for what was rightfully mine. The rest of the family, seeing what was happening, abandoned their confused guest; and finally the five of them got the turkey leg away from me. By this time, though, it was in a thoroughly inedible condition. Our guest finally went home hungry and very much disillusioned about the happy, tranquil American households one hears about.

The War Years

All my life has been spent in the midst of war or war talk. I was born September 8, 1935. Franklin Roosevelt was President. Mussolini's troops were getting ready to grab Ethiopia. The nurses and doctors of the Massachusetts Women's Hospital in Boston, my birthplace, were full of war predictions because of the large proportion of boy babies born that fall.

When I was five months old, my family—consisting only of my father and mother and me—moved to Troy, New York. We lived there only three months and then moved to Eastchester. Never have I lived such a life! We had many relatives around there who had a lot of leisure time, and I was the first baby in my generation. They took me driving, they bought me ice cream, they bought me toys, they took my picture. As soon as I was old enough to go anywhere, they took me everywhere. Besides my relatives, we were surrounded by babyless neighbors who took care of my entertainment when my relatives were busy at something else. I had a dandy time!

I made news when I was still in the crawling stage. We owned a white English bulldog, named Lovely. One day as she was lying asleep with her long pink tongue hanging out, I crawled up to her, examined her tongue for a second or so, then bit it. She snarled terribly and snapped at me viciously. She gave me a dirty look, but didn't bite me; so it remained "man bites dog."

When I was three years old, I contracted a double mastoid. I had to be operated on and was in the hospital almost a month. While I was recuperating, my mother took me to visit my Grandmother English in Gulfport, Mississippi. That was a very nice place, and I can still remember certain things about it. There was a broad beach backed by a high sea wall built in huge steps. My mother and my aunt used to sit on the beach while I would crawl around on the sea wall.

The next spring we moved to Edgemont. That was in 1939. The war was coming closer. Hitler and his goosesteppers were spreading over Europe. In the other hemisphere, Japan had almost complete rule over China. In 1940, I entered kindergarten and made many new friends. My closest friend was Alvin Day. He lives in Muncie, Indiana, now and I might not know him if I saw him, but for many years we did everything together. That winter my sister Eloise was born.

On December 7, 1941, Pearl Harbor was bombed. War was declared. I have vivid memories of the surprise and sorrow and excitement of that day. During the war, like most of the boys my age, I played war games all the time. All our toys were war toys: rifles, soldiers, tanks, even gas masks. All the boys in the neighborhood from the age of seven to fourteen were divided into two armies. We had battles and skirmishes.

My mother tired of this so she made me go into business. Our yard had seven old apple trees which really gave apples. The ground was always covered with fallen apples. If they stayed, they rotted. Then bees would come and it would all be pretty much of a mess. My mother convinced me that, since I had to pick them up, I might as well sell them. Every morning I would gather pails of apples and peddle them around the neighborhood. With the money I made I would go to the movies in the afternoon. I have always loved movies. I was only seven years old, but I would ride my bike from Evandale Road to the Scarsdale Theater every time the bill changed. I became a great friend of the ticket taker. The only rules were that I could see a show only once and that I had to sit next to the exit. That summer was a lot of fun. I kept the yard clean and at the same time felt very grown up.

In May, 1944, we moved to River Road, where we live now. This meant that I had to change from Edgemont to Greenacres School. Changing schools is always hard. You have to make a place for yourself and get used to all the new customs. In the fall of that year my second sister, Emelie, was born. The tide of the war had changed. Victory was coming, but when?

One warm spring day when I was in fifth grade, I was having a game of catch in our driveway with Maury Stein when we heard that President Roosevelt had died. Now Truman was President. It seems only a short time later that we were driving up and down Main Street in White Plains with a yelling mob, crazy with joy because the war was over.

An early type of pen. New York Public Library Picture Collection.

CHECK SHEET FOR CHAPTER 3

Analysis of Samples

1. None of the samples included information about the writers' parents. Where do you suppose they placed that information?

2. "Horace Was Right" makes a comparison between two places. How does the writer organize the piece so that he can talk about two places at the same time?

3. Which of the paragraphs seem to have the most personal style? State your reasons.

4. "First Glimpse" deals mainly with description. How does the writer organize the details to make the paragraph easy to follow?

5. In the complete chapter, what device does the writer use to unify the whole?

6. Is each paragraph in the complete chapter a separate unit? How does the writer manage to make each paragraph relate to the one preceding? The one following?

Spelling

1. acquaint, acquaintance
2. a lot (How does this word differ from *allot?*)
3. definite (Write its adverb form)
4. dependent (What is the word meaning NOT dependent?)
5. fourth (What is a homonym for this word?)
6. kindergarten
7. nearby
8. neighbor, neighborhood
9. occur, occurred (Where have we met this type of spelling change before?)
10. precocious (How many other forms of this word can you find in the dictionary?)
11. separate (Write its adverb and noun forms)
12. sibling
13. sophomore (What does the adjective form of this word mean?)
14. stepmother, stepfather

Questions for Group Consideration

1. What is the difference in meaning between these two sentences?

- **a.** My sister, who has collected snakes since she was five, seems strange to some.
- **b.** My sister who has collected snakes since she was five seems strange to some.

2. Match these sentences with the correct illustration.

- **a.** The old oak tree which is just outside my bedroom window was struck by lightning.
- **b.** The old oak tree, which is just outside my bedroom window, was struck by lightning.

3. Does either of these sentences need further punctuation?

- **a.** His sister Eileen drove him to the airport.
- **b.** Her brother the one now in Harvard is working in Washington this summer.

4. Which sentence has the better punctuation?

- **a.** Harry Truman Junior High (a monstrous factory of a building) confused me.
- **b.** Harry Truman Junior High, a monstrous factory of a building, confused me.

5. Which of these sentences needs further punctuation? Where?

- **a.** The rope hanging over the creek had a rubber tire attached to it.
- **b.** On it we would play for hours swinging happily above the often stagnant water.

6. Which of the following is a clause? What is necessary to create a clause?

- **a.** one of those people with a most unfortunate face
- **b.** who had a most unfortunate face

7. Which of the following is a phrase? What is the difference between a clause and a phrase?

- **a.** over the river and through the woods to Grandfather's house we go
- **b.** over the river and through the woods to Grandmother's house

8. Which of the following are sentences? What is the difference between a sentence and a clause?

- **a.** who wanted to use my pen?
- **b.** who wanted to use my pen.
- **c.** the person who wanted to use my pen may now have it.

9. How many clauses are in each of the following sentences?

- **a.** For Christmas I received a copy of the book, *Elizabethan Plays.*
- **b.** It is a book that I don't intend to read for some time.
- **c.** Its contents, which are intended for college students, would surely bore me to death.
- **d.** I've put it on my book shelf, hoping to be able to understand it within another year or so.

10. Which of the following sentences is written correctly?

- **a.** We arranged to meet at the Jone's house.
- **b.** We arranged to meet at the Joneses' house.
- **c.** We arranged to meet at the Jones'es house.

11. How would you punctuate the following sentences?

- **a.** Swimming has been of course the sport I have been truest to.
- **b.** Eileen had also logged seventeen rare birds in her book.
- **c.** The sisters had agreed in addition that neither would log the same rare bird.

12. What words can be deleted from the following sentences without changing the meaning?

- **a.** Algebra is very definitely on this particular list.
- **b.** Our neighbor is so old he is really antique.
- **c.** My brother had a hard time climbing up those stairs.
- **d.** We found mornings at camp to be very, very dull.

More About Commas: Rules 9, 10, 11, 12

Our previous comma rules have dealt with parts of the sentence that were, in the main, separated from each other. The new rules, for the most part, deal with commas needed to set off parts within a sentence when they interrupt the main part of that sentence. Note how, in the previous two sentences and in this one, the commas have been used so that the reader can, in No. 1, quickly connect *were* with its mother verb, *separated;* in No. 2, the subject *rules* with its verb *deal.* In the sentence you have just read, what clarity do the commas give to the sentence?

9. Use commas to set off appositives and their modifiers.

An appositive is a word or expression placed beside another so that the second explains something about the first. Since an appositive provides extra information and is usually not essential for the sentence to make sense, it is set off by commas.

A Single Appositive:

S **APPOS** **V**
Miss Smith, the teacher, began each day with a reading from the Bible.

An Appositive with Modifiers:

S **APPOS**
Jill Dahlgren, the girl who had fasci-
V
nated me, will star in the play.

Note: Short appositives, especially names or words without which the sentence would make little sense, are not set off by commas:

S **APPOS** **V**
The poet T. S. Eliot wrote "The Hollow Men."

S **APPOS** **V**
The word *moose* is of American Indian origin.

S **APPOS** **V** **O**
My sister Eileen detests our brother-in-
APPOS
law Elmo.

10. Use commas to set off parenthetical expressions.

At the Beginning of a Sentence:

As it happens, that camp was really fun.

In the Middle of a Sentence:

She was, to tell the truth, not the best-looking teacher I've ever had.

At the End of a Sentence:

He did it well, in my opinion.

11. Use commas to set off nonrestrictive adjective clauses.

A nonrestrictive clause is one which further identifies some one or thing which has already been specifically identified. It is closely akin to an appositive except that, being a clause, it has a real or implied subject and a predicate. Don't worry about the many confusing possibilities of nonrestrictive clauses and restrictive ones, which are not set off. Remember, instead, the following, usually practical, times to punctuate. Most adjective clauses that follow proper nouns are nonrestrictive.

1. Nonrestrictive clauses are set off by commas. Clauses that follow people or things which have been definitely identified are nonrestrictive. Note the examples, all correct.

- **a.** We lived then in Boston, where I learned my alphabet.
- **b.** She was Prudence Whipple, who was to marry my grandfather.
- **c.** My only brother, who often bothers me, is my favorite enemy.
- **d.** Grandpa Prut, who made a million dollars before he was thirty, established the family fortune in 1865.

2. Restrictive clauses—clauses necessary to the meaning of the sentence—are not set off by commas. Clauses beginning with the word THAT are almost always restrictive. A sensible, general rule to follow is never to put a comma before the word THAT: *Huckleberry Finn* is a book that needs to be read more than once for full appreciation of Twain's satire.

3. Nonrestrictive clauses usually begin with *who* or *which*. The *which*-clause in the middle or at the end of the sentence nearly always needs commas to set it off: The Thanksgiving dinner, which took the whole day to prepare, was fit for royalty. The *who*-clause gives the greatest worry. If the *who*-clause is necessary to identify further the person or thing it follows, do not use commas (People who live in glass houses should not throw stones.) If the clause can be left out of the sentence without destroying the essential sense of the thought, it does need commas: The Tripodis, who were our neighbors, moved to Mt. Kisco last August.

12. Use commas to set off non-restrictive phrases.

Later we will learn more specifically about special kinds of nonrestrictive phrases and how to deal with them. For the moment, consider anything which interrupts the main flow of a sentence nonrestrictive and put commas on both sides of it if it is in the middle of the sentence; before it, if it comes at the end.

Plurals and the Apostrophe

With one exception the apostrophe is NEVER used to form a plural. The exception is the plurals of numbers (He learned his 9's) and letters (*Occur* has two *c*'s in it). The apostrophe is used to show possession and in English replaces the *of*-phrase used by many foreign languages. Instead of writing "the pen of my aunt," as you would do—not using English, of course—in Spanish, French, or German, we write "My aunt's pen."

One major difficulty students have with the apostrophe is in forming the plural of surnames. Actually, surnames form their plural as do most other nouns, by adding "s" or "es": Smith/Smiths, Tanner/Tanners, Lange/Langes. Surnames ending in "s" or "x" add "es": Myers/Myerses, Fox/Foxes, Williams/Williamses. But if we want these words to be used as adjectives, to be used in a possessive form before another noun, then we proceed by the following rules.

1. The apostrophe is used for contracted words to show that a letter has been omitted: *didn't, shouldn't, Hallowe'en o'clock.*

2. The apostrophe is used to make an adjective of a noun (when the first noun possesses the second one): Barbara's dress, men's club, ladies' room, Bill's pitching. *REMEMBER,* when using the apostrophe for possession:

- **a.** The first noun must possess a second noun. In almost all cases the two nouns will follow each other—day's time, Mary's book, boys' team, Father's hat, the mothers' luncheon.
- **b.** Before adding the apostrophe, figure out whether the first noun (the one to have the apostrophe) is

going to be singular or plural: the dress of *Barbara,* the club of the *men,* the room of the *ladies,* the house of the *Smiths.* This will be easy for those who are taking a foreign language. The ′ is to English what *de* is to French, for example. What is its equivalent in the language you are studying?

3. When you have spelled the possessive word, in either its singular or plural (Barbara dress, men club, ladies room, Smiths house), follow this formula:

a. If the possessive words does not end in "s," add an apostrophe and the "s": Barbara's dress, men's club.

b. If the word ends in "s," add only an apostrophe *after* the "s"; ladies' room, Smiths' house.

Possible exception: Words of one syllable ending in an "s" sound—Mr. Burns, Jess, boss—usually add an apostrophe and an "s" in the singular because of the sound we are used to hearing. Mr. Burns's pipe, Jess's grade, my boss's tyranny. Notice how hard it would be to say "Smiths's."

Problems in Usage

1. Do not use redundant expressions: that is, do not repeat the same ideas with several sets of words. Cut out words and phrases that are not vital to your sentence. What is redundant in the following sentences?

a. For ten years Dad has commuted back and forth between New York and Wall Street.

b. Mother preferred antique furniture from old periods in history; Dad wanted something in a contemporary, modern style.

c. My sister is highly intelligent and knows a lot; she is also curious and always wants to find out about everything.

2. When the word "way" means a measure of distance, use only the singular form—"way."

wrong: We live a little ways up the street.

right: We live a little way up the street.

3. The doctor operates ON you; you graduate FROM school.

wrong: I was operated at six o'clock.

wrong: She graduated eighth grade in 1949.

right: I was operated on at six o'clock.

right: She graduated from eighth grade in 1949.

OR

She was graduated from eighth grade in 1949.

4. *Seek synonyms for GOT: learn to avoid it in formal writing.* It isn't bad, but it's monotonous, unimaginative, and sloppy —and that's often as bad as being bad. Seek the exciting verb that conveys the meaning you want.

I got wet.
better: The rain drenched me.

I had gotten sick.
better: I had pneumonia.

He got punished.
better: His parents punished him.

ASSIGNMENT 3

Write Chapter 2 of your autobiography. It will deal with your arrival, what you have been told of your earliest days, and your first recollections. Don't forget the necessary steps of research, selecting from your notes to make a rough outline, your first draft, and a careful revision before your final copy. Remember, also, to put into practice all the rules you have studied thus far. In this chapter, you will probably find it more convenient to write in the first person.

PRACTICE TEST III

Review the Check Sheets and then, without looking back, do the test. The teacher may want to check your work or to give you another test of the same sort. Each error will count as 2½ points, if anybody's counting.

I. The capitalized words in the following sentences have certain letters omitted. Fill in the correct letter to make the word appear in its correct spelling. Write only the word on your paper.

1. While I was still in KINDERGAR_EN, my sister was already

2. a SOPH_MORE in high school.

3. It then O__U__ED to me that our houses were

4. S_P_R_TED only by a tiny picket fence.

5. One of my ANCEST_RS was involved in a troublesome

6. F__D with a family that had just arrived in his

7. N__GHBORHOOD.

8. Our family is of Scotch-Irish DE__ENT.

II. Put the necessary apostrophes into the following. There will be ten. Write only the apostrophized word on your paper.

Todays paper says that Jacks arm will be in readiness for Fridays game. Jacks and Marks arms provide the pitching for our schools baseball team. In almost everyones opinion these boys are the mainstays of the team. Some mens teams dont have pitchers with the ability of these boys. Our schools lucky to have boys with ability like theirs.

III. Punctuate the following sentences. Some may need no punctuation at all. Write only the sentences that need punctuation.

1. My only sister whom we call the Tyrant was born ten years after me.

2. The maple tree that I had the tree house in was blown down in last year's hurricane.

3. Pine Grove which was a lovely picnic woods when I lived near there is now a huge housing development.

4. We often went to see Grandma Lyttle who lived in the very worst section of town.

5. It was in South Dakota that I learned to drive because then there were no laws requiring a license.

6. Soon I was only enjoying recess the time when I would be rid of the sight of that teacher's aide.

7. There has never been to the best of my knowledge a time when our family has had a serious quarrel.

8. Then I sat down and began to read *Catcher in the Rye* by J. D. Salinger.

9. "When the time came for you to be born" my mother told me "your father decided to be with me in the delivery room"

10. The house in which I was born and it is still standing in the less pretentious part of Baton Rouge had only four rooms.

IV. Rewrite four of the following groups of words that would be marked IS, RS, or CS. One needs no correction.

1. Nothing further in his life that mattered so much to him.

2. Which is to say, I was rapidly and severely spanked.

3. A spot in the woods across the river from our farm, and it was our favorite hideaway.

4. Whatever you hear, it's best to check the truth before you believe it.

5. It was a long way from Terre Haute to Denver, indeed I thought we would never get there.

V. Each of the following sentences has one error or a bad choice of words. Write on your paper the correction or improvement after the word or words which need changing.

1. Having graduated kindergarten, I felt I had already completed my education.

2. I had gotten so many toys from my grandfather that I filled up the playroom.

3. Donna sometimes cheated but got caught so many times that she has gone straight.

4. A little ways up the block lived Norbert the poodle.

5. I was told that there were twenty-two boys I am always playing with before I have gone to school.

6. After living in Utah, we moved to Calif., a state which was very different.

7. My uncle can trace his ancestry to Miles Standish, which means that we can too.

Early Lessons

The next few chapters will deal mainly with your own memories up to the present. The selections that follow deal with the childhood that others remembered. The opening poem speaks of memories as "the movie of the mind." The first prose selection covers the memories of a Puerto Rican from the time he was small to his running away from home at eleven. The next is from the pen of a highly educated man who, as a boy, detested school. It is followed by a famous writer's reminiscences of the first time she defied conformity. The selections end with a fictional account of an African's escape from a domineering father. After you have finished reading the pieces, you will be asked to review the movie of your mind before selecting and setting down your own memories.

NANCY SULLIVAN (1930–   ) teaches English at Rhode Island College and polishes most of her poetry during summers away from school. What single metaphor unites her poem?

To Remember

NANCY SULLIVAN

We travel to the memory of it.
Events in the movie of the mind
Happen in rapid scenes,
In splendid revivals
Time over time,
Cranking the brain's endless reels to find

The Moment more coveted each repetition.
We travel to the memory of it.
From the theatre of the actual night
Or morning later, we pluck at rarer sights
And plunder. Whatever happened happens after.
We travel to the memory of it.

"When I was about eleven years old and still in the first grade, I ran away for the first time."

Roberto is the fictional name given by the socio-anthropologist OSCAR LEWIS (1914–1970) to one of the Sanchez family living in the slums of Mexico City. Mr. Lewis and his assistants repeatedly interviewed and studied the family—mainly the father and his four children, one of whom is called Roberto. From his taped interviews Mr. Lewis put together one of the most highly acclaimed books of the century, *The Children of Sanchez.* In this incident Roberto talks about his childhood, his need for love, his lack of education, and his first frightening adventure. Notice how older persons are able to analyze feelings and occurrences that once baffled them. Some early happenings leave them feeling proud; others cause regret.

Roberto

OSCAR LEWIS

I started stealing things from my own house when I was small. I saw something I liked and swiped it without asking anybody's permission. Just like that. I began by stealing an egg. It wasn't that I was starving, see? because my mother fed us well. It was just for the fun of filching it, and sharing it with my friends in the courtyard, and feeling important.

I stole twenty *centavos* from my mother when I was just a little fellow, five or six, more or less. Twenty *centavos* at that time was like ten *pesos* today. My father gave us five *centavos* every day, but all my life I've always wanted more, and when I saw a twenty *centavo* piece on the cupboard, well, there wasn't anybody around and I thought I might as well take it. I bought some candy and it was my bad luck that they gave me a lot of change, all single *centavos.*

So I had a lot of money in my pocket, right? When I got home in the evening, they began to ask about the missing coin. I thought, "*Caramba!* as soon as they get the idea of fishing me they'll find the money and I'll get a licking I won't forget for ten years. I'd better go to the toilet."

The toilet, which was right inside the house, had only a half-door, so when I threw the *centavos* into the toilet bowl it made a hell of a big noise and they knew what I did. Even though I flushed the coins away forever, they knew. Now, wasn't that something? Like I said, I was a bad egg from the time I was born. So I got a real thrashing that day. My mother, my father, and my mother's mother, may she rest in peace, gave me my punishment so I wouldn't do it again.

My mother took good care of us. She was loving to me, but she loved Manuel the most. She rarely hit me, and I know she loved me a lot because she always took me with her wherever she went, me more than the others. She used to say, "Roberto, let's go and get the cake trimmings."

"All right, *mamá*, sure, let's go."

My mother and father usually got along well, except for one terrible quarrel which left a lasting impression on me. My father was hollering at my mother, may she rest in peace, and, well, he was pretty mad. My mother's mother and my aunt Guadalupe kept him from hitting her. His key ring fell on the floor during the fight and I grabbed it and ran out. It had a razor blade on it and since my father was very quick-tempered, I thought he might want to use it on my mother.

My aunt, my granny Pachita, and the servant, Sofía, all jumped in and held him off. When I came back to the house, the fight was over. My father took me with him to the Villa where he prayed to the Virgin. I saw him cry and I cried with him. Then he quieted down and bought me a *taco*.

Every year the Three Kings came on the sixth of January and left us toys in the flowerpot stand where my mother kept her favorite plants. But one sixth of January the Three Kings were unable to come to our poor house, and I felt I was the unluckiest child in the world. We children got up early, like all children do on that day, to look for our toys. We went looking in the flowerpot stand; then we looked in the brazier to see if the Kings left something for us in the ashes and charcoal. Unfortunately they didn't, so all that was left for us to do was to go out to the courtyard and watch our friends play with their toys. When they asked, "What did the Kings bring you?" Manuel and I said, "They didn't bring us anything."

It was the last sixth of January my mother spent with us before she died. After that I cried for years. . . .

I was about six when my mother died in my father's arms early one morning. Her death was a shock and a torment to me all my life, because I feel I was to blame. The day before she died, we all had gone to the Basilica with my aunt and my uncles, Alfredo and José. We were very happy. My blessed mother was always celebrating our Saint's Day and we ate pork and stuff like that, which you know are not good for you. They bring on attacks, and my mother came down with an attack on account of me.

Actually, what happened was that later that day she asked me to bring the bird cages down from the roof. My mother was very fond of birds, understand? She kept the walls covered with bird cages, just because she loved the little creatures. So I climbed on the roof and some dirt dropped over to our neighbor's side and the woman there began to throw water on me.

"You brat, why don't you watch what you're doing?"

My mother ran out to defend me and had an argument with the neighbor. If she hadn't had the argument, my *mamá* would not have died. Anyway, whether I feel guilty or not, that's what happened. . . .

I missed my mother then, and I still miss her. Since her death I felt I could never be happy again. Some people feel relieved when they talk about their troubles, but I've told this to many people and it has never helped. I feel calm only when I run away, when I go off as a vagabond, when I am alone in the country, or up in the mountains. I believe if my mother were still alive I'd be very different. Or perhaps I'd be worse.

When my mother died, my grandmother was a second mother to me. I followed her around at the time. I called her little grandmother with the same love that I had called my mother, *mamá*. She was always good to us, but was very strict and stern in character. After all, she was old and had been brought up in the old style. They were more upright in everything.

She came to live with us and took good care of us. She sold cake crumbs in the plaza and I used to visit her all the time. . . .

Manuel never wanted to go with her to buy the cake crumbs or the bread. I was the one who liked to go with her. I don't know why, I was only a kid, but I felt that if I went along with her early in the morning, nothing could possibly happen to her, and thank God, we never came to any harm. One time Manuel went with us and he made my grandmother very angry. A vendor was selling sugared crab apples on a stick, shouting, "*Tejocotes, tejocotes* one *centavo*." Manuel, who was always teasing my grandmother, began to yell, "Grandmothers, one *centavo* . . . a *centavo* a grandmother . . ." Well, she scolded him and tried to grab him, but, of course, she could never catch him. He was a fast runner. He was only fooling, but he made her cry that time, and it hurt me very much.

We were living on Cuba Street at the time, yes, on Cuba Street, because my *papá* had just gotten to know Elena, and my grandmother left our house and went to live with my aunt Guadalupe. I felt even more lonely and really missed my mother then, because as long as my grandmother was there, I didn't feel as though my mother was gone.

When Elena came to be my stepmother I went to my granny Pachita to complain, telling her Elena this and Elena that. My grandmother was my crying towel in those days. I really unburdened myself with her. I even stole the plants and, well, I didn't steal them, they were my mother's and I didn't want Elena to touch them, so I would bring them to my grandmother or to my aunt. But I lost my poor little grandmother too, for she died soon after.

From the beginning, my stepmother didn't like me and I didn't like her. We did not get along very well, my young stepmother and I. For me there was only one mother in all the world, and even though a hundred others came along and wanted to act like my mother, it was not the same thing. Besides, I had learned from my friends that stepmothers were bad.

Elena was about eighteen years old, I think, or less. Anyway, she was too young and lacked experience to take care of a widower with four children. She didn't know how to get us to obey her, especially me, for I was the wildest. If she had spoken to me nicely, I would have been putty in her hands, but she always wanted to control me, to order me around, to dominate my life. Ever since I was small, I didn't like to have anyone but my mother or father order me around. If Elena laid a hand on me I would fight back. I always defended myself physically, I never knew how to defend myself with words. . . .

Although I haven't been able to show it, I not only love my father, I idolize him. I used to be his pride and joy when I was a kid. He liked me more than my brother, because when he'd go anywhere, he took me first. Many times just the two of us would go to the Basilica or to the movies or just take a walk in the evening. He still loves me with the same deep love, except that he doesn't show it any more because I don't deserve it.

My father was always very dry with us; he didn't talk much and we could never discuss our problems with him. I tried to be close to him. I wanted him to treat us in a special way, like other *papás,* to talk with us, to fuss over us. I liked so much the way we used to kiss his hand when he came home, or hug him. I felt my father understood me better in those days, although even then I missed a sign of affection, a word of encouragement.

Only twice in my life did my father speak intimately to me. He asked me, "Son, what troubles you? What is the matter? Tell me your troubles." I felt the most important and happy person in the world to hear him call me "son" so affectionately. Usually he called me Roberto or "you," and scolded me with bad words.

I have always disliked it when a son raises his voice to his father. Whenever my father scolded us or even just talked to us, it was impossible to look him in the eye, because he had a fierce expression. When I wanted to explain myself or at least clear up the truth a bit, he would not let me speak. "You, shut your mouth," and, "The only thing you are good for is this or that." I have never answered him back when he bawled me out. Instead I reproached myself. I told my brother and sisters that if my father was not good with us it was our fault. A father is sacred, especially mine. He is a good, fine person. There isn't another like him.

My father never beat us unless there was a good reason. He hit us with a broad belt he still wears. It was double thick and he'd hit us hard, especially me. He whacked us so much we sort of got hardened and didn't feel it any more, even though when he was angry he laid it on. Unfortunately for me, I had the [worst] habit. When I was being whipped, I'd knock my head against the wall or the wardrobe or something else. I kept whacking myself on the head, without knowing why.

Then, when I was about ten years old, my father took to using an electric cord, a very thick one, two meters long. He folded it in four parts and tied a knot in it. Wow! then we could feel the punishment. Every time he gave us a lash, it raised a welt. And my father wasn't the type who stopped with the one who did it, he went after both of us alike. He was impartial that way.

My father always urged me to go to school. How stupid I was not to have listened to him! I could never explain to myself why I didn't like school. When my classmates were sent to the blackboard they did their exercises quickly and were sure of themselves, but when I was called up, I felt a weight on my back because I knew everybody's eyes were on me. I thought they were whispering about me. I wanted to be way ahead of them and because of this I couldn't concentrate and it took me longer.

My mother, my aunt, or my grandmother would take me to school; sometimes they had to drag me there. I had a feeling of desperation about them leaving me alone with all those boys and girls. I felt inferior compared to so many people.

I was in the first grade for four years, not because I was stupid but because I played hooky. I did second grade in one year but when I passed to the third grade I attended only two or three months and never returned. Because of my friends and perhaps because I had so little liberty in my home, I enjoyed playing hooky and often went to Chapultepec Park. My father was notified when I missed school and would be waiting for me with the strap when I got home.

When we were children, my brother and I were closer to each other. He always protected me; for years Manuel was the handkerchief I dried my tears on. I used to be quite a coward and a crybaby, very *rajón*, as we say in Mexico, because if somebody would just shout at me, I'd start crying. I was afraid of the older boys. They'd threaten me and I'd cry; if anyone touched me, I'd scream. Right off I'd go running to my brother and he, poor fellow, had a lot of fighting to do on account of me.

I was in the third grade when Manuel graduated. I didn't have the courage to face all those boys without him and that is why I quit school.

I don't know why but I have always felt less than a nobody. Never in my whole life did I feel that there was anyone who paid attention to me. I have always been sneered at . . . belittled. I always wanted to be something in life, to do whatever I felt like and not have to take orders from anyone. I wanted to make a kite of my life and fly it in any field.

I wanted to be somebody in athletics, to be a great automobile driver or motorcyclist and compete in races. I have always wanted to be an aviator. One day my *papá* took me to the Lagunilla Market to buy me a cap. He said, "Which cap do you want?" I immediately asked for one with goggles, the kind aviators use.

When I played with my friends, the game was always aviation. To make it more real, I would lower my goggles and go up on the roof to run there like a plane. Or I would go running around the courtyard. I'd tie ropes to the water pipes and make a swing. That was my airplane and I really felt as if I were flying. That was one of my dreams. Whenever a plane flew by, even to this day, I keep watching it, longing to fly one some day.

My head was cracked open because I wanted to fly. My cousin Salvador, my aunt Guadalupe's son, may he rest in peace, was very playful and liked to fool around with us. One time I asked him to give me an airplane ride, that is, to swing me around and around. He always did whatever we wanted and so he took hold of my wrist and ankle and began to whirl me around. He suddenly lost control, and wham! I was dashed against the wall. My head was opened and when I came to, my *mamá* and *papá* and everybody were very alarmed. I was covered with blood but I didn't get scared. Actually, I enjoyed the fact that I was bleeding. It left a scar here on my head.

I am full of scars. I was always getting banged up. My head was opened other times, by falling off the roof or getting hit in stone fights, in wars, with my friends. Once I nearly lost an eye and I bled so much I thought I was going to die. I was running and fell on a sharp little toy shovel I was carrying. It went right into my left eye,

Background: Jay Lurie, Black Star. Insert: Nicholas Sapieha, Stock Boston.

but they took me to a doctor and I can still see out of it pretty well. The worst scar and one of the worst frights of my life was when I was bitten on the arm by a dog.

I learned to swim before my brother did even though he had gone often with his friends. I sort of hung around them hoping they would take me. I used to play hooky to go swimming in a pool not far from my house. There was an attendant there, José, whom I admired very much because he was a good swimmer and a nice guy. He was tall, strong and very husky. I don't mind telling you, he had some body. I wanted to be like him, nice, big, strong, and able to get some recognition. He used to talk to us about how he had been all over the Republic. . . .

When I played hooky, or when my father sent me to the Lagunilla Market to carry home the things he bought, I got into the habit of taking my little sister Marta with me. I have always liked her better than the others. I don't know whether it was because she had never known our mother or because she followed me wherever I went.

I taught Marta how to hitch rides by jumping on the bumpers of the trolley and holding tight. I used to take a little white dog from the Casa Grande too, because he followed me everywhere. There we would be, comfortable and happy, sticking like flies to the back of the trolley, with the dog running after us. Everybody would stop to look at us, people would put their heads out of the cars and buses to see the spectacle. I thought they were admiring us and I enjoyed it.

I liked to jump while the trolley went at full speed. Marta was very brave and learned to do it too. I not only risked my life, I risked hers, but she enjoyed it so much that it made quite an impression on me. I believe that's why I preferred her to Consuelo and Manuel. . . .

There was a big difference between Marta and Consuelo. Consuelo was more intelligent and persistent and liked to study. When she decided to do something she stuck to it. She never played with boys like Marta and was very reserved even with girls. She was nice and quiet, and very thin and frightened-looking.

When we were little, I got along well with Consuelo. Later, I was surprised at how my sister changed. She blew up at practically nothing and would create a tempest in a glass of water. She had an uneven temperament and seemed to me to be unsociable, secretive and irritable. She was very dry and didn't have much to do with people. But apart from that, she was good, all good.

The trouble between Consuelo and me began after my stepmother came to live with my father. I ate breakfast late, after the others, because, I don't know why but ever since I was little, I was ashamed to sit at the table without doing some chore. I always did work around the house, like lighting the charcoal fire, putting up the coffee, cleaning the bird cages and feeding the birds. No one told me to, but it pained me not to do something before I ate.

When we moved to the Casa Grande I was still quite small. Our first room there was very tiny and in terrible condition. The floor was full of holes, out of which came large rats. We would lose lots of things down those holes, money, marbles, combs. There was no electricity there then, until my father paid to have them connect it up. I liked being in the dark, or having only candlelight, but my father has always insisted on modern comforts. He liked a place to be roomy and very clean, and that is why we moved into a larger room. . . .

The law in the Casa Grande was . . . new tenant . . . new fight. To get into the gang, I had to pass through a number of tests. They put their best *gallos* or fighters on the new boy, to see if he was acceptable as a friend. Before, families moved in and out wholesale and there were lots of free-for-alls. Anyone who saw me in the courtyard would hit, pinch, or throw stones at me. If I was carrying something from the store, they would knock it down, and then I would get punished again at home. And so, as the amount of pain the human body can stand has its limit, so patience has its limits, and you find yourself obliged to fight.

One day I was walking by and there in the courtyard, waiting for me, were my brother and the four Ramírez boys. They were waiting for that decisive bout. Manuel had felt obligated to propose me as a member of the gang. But I wasn't going to be their butt just because I was new. My brother said, "Come on, fight." Daniel was going to be the one to test me. I called out to Manuel, but it made him mad that I should be such a coward. "Don't be a slacker. Defend yourself. I won't be fighting for you all your life."

Then they threw Jorge Ramírez at me, and they said, "Mix it up with him or we'll beat . . . you." So, whether I wanted to or not, because I was so . . . afraid of those guys, Jorge lasted two or three punches and went away crying. I drew blood. After that I fought Hermilio and Daniel . . . all good friends . . . as these were friendly fights, even though they seemed very real. I fought every one of them until I got to the main *gallo,* and beat him. I figured that was it, but neighbors kept moving in and I had to test them, to make them come into our circle. If they didn't, they were led a miserable life.

I began to like fighting. I didn't go complaining when they hit me, but would tangle with anybody immediately. Thus, I relieved my brother of the responsibility of having to fight for me. Actually, I never wanted to fight with anybody, but they kept looking for it. I had to defend myself and continued to do so all my life. . . .

When I was about eleven years old and still in the first grade, I ran away for the first time. I went to Veracruz with no more than the clothes on my back. I had no money to start out with. In those days, I never got to have a whole *peso* in my pocket all at once. I was limited to the five *centavos* my father would put under our pillows each morning before he went to work. On Sundays, we got twenty *centavos* each. But I usually spent my money right away and never had any in my pocket. On the road all the money I had was what one driver gave me.

My excuse for running away was that my father scolded me, but in reality, he always scolded me. The main reason was that I heard the boys talking about their adventures and I wanted to find out for myself. So I went to Veracruz. . . .

Right off the bat, I walked about twenty-three kilometers on the Mexico-Puebla highway. I have always liked the road; walking is my life. I've walked from Maltrata all the way along the railroad tracks as far as Orizaba (about seventy kilometers), just to see the vegetation and the fantastic view. The train would pass by and I could have jumped it (I don't have the old-fashioned bad habit of paying fares) but I preferred to walk along, admiring the scenery. I like to walk day and night, until I fall down with exhaustion. Then I go to sleep at the side of the highway. I can find grass anywhere and I'd cut a pile of it for my bed.

On the highway I felt happy and carefree. The problem of food didn't worry me. It was easy for me to go up to a shack and ask for work to do in exchange for a *taco*. Everybody gave me something to do, draw water from the well, chop wood, or any simple thing like that, and then they'd give me something to eat. Lots of people would tell me to sit down to eat first, and then they wouldn't let me do anything for them. They would fix up a pack of *tortillas* and salt and off I'd go. . . .

I traveled alone. I never wanted to take along friends because I have always preferred to go on my own. It is easier for me to get around by myself. I would ask people the way. By asking, you can get to Rome.

When I left home, I felt as though a great weight was lifted off me. To live with other people is hard. I never wanted to be tied to the family again. Sometimes I would ask for lodging for a night and I would stay with a family for a few days. But I wasn't comfortable because what I was looking for was to be free. And so I went, like the air, without difficulty, without direction, free . . . People would ask, "Why did you leave home?"

"Because my father scolded me. I have a stepmother." How I used

Elena as an excuse! I think that was why I was always making her mad, so that I could use her as a pretext for my lies. I had the luck of a canaille, for I achieved my ends for the moment. I call myself canaille, because I used another person to cover up my lies. What I have gone through is nothing, compared to what I deserve.

Like all adventurers, when I arrived in Veracruz, I asked the way to the sea. I reached it and sat on a navy dock all day looking at its vastness. The sea was beautiful, overpowering. I was there all day and saw how the tourists and the watchmen, who guard the docks and the cargoes, had nothing else to do but fish. When it was nightfall I wondered where I was going to sleep. That is the least problem there, because it is very hot. I decided to stay on one of the beaches, the best and softest one. At night the tide rises, so I stayed some distance from the sea.

The next day I felt like eating. I hadn't eaten anything the day before. I was so entranced, watching the sea and the fishing. I went over to the docks, because of the cargo boats anchored there. I saw a lot of people walking back and forth. They were a rough bunch, dark-skinned guys . . . . I approached the boat cook and asked if he didn't have any work for me in exchange for a *taco*. He felt sorry for me and it was because of that cook that I worked as a longshoreman for the first time in my life. I carried any little stuff and they would give me meals in return. We started work at eight and stopped at twelve, then began at twelve-thirty and quit at four-thirty. That was the way I got my food and lodging, for they gave me permission to sleep on the boat.

After a while, it didn't look like such a good setup for me. A boat would come in and I would stick to it like a leech. But the next day it would pull out and I would be homeless and without food again. I was always having to look for a place to eat and sleep. But I knew that if anybody died of hunger it was because he was lazy. If you helped the fishermen on the free beaches pull in their nets, you wouldn't get money but they'd give you a few fish. In one casting, they get all kinds of things, from sharks to turtles. I sold the fish, keeping one or two which I'd ask the fishermen's wives to cook for me.

I was willing to work at whatever came along, so I could eat. I never earned a copper working, they just gave me fruit, for the most part. I even ate wild greens and there were times when I didn't taste bread for two weeks. When I had nothing to eat, I would ask the watchmen to let me take a few pieces of coconut. When ships came in from Tabasco, or from places where they grew fruit, I had a feast day! . . .

About three months passed like this. The time came when I felt like going home. I thought of the family only once in a while, but when I did, I felt like getting back home as fast as I could. There were moments when I felt brave enough to leave, then I would lose heart. I never wrote home, because I didn't know how to write a letter and I didn't want them to know where I was. I imagined that if my *papá* found out he would come and beat me to death. That is what I thought, but I went home anyway.

The return trip was hard because I had to walk from Veracruz to Puebla. It took me eight or nine days. I walked day and night, as no . . . truck would pick me up. I took the Córdoba road and came to the police booth at the entrance of the city of Puebla. My shoes were all worn out, strong miner's boots that my father always bought for us. I asked the truck drivers for a lift, but they refused. Some of them made fun of me. I paid no attention to them but I felt lonely for the first time, alone as a feather flying through the air. I sat at the side of the road, crying.

Finally, the police stopped a truck and said, "Take care of this kid adventurer. He is headed for Mexico City." I got on and we arrived late at night, at the Merced Market, near the Zócalo, the central square at Mexico City. Imagine, it was my first time there. I had been to Veracruz but had never seen the Zócalo! When I crossed in front of the National Palace, I saw the great big clock in the Cathedral as it struck three. There I was, all alone in the plaza. I hurried home, knocked at the *vecindad* gate and the *porterà* let me in.

Outside our door I sat, wondering whether or not to go in. I expected a terrific beating. I started to knock, but sat down again. Then something strange occurred. I am not superstitious, but if you had seen what I have, you would consider me a superior being. Sitting there, at that hour, I saw someone dressed like a *charro*, a cowboy, come down from the roof near the water tank. He lit something, a cigar, I think, because the fire was so big. I kept staring and wondering what the man was looking for. Then the cigar fell to the ground and the man disappeared . . . just like that. I figured he must have been kidding around . . . but where did he go?

I have always liked danger and strong emotions and when there is something unfamiliar, I want to know more about it. So I climbed up to the water tank, way up to the top. I went to the little garden and to the bathhouse. Rumors had gone around the *vecindad* that these places were haunted. Well, if I were superstitious, I would be dead now, because as I went to the bathhouse I heard a tremendous noise, a crash, as though something had broken. I got panicky and ran back to our door and knocked. They called out, "Who is it?" and I said, "Me, *papá*."

My father opened the door immediately. "So you finally got back, son. Well, come on in." He was very nice. I thought he would meet me with a belt in his hand and give me the hiding of the ages. But he said to me, "Did you have any supper?" We had no kerosene stove then, just a charcoal brazier, so he got himself to work and lit a fire. He heated the beans and coffee and said, "Eat. When you are finished turn out the light." Then he went back to bed. As I knew he left for work early and that he was a light sleeper, I turned out the light and there I was eating in the dark. Then I went to sleep . . . and he hadn't scolded me or hit me or anything. . . .

Vocabulary

we looked in the *brazier* to see if the Kings left something for us in the ashes and charcoal . . . . . (64:30); I have never answered him back when he bawled me out. Instead I *reproached* myself . . . . . (67:7); he went after both of us alike. He was *impartial* that way . . . . . (67:24); Never . . . did I feel that there was anyone who paid attention to me. I have always been sneered at . . . *belittled* . . . . (68:14); She blew up at practically nothing. . . . She had an uneven *temperament* . . . . . (70:37); How I used Elena as an excuse! I think that was why I was always making her mad, so that I could use her as a *pretext* for my lies. . . . . . . (73:3); I was so *entranced*, watching the sea and the fishing . . (73:17); A boat would come in and I would stick to it like a *leech* . . . . (73:29)

Study Questions

1. The strongest characterization in this selection is obviously that of Roberto, the fictional name of the man who spoke his story to Oscar Lewis, who then transcribed the tape into print. Make a list of as many of Roberto's traits as you can find. Then try to find whether Roberto feels that they are good or bad traits. Do you agree with his assessment of his traits?

2. A proverb states, "Spare the rod and spoil the child." It is one in which Roberto apparently believes, at least in part. In your own review of Roberto's experience with punishment, does the proverb seem apt or not?

3. Roberto's lack of formal education is probably in part responsible for his being able to recall tragic personal happenings with astonishing clarity and lack of sentimentalism. In the eleven years of his life covered by the selection, what tragic events have been part of his life?

4. Roberto is capable of making unusual metaphors. "I wanted to make a kite of my life and fly it in any field," he says. What other examples of his vivid metaphors can you find?

5. Roberto has a deep sense of what is right and what is wrong. List the rights and wrongs he believes in. What are his feelings when he violates one of his own rules of good conduct?

6. Elena the stepmother is certainly not one of Roberto's favorite people. What valid evidence does he give to support his reasons for disliking her?

7. In one place Roberto says that he idolizes his father. What evidence can you find to show that the son has modeled himself after his father? Is there any evidence that his behavior toward Elena or his running away is founded on his feelings toward his father?

8. Roberto says he dreamed of becoming an aviator. Knowing his background and family, what chances would you give him of achieving his goal? How seriously do you think he took his own dream?

9. Though formal education was not much a part of Roberto's life, he was a well experienced boy at eleven. What had he learned about life, and how had he learned it?

"In any and all its forms, the boy detested school, and the prejudice became deeper with years."

HENRY BROOKS ADAMS (1838–1918) had as his great-grandfather the second President of the United States, as his grandfather the sixth President, and as his father a man who had unsuccessfully aspired to the same office. Though his own ambitions never soared so high, Henry Adams was much influenced by the family heritage in his own distinguished career as diplomat and college professor. In this selection, writing about himself in the third person, he talks of the educational influences upon, if we dare use the word in this country, the aristocratic Bostonian in 1850. As you read the selection, ponder the influence your heritage has had upon your present thinking and may have upon your future.

"Boston" (1848-1854)

From *The Education of Henry Adams*

HENRY ADAMS

As the boy grew up to be ten or twelve years old, his father gave him a writing-table in one of the alcoves of his Boston library, and there, winter after winter, Henry worked over his Latin Grammar and listened to these four gentlemen discussing the course of anti-slavery politics. The discussions were always serious; the Free Soil Party took itself quite seriously; and they were habitual because Mr. Adams had undertaken to edit a newspaper as the organ of these gentlemen, who came to discuss its policy and expression. At the same time Mr. Adams was editing the "Works" of his grandfather John Adams, and made the boy read texts for proof-correction. In after years his father sometimes complained that, as a reader of *Novanglus and Massachusetts,* Henry had shown very little consciousness of punctuation, but the boy regarded this part of school life only as a warning, if he ever grew up to write dull discussions in the newspapers, to try to be dull in some different way from that of his great-grandfather. Yet the discussions in the *Boston Whig* were carried on in much the same style as those of John Adams and his opponent, and appealed to much the same society and the same habit of mind. The boy got as little education, fitting him for his own time, from the one as from the other, and he got no more from his contact with the gentlemen themselves who were all types of the past. . . .

The boy naturally learned only one lesson from his saturation in such air. He took for granted that this sort of world, more or less the same that had always existed in Boston and Massachusetts Bay, was the world which he was to fit. Had he known Europe he would have learned no better. The Paris of Louis Philippe, Guizot, and de Tocqueville, as well as the London of Robert Peel, Macaulay, and John Stuart Mill, were but varieties of the same upper-class *bourgeoisie* that felt instinctive cousinship with the Boston of Ticknor, Prescott, and Motley. Even the typical grumbler Carlyle, who cast doubts on the real capacity of the middle class, and who at times thought himself eccentric, found friendship and alliances in Boston—still more in Concord. The system had proved so successful that even Germany wanted to try it, and Italy yearned for it. England's middle-class government was the ideal of human progress. . . .

Viewed from Mount Vernon Street, the problem of life was as simple as it was classic. Politics offered no difficulties, for there the moral law was a sure guide. Social perfection was also sure, because human nature worked for Good, and three instruments were all she asked—Suffrage, Common Schools, and Press. On these points doubt was forbidden. Education was divine, and man needed only a correct knowledge of facts to reach perfection:

"Were half the power that fills the world with terror,
    Were half the wealth bestowed on camps and courts,
Given to redeem the human mind from error,
    There were no need of arsenals nor forts."

. . . Of all the conditions of his youth which afterwards puzzled the grown-up man, [the] disappearance of religion puzzled him most. The boy went to church twice every Sunday; he was taught to read his Bible, and he learned religious poetry by heart; he believed in a mild deism; he prayed; he went through all the forms; but neither to him nor to his brothers or sisters was religion real. Even the mild discipline of the Unitarian Church was so irksome that they all threw it off at the first possible moment, and never afterwards entered a church. The religious instinct had vanished, and could not be revived, although one made in later life many efforts to recover it. . . .

The children reached manhood without knowing religion, and with the certainty that dogma, metaphysics, and abstract philosophy were not worth knowing. So one-sided an education could have been possible in no other country or time, but it became, almost of necessity, the more literary and political. As the children grew up, they exaggerated the literary and the political interests. They joined in the dinner-table discussions and from childhood the boys were accustomed to hear, almost every day, table-talk as good as they were ever likely to hear again. The eldest child, Louisa, was one of the most sparkling creatures her brother met in a long and varied experience of bright women. The oldest son, John, was afterwards regarded as one of the best talkers in Boston society, and perhaps the most popular man in the State, though apt to be on the unpopular side. Palfrey and Dana could be entertaining when they pleased, and though Charles Sumner could hardly be called light in hand, he was willing to be amused, and smiled grandly from time to time; while Mr. Adams, who talked relatively little, was always a good listener, and laughed over a witticism till he choked.

By way of educating and amusing the children, Mr. Adams read much aloud, and was sure to read political literature, especially when it was satirical, like the speeches of Horace Mann and the "Epistles" of "Hosea Biglow," with great delight to the youth. So he read Longfellow and Tennyson as their poems appeared, but the children took possession of Dickens and Thackeray for themselves. Both were too modern for tastes founded on Pope and Dr. Johnson. The boy Henry soon became a desultory reader of every book he found readable, but these were commonly eighteenth-century historians because his father's library was full of them. In the want of positive instincts, he drifted into the mental indolence of history. So, too, he read shelves of eighteenth-century poetry, but when his father offered his own set of Wordsworth as a gift on condition of reading it through, he declined. Pope and Gray called for no mental effort; they were easy reading; but the boy was thirty years old before his education reached Wordsworth. . . .

Home influences alone never saved the New England boy from ruin, though sometimes they may have helped to ruin him; and the influences outside of home were negative. If school helped, it was only by reaction. The dislike of school was so strong as to be a positive gain. The passionate hatred of school methods was almost a method in itself. Yet the day-school of that time was respectable, and the boy had nothing to complain of. In fact, he never complained. He hated it because he was here with a crowd of other boys and compelled to

Henry Adams, Culver Pictures.

learn by memory a quantity of things that did not amuse him. His memory was slow, and the effort painful. For him to conceive that his memory could compete for school prizes with machines of two or three times its power, was to prove himself wanting not only in memory, but flagrantly in mind. He thought his mind a good enough machine, if it were given time to act, but it acted wrong if hurried. Schoolmasters never gave time.

In any and all its forms, the boy detested school, and the prejudice became deeper with years. He always reckoned his school days, from ten to sixteen years old, as time thrown away. Perhaps his needs turned out to be exceptional, but his existence was exceptional. Between 1850 and 1900 nearly every one's existence was exceptional. For success in the life imposed on him he needed, as afterwards appeared, the facile use of only four tools: Mathematics, French, German, and Spanish. With these, he could master in very short time any special branch of inquiry, and feel at home in any society. Latin and Greek, he could, with the help of the modern languages, learn more completely by the intelligent work of six weeks than in the six years he spent on them at school. These four tools were necessary to his success in life, but he never controlled any one of them.

Thus, at the outset, he was condemned to failure more or less complete in the life awaiting him, but not more so than his companions. Indeed, had his father kept the boy at home, and given him half an hour's direction every day, he would have done more for him than school ever could do for them. Of course, school-taught men and boys looked down on home-bred boys, and rather prided themselves on their own ignorance, but the man of sixty can generally see what he needed in life, and in Henry Adams's opinion it was not school.

Most school experience was bad. Boy associations at fifteen were worse than none. Boston at that time offered few healthy resources for boys or men. The bar-room and billiard-room were more familiar than parents knew. As a rule boys could skate and swim and were sent to dancing-school; they played a rudimentary game of baseball, football, and hockey; a few could sail a boat; still fewer had been out with a gun to shoot yellow-legs or a stray wild duck; one or two may have learned something of natural history if they came from the neighborhood of Concord; none could ride across country, or knew what shooting with dogs meant. Sports as a pursuit was unknown. Boat-racing came after 1850. For horse-racing, only the trotting-course existed. Of all pleasures, winter sleighing was still the gayest and most popular. From none of these amusements could the boy learn anything likely to be of use to him in the world. Books remained as in the eighteenth century, the source of life, and as they came out—Thackeray, Dickens, Bulwer, Tennyson, Macaulay, Carlyle, and the rest—they were devoured; but as far as happiness went, the happiest hours of the boy's education were passed in summer lying on a musty heap of Congressional Documents in the old farmhouse at Quincy, reading "Quentin Durward," "Ivanhoe," and "The Talisman," and raiding the garden at intervals for peaches and pears. On the whole he learned most then.

Vocabulary

his father gave him a writing-table in one of the *alcoves* of his Boston library . . . . . . (76:2); The boy naturally learned only one lesson from his *saturation* in such air . . . . . (77:8); The Paris of Louis Philippe . . . as well as the London school of Robert Peel . . . were but varieties of the same upper-class *bourgeoisie* . . . . (77:14); three instruments were all she asked—*Suffrage*, Common Schools, and Press . . . . (77:26); he learned religious poetry by heart; he believed in a mild *deism* . . . . (77:37); Even the mild discipline of the Unitarian Church was so *irksome* that they all threw it off at the first possible moment. . . (77:39); The children reached manhood without knowing religion, and with the certainty that *dogma*, metaphysics, and abstract philosophy were not worth knowing . . . . . (78:3); The boy Henry soon became a *desultory* reader of every book he found readable . . . . (78:27); In the want of positive instincts, he drifted into the mental *indolence* of history . . . . (78:30); For him to conceive that his memory could compete for school prizes with machines of two or three times its power, was to prove himself wanting not only in memory, but *flagrantly* in mind. . . . . . (80:5); For success in the life imposed on him he needed . . . the *facile* use of only four tools; Mathematics, French, German, and Spanish . . . . (80:14); they played a *rudimentary* game of baseball, football, and hockey . . . . (80:33); a *musty* heap of Congressional Documents in the old farmhouse . . . . . (81:4)

Study Questions

1. Which of the following do you think young Adams resented most?

a. His feeling that his education was little different from that of a boy of his culture a hundred years previous to his time

b. The smugness with which his class accepted the idea of the education they were getting

c. His feeling that he was receiving no spiritual guidance in religion

d. The methods used in the schools he attended

e. The curriculum he was expected to study in his schools

2. What do you find Adams accepting as the real education he received in his youth?

3. Reread carefully the third from the last paragraph, the one beginning "In any and all forms. . . ." Do you agree with all, part, or none of his statements? Be prepared to argue your case.

4. Of his brother, Henry writes that John was "perhaps the most popular man in the state, though apt to be on the unpopular side." How do you explain this apparent paradox?

5. Henry Adams writes about himself when he was approximately the same age as Roberto in the previous selection. How might he have profited from Roberto's education?

6. How many of Henry's charges against the education of his time do you find applicable to the education of your own time? Explain.

EMILY HAHN (1905–   ), like the narrator in the selection that follows, was born in St. Louis, Missouri. Like the narrator, also, she has a daughter Carola. After completing her education at the University of Wisconsin, Columbia, and Oxford, she became a writer and journalist. Eventually she traveled to China, where she taught English in college. In that land, when World War II broke out, she was one of the several Americans interned by the Japanese for the war's duration. She has written numerous books, many of them biographies, and many of her short stories have appeared in *The New Yorker* magazine, where the following selection was first published. It is a short story rather than straight autobiography, but except for eight paragraphs it reads like autobiography. Despite its humor, it centers upon a serious topic, the price one pays for not following the crowd. Studying its style may help you make your own serious writing wittier.

Be Not the First

EMILY HAHN

My little daughter, Carola, aged three and a half, was raising a considerable stink. "I wanna wear it!" she yelled, and jumped up and down, kicking at the floor in a rage. "I wanna wear my new dressing gown! I want to, Mommy!"

"Listen, darling," I said, "you can't wear your new dressing gown to school. You've got a lot of good, hard work to do at school. You've got to climb all over that nice progressive equipment, and a dressing gown would only be in your way. And there's finger painting. You've got to have perfect freedom for your creative instincts, and I don't have to tell *you* what that means, Carola. You know all about you and finger paint. Personally, I don't see eye to eye with the school on that, but never mind. Suffice it to say that you wouldn't want to wear your new dressing gown when you do finger painting. In short, Carola, you don't want to wear your nice new expensive dressing gown to school."

Carola jumped up and down with fresh abandon. "I do!" she said. "I *want* to!"

"Listen, darling," I said. "Let's start over again from a new angle. Maybe what you want to do isn't the point. Maybe *Mommy* doesn't want you to wear your new . . ."

All of a sudden it came over me, just like that, and I remembered my school in 1920. Of course, I was a good deal older than three and a half then. I was fifteen going on sixteen. I was what they still call young for my age—not boy-minded, and well padded with puppy fat. One's figure at fifteen didn't matter very much in St. Louis, but we moved to Chicago that year and plunged into a world of dizzy sophistication. Being fifteen in Chicago was a serious matter. But then, even thirteen, in Chicago, seemed to call for a degree of poise and experience that my kid sister, Dauphine, could not achieve overnight, and we talked about this bitterly whenever the rest of the family would listen to us, which was not often.

The family's emigration had been hardest on us, the two youngest children. We had to *live* there, whereas our older sisters, the lucky ones, would be away from home at various universities. We both hated Chicago and for a long time made only the most reluctant efforts to adjust ourselves. First of the difficulties was a puzzling row about schools. Back in St. Louis, nobody had any notions about education; you went to the neighborhood public school and that was that. In Washington School, the teachers had practically been old family retainers, because all six of us children had attended the school from kindergarten on. Now and then, a teacher would get us a little mixed up and would call me Helen, for example (Helen was the fourth), or Dorothy (the third), but that was only natural. Even my father did that occasionally; none of us ever dreamed of resenting it. The important point was that you went to public school. Everybody did. I suppose there were private schools in St. Louis; there must have been. But we thought of private schools only as places for children who had something the matter with them—feeblemindedness or divorced parents.

Therefore we were shocked, after our arrival in Chicago, by my eldest sister Rose's report on educational methods there. She had been asking around among her classmates at Smith. "The city schools are terrible, Isabel says," she announced. "Those children haven't got the right background, and incidentally the teaching isn't any good either. Isabel says we just simply can't send the kids anywhere but Francis Parker."

We all gasped. Mother said, "Francis Parker? Isn't that a *private* school?"

Rose turned pink and squared her shoulders. "This is a much bigger city than we've been used to, Mother," she began. "We'll have to readjust our ideas. We've got to remember that people of our class . . ."

Really, Rose should have known better. It wasn't as if she didn't know all about Mother's democratic principles and wasn't locked in grim battle with her most of the time on one point or another. Rose was a girl of her times, but Mother was ahead of hers. Mother was not a career woman only because career women had not yet been developed. She showed most of the earmarks of the species in its earliest phase—she wrote a paper once a month for her club, and every four years she objected, without fail, to my father's Presidential choice, arguing with him each evening at the dinner table for a full month before the election. She also took an intelligent and humane interest in such matters as fur trapping in Canada. As long as we girls lived at home, none of us was permitted to use fur or feathers on our clothing. However, aside from the Presidential elections, she didn't pay any attention to politics. That would have been going too far, even for a free-thinking female like Mother.

She had other convictions, strong ones. We girls were all going to have college educations or she would know the reason why. My brother's education was taken for granted. Mother was far more interested in seeing to it that her daughters were emancipated females, and this caused trouble between her and Rose. Rose didn't much care about being emancipated. Like Dauphine, she was more her father's girl, but Dauphine was easygoing and Rose wasn't.

Dad constantly frustrated Mother, not only by being unsympathetic but by not offering opposition. He didn't give her restless spirit the exercise it craved. He was a quiet man who loved to read. Mother, though she was a perfect lady and glad of it, just had to be arguing with somebody. She worked out some of her energy on our aunts. They usually considered Mother a harmless madcap, but sometimes they thought her downright dangerous—Rights for Animals, for Women, for Enslaved Peoples, Religious Tolerance. . . . The aunts were sorry for Dad and Rose, but I wasn't.

I thought Mother was just about perfect. It wasn't only that I agreed with her all the time, and burned to go out and save a few trapped fur-bearing animals myself; it was also that she had such excellent moral reasons for diving into battle, and had a hell of a good time doing it. Mother always did exactly what she wanted to do, but she always richly justified herself in advance. For example, there was her job before she married, which I loved to hear about. Mother had gone out and got herself a business training and worked in an office, long before most girls dared have such excitement in their lives. She had refused to stay home and cook; she had two sisters who could cook, she argued. And why had the headstrong girl done this, nearly breaking her poor old parents' hearts and dragging down their heads with the shame of it? Because women have the same right to earn a living as men have, that's why, and it was Mother's moral duty to demonstrate this. She hated housework, anyway. Deciding to marry Dad and to keep house must have been a struggle, but she was in love. That wasn't why she married him, of course. Mother married Dad because he was an orphan.

Mother approved highly of the democratic principles set forth in the Constitution. Now here was her own daughter talking about this class and that class, just as if she hadn't been brought up a good American. It was a shock to Mother, but it gave her a long-desired chance for a little legitimate excitement. She exploded, and they had one of their good old-fashioned arguments. At the end of it Rose retired to her bedroom and wept, while Mother, flushed with the pure emotion of the crusader, put on her hat and went out to enroll Dauphine and me in the nearest high school.

The only flaw in the setup was that Rose seemed to be quite correct in her opinion; the nearest high school was a pretty bad school.

Dauphine and I didn't suffer more than most other children from inadequate teachers and a poorly planned schedule, because there was something wrong in those days with the American high-school system in general, and we would probably have been just as bored and badly informed in any other institution. The real difficulty for us was social. We couldn't get the hang of this new crowd of schoolmates, and they didn't care so much for us, either. Some of the males looked like thugs. In time, I am sure, they became genuine professional thugs on a highly successful scale. They were the social leaders of the school. Their little group was exclusive and only the highest-ranking, most enviable people were admitted. They were the élite and we recognized their position at once.

It was the period just after the success of "The Sheik," when "This Side of Paradise" was a best-selling novel and people were dancing to the strains of "Dardanella." Our high-school men—one couldn't call them boys—shaved every day, and sported the lacquered hair and bell-bottomed trousers of the current John Held drawings. I suppose we called them parlor snakes. I'm not sure. Dauphine and I, wholesome little girls from St. Louis, thought them absolutely beautiful and just about as unattainable as gods. And they were indeed unattainable. We would have been more profitably employed in dreaming of and yearning after football stars and swimming-team champions. The high school had its quota of those, too, but they didn't have the glamour of the bad boys or their girls. Those girls! I wonder where they are now. I can make a shrewd guess. I don't know what their mothers were like, but I'm sure they didn't look any older or more sinful than their little daughters. The accepted costume for class attendance was a skimpy black satin dress, black silk stockings rolled to the knee, opera pumps, and a tight cloche hat, worn over a frizzy hairdo. The girls also went in for what we still knew as "paint," thick spread on their tough little faces.

I can't say honestly that Dauphine and I were shocked by them, because we were not. We were merely thrilled to death. We would go down to the corner candy store at twelve o'clock and buy our lunch there just because that was where the glamour boys and girls went. We listened eagerly to their talk as we munched hamburgers and dill pickles, wondering what the cryptic phrases meant. "Helen's some vamp, huh?" "You'd be surprised." "Oh, boy! No future, but what a past!" "Come awn, come awn, don't hang on to that canteen all day. I gotta rench my mouth."

Mother couldn't understand why we never brought any little friends home. "The house in St. Louis was always full of young people," she said wistfully. "What do these children do after school? I suppose they go and sit in the movies."

"Maybe," I said doubtfully. It was my private opinion that they were out cracking safes somewhere or rolling around on the floor of some opium den.

"Well, I don't approve of that," said Mother. "I'm suprised that you children aren't more sociable, though. We always wanted to know your friends. We want them to feel welcome to come in any time."

Dauphine finally put in a request, without much hope, for a black satin dress; she didn't get anywhere. So she and I went our unobtrusive ways in Chicago, skating in the park when the weather permitted and sighing after strange gods. Nobody at home realized how very strange they were.

When Mother saw an advertisement for knicker suits in the paper, she probably didn't realize what a delicious upset she was in for. Ostensibly, knickers for her two young daughters were just a good, practical idea. They seemed to settle the long-standing problem of how to dress us so that we could attend school and then go straight out to play rough games without ruining our clothes. Actually, it was a matter of deep calling to deep. Mother, in her young, office-going days, had created a mild scandal in St. Louis by wearing bloomers for bicycling, and she was hurt and puzzled that Dauphine and I scorned bloomers. The knickers, however, met with our approval. They looked just like the clothes little boys wore before they graduated to long trousers, and, as successors to the comfortable rompers we had worn in childhood, they seemed pretty good. In 1920, remember, slacks had not yet been invented, and nobody wore pajamas in public except as Oriental fancy dress.

We were completely innocent about it, all three of us. Mother went downtown and bought the knicker suits, and one morning Dauphine and I put them on and started out for school.

On our way to the streetcar line, it began to be apparent that the public was going to consider the costume startling. A man driving a delivery truck reined in his horse and asked us if we had not forgotten something. It took us a little while to catch on. Then we flounced off indignantly, blushing. A group of street urchins followed us, making loud remarks. By the time the streetcar came, we were suffering badly from jitters.

"Do you think maybe there's a law against it?" whispered Dauphine.

"Of course not, or Mother wouldn't have let us wear them," I said. "Why, they couldn't have sold them in the store. These crazy people!"

The other passengers in the streetcar took a lively interest in our appearance. We stared ahead of ourselves with grim and rigid dignity. "Don't you let them scare you," I counselled Dauphine. "I guess we've got a right to wear knickers if we want to."

Fortunately, a group of girls from school boarded the car a few stops along the line, and they broke the tension. They were squealingly enthusiastic about the innovation, making blithe, clearly insincere plans to convert their mothers to the idea. Though they weren't representatives of the bright young set, the support of anybody, however obscure and dull, meant a good deal just then. We clung to them with pathetic eagerness all the rest of the way.

By the end of that first morning, my sister and I had learned a lot. We had tasted the sweets as well as the bitterness of notoriety. There was now no doubt that the high school was aware of us. We knew what to expect from people approaching us in the narrow corridors. We became all too well acquainted with the first startled jump, the second glance, the amused stare, the craned head, the animated discussion between bystanders, as each of us made her lonely way from class to class. It might have been less painful if we had been able to go together.

Most of my teachers, timid by nature, took the easy way out and ignored my knickered legs. Only one of them, an elderly spinster soured by too many years of teaching history, spoke about the costume when I entered her room. "What, Emily, is that extraordinary outfit?" she demanded. "What do you call it?"

In a husky voice I told her what it was called and where it had been bought. I really thought at first that she must want a pair.

"Looks completely ridiculous," she said in hearty tones. "All you need is a red parasol for the finishing touch. Reminds me of one of those Africans the missionaries talk about. Tell your mother I said so."

"My mother likes knickers," I said. "She would like to wear them herself. She said she was sorry she's too old."

"Well, that settles it, of course," said the history teacher.

"Yes, Ma'am," I muttered, and buried my flaming face in a book. Neither Dauphine nor I had bargained on the teachers. We had never thought that teachers would have opinions about clothes.

There was a choice of two paths. We could give in and try to live down the knickers, or we could brazen it out by insisting on our rights and wearing the things again. On that first day two newspaper photographers lay in wait for us as we came off the school grounds. We should have gone over to the basketball field, for now was the moment to justify and vindicate those knickers by playing games with all the freedom and grace we were expected to feel. We didn't though. We made for home like scared rabbits.

"Are we going to tell Mother?" Dauphine asked on the streetcar.

"Tell her what?" I asked haughtily. "That a few fools looked twice at us? I guess she'd expect that, anyway. *She* wouldn't pay any attention to that."

"Oh," said Dauphine, and at her forlorn tone I looked sharply at her. "Then you're going to wear 'em tomorrow?" she asked.

"Aren't you?" I turned on her and she shrank back.

"I wanted to wear my pink dress," she faltered. "I never meant to stop skirts altogether. We've got a lot of dresses to wear out. . . . Well, all right. If you do, I guess I will, too."

The next day there was a piece in one of the evening papers, along with photographs. The Board of Education had refused to make any statement about knickers, and some enterprising reporter had tried to discover whether there was any ordinance on the subject of proper clothing for public-school students. He couldn't find any. There was only a vague city ruling about immodest attire.

Robin Forbes.

"Immodest?" cried Mother, her face lighting up with the familiar glow of battle. "Do they dare to call these suits immodest? Why, the girls are covered from head to foot with good, thick wool! When I see some of those skimpy little things, with their rolled stockings and their low necks, I'm very proud of our girls. Isn't that so?"

"Of course it's so," I said heartily. Dauphine did not reply, nor did my father, but then he wasn't listening.

Dauphine and I continued to wear our knickers to school. The excitement among the students soon died down, and the teachers managed to relax and pay attention to their jobs. A few girls in knicker suits were seen in the streets, and the newspapers worked up more and more interest in them. My Aunt Lillie made a trip from the suburbs to speak her mind to Mother about it. "I may be old-fashioned," she said, "but if the good Lord had meant girls to wear pants, they'd be born with 'em on."

Mr. Clarke, our principal, called an assembly one day, and, as usual, there was free speculation about its object. Mr. Clarke knew the authoritative value of the dark hint, and in the discharge of his duties he was always mysterious. I may be maligning him in saying his actions were the result of deliberate policy. They may have been the result of not quite knowing what to do next. In the *affaire des* knickers, for example, he was definitely up against it, because Mother had him on toast and we all knew it. Mr. Clarke had stuck his neck out; he had written her a letter signifying his disapproval of our costumes, and Mother was joyfully able to point out that his disapproval was purely private and personal. Besides, the newspapers had already made it clear that the Board of Education, upon due examination of its rights in the matter, had admitted that it couldn't expel Dauphine and me from class or dictate what we were to wear as long as we didn't come to school in a state suggesting nudity. Mr. Clarke didn't reply to the letter.

An assembly was a sort of emergency function in the auditorium, to which the entire school personnel (with the possible exception of the janitor) was peremptorily invited. In spite of the principal's cumbersome secrecy, I had a pretty good hunch that he intended to be pompous about knickers. It would be his only way to talk back to Mother.

Against Dauphine's protests, I dragged her down to the front row that afternoon and sat her next to me, directly below the rostrum. I was quite right in my hunch.

Mr. Clarke stood alone on the platform, a solid, stubby man with impressive thick white hair. After the rustling and whispering and the squeaking of folding seats had subsided, he still stood there in silence, solemn and awe-inspiring. He always started out that way, no matter what the occasion. He would lower his white head and stare at us fiercely, lips compressed and nostrils dilated, until our nerves were definitely strained. Then he would open his mouth and speak.

This day he was slow about opening his mouth, and from where I sat, bright-eyed and expectant in my knickers, I could detect a certain lack of assurance. Obviously, Mr. Clarke didn't quite know what he was going to say. At last he raised his head, placed his feet a little further apart, and declaimed, while avoiding our eyes.

"The immortal Shakespeare always has something pertinent to say," he began. "I cannot do better than to quote his deathless lines

> 'Be not the first by whom the new are tried,
> Nor yet the last to lay the old aside.'

I am grieved to tell you that our school's fair reputation has suffered. Owing to an ill-advised experiment made by two of our young women, who think themselves, no doubt, very modern. . . ."

Mr. Clarke loved to speak in a deep stern voice that could swell to a roar. On this occasion he let himself go, but he didn't really say anything in an entire half-hour except that knickers where immodest and that any girl wearing them rendered herself ludicrous and unwomanly. He did not, I marked with interest, forbid them. He didn't say anything that Dad would have to resent legally. He merely advised females against wearing pants, on the general grounds of morality, world civilization, and taste. Then he came to a stop, blew his nose, and started off the stage, with an avuncular wave of the hand to signify we could adjourn. An English teacher ran up the steps and whispered to him frantically. Mr. Clarke clapped his hands to call us back, and walked to the center of the platform.

"I have just been informed—that is, reminded," he said, "that it was not Shakespeare, as a matter of fact, who penned those immortal lines. It was Pope—Alexander Pope, Miss Jensen?" Miss Jensen, hovering offstage, nodded. "Yes," said Mr. Clarke, "it was Alexander Pope who wrote those words, as it happens. However, they are so wonderful that they might have been written by Shakespeare. And with that thought I will leave you."

"Well?" asked Dauphine as we walked out, last in the line of students. The others were looking back to see how we had taken it. My mouth was stiff from smiling carelessly.

"Well," I said, "what?"

"You wearing them tomorrow?" asked Dauphine.

"Sure," I said. "Aren't you?"

"Of course," she said savagely. "He doesn't give us any choice. Oh, dear, and I'm so tired of this color."

"Mine are wearing out," I said. There was a traitorous note in my voice, a note of hope.

"You don't want to wear your new dressing gown to school, Carola," I said, "and I'll tell you why."

"Why?" asked Carola.

"Because," I said, "the other children will laugh at you. Nobody wears dressing gowns to school. They'll *laugh* at you. Think of that! You wouldn't want the other children to laugh at you, would you, Carola?"

Silently my daughter put down the dressing gown she had been clutching to her breast, allowed me to put a dress on her, and trotted off to nursery school meek as a lamb.

Vocabulary

She also took an intelligent and *humane* interest in such matters as fur trapping in Canada . . . . (84:16); She had refused to stay home and cook; . . . And why had the *headstrong* girl done this . . . . . (85:6); it gave her a long-desired chance for a little *legitimate* excitement . . . . (85:18); Some of the males looked like *thugs*. . . (85: 32) ; We listened eagerly . . ., wondering what the *cryptic* phrases meant . . (86: 19) ; she and I went our *unobtrusive* ways in Chicago . . . . (86:34); wearing *bloomers* for bicycling . . . . . (87:3); *blithe*, clearly insincere plans . . . . (87:32); We had tasted the sweets as well as the bitterness of *notoriety* . . . . (87:38); an elderly *spinster* soured by too many years of teaching history . . . . . (88:4); now was the time to justify and *vindicate* those knickers . . . . (88:24); some enterprising reporter had tried to discover whether there was any *ordinance* on the subject of proper clothing for public-school students . . (88: 40) ; the entire school personnel . . . was *peremptorily* invited . . . . (90:19); he intended to be *pompous* about knickers . . . . (90:21); knickers were immodest and . . . any girl wearing them rendered herself *ludicrous* and unwomanly. . . . . (91:7); an *avuncular* wave of the hand to signify we could adjourn . . . . (91:12)

Study Questions and Activities

1. The real story in this selection is enclosed by an anecdote concerning the narrator and her daughter. How is the anecdote pertinent to the story it encloses? How would you complete the following analogy? dressing gown:Carola :: _______: Carola's mother

2. The family that moved to Chicago was fairly large. How does the author give us this information?

3. Besides the narrator, we get to meet only five members of her family: Carola, Dauphine, Rose, the mother, and the father. What characteristics would you give each of them? Which do you find most memorable? Argue your choices by clear reference to the selection. How would you complete this analogy? _______:her mother :: _______:her father

4. The selection deals in part with the problems of moving to a new place. Whom do the girls seem to envy in their new school? How has the narrator changed her opinions about them in her mature years?

5. Rose shocked her mother by saying the new schools were "terrible." Later, the narrator says, ". . . the nearest high school was a 'pretty bad' school." What did Rose mean by her remark? The narrator by hers? What evidence does the narrator supply to let readers positively know that her meaning was not the same as Rose's?

6. The narrator remembers that her mother in her youth had caused a stir by appearing in bloomers. How do bloomers differ from knickers? What would be the reaction today if a student wore either knickers or bloomers to your school?

7. "By the end of that first morning," the narrator writes, "my sister and I had learned a lot." What had they learned about their schoolmates? Their teachers? The alleged advantages of knickers? What had the narrator learned that she could use to help her own daughter?

8. Why doesn't the principal expel the girls? What is his purpose in calling the assembly? What is the reader likely to think of the principal after the assembly? Why?

9. What is the immediate result of the assembly upon the sisters? How does the author use the incident to close her narrative gracefully?

10. What is the predominant tone of the selection? (No answer among the choices is absolutely right. Choose one and argue your choice by reference to the text.) (**a**) humorous (**b**) satirical (**c**) partly serious (**d**) melancholy (**e**) reflective

11. Probably some in your class remember changing locations. Let them form a group and discuss their experiences while the class listens. On the whole, are their remembrances similar to or different from those of Carola's mother?

"That is how I became Father Gilbert's boy."

TOUNDI ONDOUA is the fictional protagonist from the novel *Boy!*, described as "neither a true autobiography nor a complete fiction," by FERDINAND OYONO (1929–). Like Toundi, Mr. Oyono was born and raised in the French Cameroun; unlike Toundi, his creator went to France to complete his education and is today a distinguished novelist and diplomat for the now independent Federal Republic of Cameroun. In this incident Toundi defies his father and defects to the French administration of his district. Some of the customs and habits familiar to Toundi may be strange to you. But were all of your present habits a part of you from early childhood? What was your reaction when first confronted with something strange that you later became accustomed to?

August

FERDINAND OYONO

Father Gilbert says I can read and write fluently. Now I can keep a diary like he does. Keeping a diary is a white man's custom and what pleasure there is in it I do not know. But I shall try it out.

While my master and benefactor was hearing confessions, I had a look into his diary. Ah, it is a grain-store for memories. These white men can preserve everything. In Father Gilbert's diary I found the kick he gave me when he caught me mimicking him in the sacristy. I felt my bottom burning all over again. It is strange, I thought I had forgotten all about it. . . .

My name is Toundi Ondoua. I am the son of Toundi and of Zama. When the Father baptized me he gave me the name of Joseph. I am Maka by my mother and Ndjem by my father. My ancestors were cannibals. Since the white men came we have learnt other men must not be looked upon as animals.

They say in the village that I was the cause of my father's death because I ran away to a white priest on the day before my initiation when I should have met the famous serpent who watches over all the men of my race. Father Gilbert believes it was the Holy Spirit that led me to him. In fact I just wanted to get close to the white man with hair like the beard on a maize cob who dressed in woman's clothes and gave little black boys sugar lumps. I was in a gang of heathen boys who followed the missionary about as he went from hut to hut trying to make converts to the new religion. He knew a few words of Ndjem but his pronunciation was so bad that the way he said them, they all had obscene meanings. This amused everybody and his success was assured. He threw the little lumps of sugar to us like throwing corn to chickens. What a battle to get hold of one of those little white lumps! They were worth all the scraped knees, swollen eyes and painful cuts. Sometimes these distributions of sugar turned into brawls between our parents. One day my mother got into a fight with the mother of my friend Tinati because he had twisted my arm to make me let go of two lumps of sugar which I had won at the cost of a bleeding nose. That battle nearly came to bloodshed. My father had to be restrained by the neighbours from splitting open the head of Tinati's father, while Tinati's father was threatening to put his assegai through my father's stomach. When they had both been calmed down, my father, armed with a cane, invited me to follow him behind the house.

'You, Toundi, are the cause of this whole business. Your greediness will be the ruin of us. Anyone would think you don't have enough to eat at home. So on the day before your initiation you have to cross a stream to go begging lumps of sugar from some white man-woman who is a complete stranger to you.'

My father however was not a stranger and I was well acquainted with what he could do with a stick. Whenever he went for either my mother or me, it always took us a week to recover. I was a good way from his stick. He swished it in the air and came towards me. I edged backwards.

Are you going to stop? I've not got legs to go chasing you. You know if I don't get you now I will wait for you for a hundred years to give you your punishment. Now come here and get it over with.'

'I haven't done anything to be beaten for, father,' I protested.

'Aaaaaaaaaakiaaaaay!' he roared. 'You dare to say you haven't done anything? If you weren't such a glutton, if you hadn't the blood of the gluttons that flows through your mother's veins you wouldn't have been in Fia to fight like the little rat you are over the bits of sugar that cursed white man gives you. You wouldn't have got your

Marc & Evelyne Bernheim from Woodfin Camp & Assoc.

arm twisted, your mother wouldn't have had a fight and I wouldn't have wanted to split open Tinati's old father's head. . . . I warn you, you had better stop. If you go one more step backwards, that will be an insult to me. . . .'

I stopped. He flung himself on me and the cane swished down on to my bare shoulders. I twisted like a worm in the sun.

'Turn round and put up your arms. I don't want to knock your eye out.'

'Let me off, father,' I begged, 'I won't do it again.'

'You always say that when I start to give you a thrashing. But today I'm going to go on thrashing and thrashing until I'm not angry any more.'

I couldn't cry out because that might have attracted the neighbours. My friends would have thought me a girl. I would have lost my place in the group of 'boys-who-are-soon-to-be-men.' My father gave me another blow that I dodged neatly. . . .

'I have not insulted you . . . and I won't be beaten any more, so there.'

'How dare you speak to me like that! . . . Unless you stand still at once, I shall curse you.'

My father was choking. I had never seen him so furious. I went on backing away from him. He came on after me, down behind the huts, for a good hundred yards.

'Very well then,' he said. 'We'll see where you spend the night. I will tell your mother you have insulted us both. . . .'

With that he turned his back. I did not know where I could go. I had an uncle I did not like because of his scabies. His wife smelt of bad fish and so did he. I hated going into their house. It was growing dark. You could begin to see the flashing light of the fireflies. The thud of mortars announced the preparation of the evening meal. I went back softly behind our house and peered through the cracks in the mud wall. My father had his back to me. My unpleasant uncle was facing him. They were eating. . . . The aroma of porcupine made my mouth water. It had been caught in one of my father's traps and we had found it half eaten by ants two days later. My mother was famous in the village for her cooking of porcupine.

'The very first of the season,' said my uncle with his mouth full.

My father did not speak but pointed with his finger above his head to where the skulls of the animals he had taken in his traps were hung up in a row.

'You can eat it all up,' said my mother. 'I've kept some for Toundi in the pot.'

My father leapt up, stammering with rage. I saw there would be a storm.

'Bring Toundi's share here,' he shouted. 'He's not to have any of this porcupine. I will teach him to disobey me.'

'But he hasn't had anything since this morning. What will he eat when he gets in?'

'Nothing at all,' said my father.

'If you want to make him obedient,' added my uncle, 'take away his food . . . this porcupine is really delicious.'

My mother got up and fetched the pot. I saw my father's hand and my uncle's hand go in. Then I heard my mother crying. For the first time in my life I thought of killing my father.

I went back to Fia . . . and after hesitating for a long while I knocked at the white priest's door. I found him in the middle of his dinner. He was very surprised. I tried to explain through signs that I wanted to go away with him. He laughed with all his teeth so his mouth looked like a crescent moon. I stood shyly by the door. He made signs that I should come closer and he offered me what was left of his meal. I found it strange and delicious. We continued a conversation by signs. I knew I had been accepted.

That is how I became Father Gilbert's boy.

My father heard the news next day. I was afraid of how angry he would be . . . I explained to the priest, still using signs. He was amused. He gave me a friendly pat on the shoulder. I felt protected.

In the afternoon my father came. All he said to me was that I was still his son . . . and that he bore me no grudge. If I came home, everything would be forgotten. I knew just how much trust I could put in a speech like this made in front of the white man. I put my tongue out at him. The look came into his eye that always came when he was going to 'teach me how to behave'. But I was not afraid while Father Gilbert was there. Father Gilbert's eyes seemed to cast a spell over my father. He lowered his head and went out crestfallen.

My mother came to see me that night. She was crying. We cried together. She told me I had done well to leave my father's house and that my father did not love me as a father ought to love his son. She said that she gave me her blessing and that if ever I fell ill I had only to bathe in a stream and I would be cured.

Father Gilbert gave me a pair of khaki shorts and a red jersey. All the boys in Fia were so impressed by these that they came to ask Father Gilbert to take them on as well.

Two days later Father Gilbert took me on his motorcycle. We spread panic through the villages by the noise we made. His tour had lasted a fortnight and now we were on our way back to the Saint

Peter's Catholic Mission at Dangan. I was happy. The speed intoxicated me. I was going to learn about the city and white men and live like them. I caught myself thinking I was like one of the wild parrots we used to attract in the village with grains of maize. They were captured through their greediness. My mother often used to say, laughing, 'Toundi, what will your greediness bring you to . . . ?'

My parents are dead. I have never been back to the village.

Vocabulary

Father Gilbert says I can read and write *fluently* . . . . . . (93:1); I just wanted to get close to the white man with hair like the beard on a *maize* cob . . . . . . (94:6); He knew a few words of Ndjem but his pronunciation was so bad that the way he said them, they all had *obscene* meanings . . . . . (94:11); Your greediness will be the ruin of us. . . . If you weren't such a *glutton* . . . . (94:40); The thud of *mortars* announced the preparation of the evening meal . . . . . (96:30); He laughed with all his teeth so his mouth looked like a *crescent* moon . . . . . (97:17); He lowered his head and went out *crestfallen* . . . . . (97:32); His tour had lasted a *fortnight* . . . . . (97:43)

Study Questions

1. Study the final sentence of paragraph 3 and then reread paragraph 2 carefully. What subtle satire do you find? What other examples of the same sort of satire can you find in the rest of the passage?

2. Toundi undergoes an initiation of his own choosing and misses the one the tribe had made a ritual. What initiation does he miss? What is his chosen initiation? Which would you have preferred? Why?

3. When we lose our tempers, we often do so because we ourselves have acted foolishly and we transfer our anger with ourselves by trying to inflict pain upon others. How does Toundi's father's attack upon his son illustrate the truth of the above statement? By using the same logic, how might Toundi—had he been given the chance—have answered his father?

4. Toundi holds a grudge against both his father and his uncle. Which does he characterize as the more odious? Be prepared to argue your answer.

5. Which of the following statements seems to you to have the most truth?

a. Father Gilbert acted with complete charity in rescuing Toundi.

b. Father Gilbert might have made a wiser decision had he released Toundi to his family when his father's anger had cooled.

c. Father Gilbert's reputation with the natives was such that Toundi's future success and good fortune are assured.

d. Father Gilbert rescued Toundi only because he wanted to acquire an inexpensive laborer.

e. Father Gilbert rescued Toundi in order to teach and demonstrate to him the superior religion and civilization of the white world.

6. Read carefully the next to the final paragraph of the passage, which foreshadows the future of Toundi. What do you think the answer to the mother's question will be? Be prepared to argue your answer. (To learn the answer, find the novel and read it.)

New York Public Library Picture Collection.

VOCABULARY: SENTENCE COMPLETION

Review the vocabulary. Then try answering the following questions. Each sentence has one or two words left blank. The choices that follow the sentence contain a word or a pair of words to complete the blank or blanks. Choose the word or pair that makes the best fit and write the appropriate letter on your paper.

1. The moon was a silver ______ in the sky.
(**a**) dogma (**b**) crescent (**c**) palaver (**d**) maize

2. The ______ in the restaurant was reserved for ______ who liked their meals to continue for three hours.
(**a**) brazier—temperaments (**b**) camouflage—aesthetes (**c**) mortars—gluttons (**d**) alcove—gourmands

3. The young girl's ______ was great when her teacher ______ her.
(**a**) anguish—belittled (**b**) humiliation—lavished (**c**) pretext—confronted (**d**) suffrage—endowed

4. The judge charged the jury to make an ______ decision.
(**a**) impartial (**b**) anguished (**c**) irksome (**d**) unseemly

5. The tourists found New York City buildings ______, dwarfing them completely.
(**a**) desultory (**b**) Gargantuan (**c**) gluttons (**d**) Lilliputian

6. The father frequently ______ the boy for his ______.
(**a**) entranced—pretext (**b**) repressed—psyche (**c**) reproached—indolence (**d**) lauded—impiety

7. By ______ given to sloth, the young man had slovenly habits.
(**a**) repression (**b**) affectation (**c**) dogma (**d**) temperament

8. In her maturity Mabel's ______ caused her to loathe any display of ______.
(**a**) ulcer—bourgeoisie (**b**) anguish—languor (**c**) asceticism—voluptuousness (**d**) impartiality—equivocation

9. Women in most parts of the world were not granted the rights of ______ until this century.
(**a**) saturation (**b**) suffrage (**c**) deism (**d**) sensuousness

10. In his bestiary the author discusses unicorns, behemoths, and other ______ monsters.
(**a**) ephemeral (**b**) flagrant (**c**) desultory (**d**) fabulous

An early type of fountain pen. New York Public Library Picture Collection.

4

Getting Personal—Preschool Childhood

Now that you have explored things about your past which have required research, it is time to begin putting down memories. In this chapter, you can write of those things you remember happening before you went to school. You may need to check some facts with your parents, but most of what you remember will come easily once you begin thinking about your early childhood.

Organization of this chapter can be a bother unless you plan carefully. For one thing, remember that the next chapter can be reserved for the first day of school and other less carefree incidents. Then, as you plan, it is a good idea to write down on scratch paper brief titles of incidents you can remember. After you have finished this sheet, sort the incidents. Some you will find that you have no room for; these you must be prepared to discard. Others will fit into some sort of organization. One way to organize is to group your items from the scratch paper under headings, such as Early Fears, Embarrassments, Disenchantments. Doing this will allow you to form paragraphs with more facility.

Getting Started

Form a group and begin your session by talking about early memories of the characters you have been learning about in your supplementary reading. Think not only of the memories but of the ways the writers managed to convey these memories. Some of your group may want to read aloud short passages to illustrate their ideas.

What follows is a list of topical headings with questions under each topic. Explore the answers you and others can give these questions. Make notes of experiences that you feel worthwhile to include in the story of you.

MEMORIES: What are your earliest memories? After you think that you have found the earliest ones, let your senses explore further. Can you discover any that have been buried? What sounds, odors, touch sensations, and pictures are associated with these memories?

EARLIEST INCIDENTS: I win a set of doll dishes at the fair; the teapot breaks. Blowing soap bubbles and wondering what makes the colors. In the back seat of Uncle's station wagon on a dark night with all the fishing equipment.

FEARS: Dread of strangers, jails, policemen, animals, a cat that had fits. Catching fear of the dark from someone else. How rational were your fears? How did you master those fears?

WONDERING: What did the boys find so interesting in my sister? Why do people always say, "He can't understand"? Why do little pitchers have big ears?

NEW IDEAS: Keeping minutes with the clock. Burying feathers and bones so that chickens and sheep would grow.

MISTAKES: I thought I could find the store by the lawn mowers outside, but someone had taken them in. I believed that people went to war to kill flies.

ENLARGING HORIZONS: My first runaway from home. No Santa Claus? No tooth fairy? I learn that nuns in white are not really ghosts. I discover certain words that aren't to be said in company.

DRAMATIC MOMENTS: When I was five my brother Jack brought home his wife, Elizabeth. She said, "There are possibilities in the house." I live through my first dangerous experience. I learn that some people cannot be trusted.

SADNESS AND MISERY: What experience before school caused you great sadness? Have you ever been miserable because a place was too clean, too neat?

Too quiet or too noisy? Too ugly? What sorts of things made you sad and miserable: People? Food? Moving? Criticism?

HAPPINESS: What was the happiest moment of your life before school began? Have you ever been happy in a place because it was restful and you were very tired? Because a great pain ended? Because you did something well and were praised? Because you made a mistake and were not caught? Because you could read, or draw, or swim better than someone else?

PLACES AND THINGS: What house, yard, city, or farm can you recall from your preschool days as especially wonderful? As especially loathsome? Can you remember anything you felt was especially beautiful? Lonely? Mysterious? Did you ever possess something you valued more than gold? A blanket? A picture? A piece of jewelry? A doll?

Nikki Giovanni, self-portrait.

THE FORMING MIND: What was your first real feeling? Opinion? Hatred? Love? When did you first feel thoroughly ashamed of yourself? Proud? When did you have your first feeling of responsibility? When and how did you learn that people approved and/or disapproved of you? When did you first feel inferior? Superior?

TALENTS: What did you enjoy doing? Any special sport? Drawing? Reading and writing? Building with blocks? What did you feel especially stupid about doing? Why did this make you feel stupid?

Illustrations

Keep up the hunt for photographs and samples of your early handiwork. Remember that now, as you are bringing others into the story, you can use pictures of them. Think of new ways to illustrate your ideas. Draw a picture of the world as you saw it when you were five. Did you know a state from a country? A city? Make a caricature of the dreaded dog next door. Revisit some place that seemed awesome to you then; draw what it looked like to you and then photograph or draw it as it is today.

A Chart for Future Reference

Now is the time to begin another type of reference sheet. We can call this a Then and Now chart. Simply take a piece of paper, run a line perpendicularly through its center, title the left side THEN; the right side, NOW. As you put down the discoveries you make about yourself before the present, list them under THEN. On the other side make notes as to how you have changed, reasons for the change, or reasons that have caused you not to change. Add to the pages as you continue writing. As you come to your final chapters of self-evaluation, you will find this chart useful.

A Long Anecdote from "**The Good Companions**"

Our most interesting pets we didn't exactly love, though. We had a neighbor who was very fond of us, and she had her brother in Florida send us a present. There was great mystery about it, and when the wooden crate arrived we stood about hoping it would be candy. It wasn't. Jeanne ripped off the last board, and out crawled two of the ugliest looking alligators one could hope to see. Dad had to build an alligator pit for them. He lined it with bricks and put a screen on top. I guess he forgot that alligators can stand right up on their tails, so he didn't make it deep enough. The beasts kept pushing the screen off. Then they would go swimming in the rectory pool and eat the goldfish. We had to weight the screen with a stone.

One day Mother had a garden party—a lot of ladies from the church. My sister and I were all dressed up. The ladies admired us and admired the garden, and it was all very dull. So I pushed a certain stone—just a little! All of a sudden one of the ladies slid her gaze past the rose garden. Her eyes bulged in unbelieving horror. She uttered a strangled shriek. Alexander, the biggest alligator, lay there in the grass with his big mouth wide open, hissing evilly at her. The party broke up in a hurry.

A Harrowing Experience from "**Cloudy Days**"

I was badly frightened again when I visited a little Russian girl who lived nearby. My mother sent me over with Bertha, my sitter, who left me there under the impression that Kathy and I would have a pleasant afternoon playing with dolls. But as soon as we were alone, Kathy locked me in a closet with her and started choking me. Her mother, hearing my screams, rushed in and saved me. I couldn't talk when Bertha came back so she thought I had had a wonderful time, and I was forced to spend many other similar afternoons with Kathy.

A Paragraph on the Discovery of Discipline from "**Toddler to Teen**"

I will always remember my first movie, which I never saw. My grandmother was taking my two cousins to a special matinee showing of a musical entitled *The Tin Soldier,* and I was invited too. I had never seen a movie and had no idea of what it would be like. They were going to pick me up at two o'clock, and I already had on my best dress when we started lunch at one. We had a casserole of Spanish rice, a dish I didn't like. After Dad had gone back to the office and Mom to the living room, I was still at the table with that dish of dreadful Spanish rice in front of me. I sat picking at it when Mom came in and told me if it wasn't eaten in five minutes, no movie. I didn't think she meant it, and after five minutes rice still covered the plate. I'll never forget it. Mother picked up the plate, took it into the kitchen, and then went to the phone. She took up the receiver and said "5—0" to the operator. When a voice answered on the other end, Mom said that I wouldn't be able to go. The voice said it was sorry and hung up. Oh, I had lost my faith in mothers! I spent the whole afternoon in tears, and I had Spanish rice for supper. I wonder if it was a good movie.

A Paragraph of Introspection from "**Combined Operation**"

As a child my imagination stretched very far. From the age of four to seven, instead of taking a teddy bear to bed like the average child, I would take my imagination with me. For about an hour each night, I would pretend to be working as a radio repairman for my imaginary boss, Mr. Spinach. I would dramatize the story so well that my brother even believed me. I sometimes wonder if I did not believe my story myself. It was always my habit to talk out loud to myself about how I went to work after my brother fell asleep. I used to hide my imaginary radio under my bed and say that I had it down to my place of business and was going to repair it. I also told our next-door neighbor's daughter Ruth about my "work," and one day she asked Mother if I really went to business. It was through Mother's honesty that I outgrew this fantasy.

A First Paragraph of "**From Pram to Primer**"

I had wings, a halo, and a heart of gold; but sometimes my halo slipped and my wings got tangled up. "Tangled up in what?" you may ask. I answer, "In my imagination." You may laugh and wonder how this has anything to do with you or me. The only answer I can give is that you will need imagination during the time you read this, and I needed imagination—along with some facts—to write it.

My Heart Was Young and Gay

Although I spent most of my early childhood in France, some of my recollections center around Russelville, a small town in northern Alabama, where I spent two of my early years. I was two when we first moved to this town, and we spent a very cold winter there. I spent most of it in bed with pneumonia. It was fairly uneventful and most unpleasant. The following winter, all of my family moved to France.

There our mansionlike house seemed very strange to me at first. I was always scared of the big atticlike third floor, where my brothers liked to play. I can remember the tin can telephone which they installed between the roof of our house and the ground below. I always wondered how it worked.

Another incident I can remember very clearly was the time when I went out picking flowers in our huge garden. My mother had brought out a bowl, into which we were putting the pansies as we picked them. I soon tired of bending over the flower bed so I sat down right in the pansy bowl. I started crying and Mother started laughing. I didn't break the bowl, but I certainly am glad that there wasn't a frog in it.

I also remember a happening which took place when I was left alone with our maid, a French girl who could speak no English, and one of my parents' friends, an American who couldn't speak French. I acted as translator and mediator for several hours, but I soon tired of the work. Most politely I ended my duties by saying, "Alice, there is a dictionary upstairs in the library."

The following year we moved back to Alabama. I can remember going out to pick blackberries in a vacant lot and then selling them to the lady who owned the lot. Once I was out there picking berries when a strange odor drifted to my nostrils. I commented on it to a friend who was there with me. He said, "We'd better be careful. Rattlesnakes often stay in berry patches, and they always smell strange." The next thing I remember, I was at home, all out of breath, with the door locked securely behind me.

CHECK SHEET FOR CHAPTER 4

Analysis of Samples

1. The fourth sentence of the first sample consists of only two words. Why is it effective?

2. What tone does the writer of the first sample adopt toward her material? Back up your answers by references to the anecdote.

3. Have you ever thought of how cruel even little children can be to one another? Do children use this cruelty casually or with malice aforethought? Read again the second sample and think of some times when you have been cruel to others and they to you. Do you think the malice was intentional?

4. Sample 5 states that "I needed imagination—along with some facts—to write it." How do we all have to use imagination as we write these autobiographies?

5. The complete chapter that ends the samples is clearly coherent. What words or phrases in each paragraph serve to link that paragraph to the one which preceded it?

Spelling

1. bawl (How does this word differ from ball?)
2. breathe, breathes, breathed
   breath, breaths (When do we use each of these words?)
3. carry, carrying, carried (What spelling rule does this word illustrate?)
4. catastrophe
5. clothe, clothes, clothed
   cloth, cloths (How is this word like those in No. 2?)
6. despite
7. dine, dining, dining room
8. immediate (Write its adverb form)
9. lead, led, led (Which of these words has another meaning when given a different sound?)
10. pastime
11. picnic, picnicking, picnicked
12. undoubtedly (What is the stem of this word? What do we call its other parts?)
13. whine, whining, whined
14. win, winning (Why does this word have a double "n" whereas words 7 and 13 do not?)

Questions for Group Consideration

1. What is the difference between a phrase and a clause?

2. What is a participle? Review Chapter 2 if necessary.

3. How would you punctuate the following sentences?

- **a.** Having finished our work we sat down to plan our evening.
- **b.** We sat down to plan our evening having finished our work.
- **c.** We sat down having finished our work to plan our evening.

4. Which of the following sentences need punctuation?

- **a.** When Mother is in one of her many good moods she frequently talks to me about her childhood in India.
- **b.** My mother when she is in one of her many good moods frequently talks to me about her childhood in India.
- **c.** My mother frequently talks to me about her childhood in India when she is in one of her many good moods.

5. What do you find funny about these sentences? How can you make them say what their authors intended?

- **a.** Covered with chocolate sauce, you will enjoy this kind of ice cream.
- **b.** Wanted: Antique table by antiquarian with intricately carved legs.
- **c.** He never really likes that sauce unless thoroughly boiled.

6. Which of these sentences needs further punctuation?

- **a.** To understand the problem one needs to study the lesson carefully.
- **b.** One needs to study the lesson carefully in order to understand the problem.

7. Which of these sentences needs further punctuation?

- **a.** While carrying the pail down the hill Jack and Jill both fell.
- **b.** Jack and Jill both fell while carrying the pail down the hill.

8. Write the following sentence in two different ways, punctuating properly.

We were prevented from finishing our math test because the fire alarm sounded.

9. Write the following sentence in two different ways, punctuating properly.

Having seen the Wax Works Museum, we decided we'd had enough horror for the day.

10. Most people would find the following sentences poor examples of Standard Written English. Can you put them in better form?

- **a.** It was because of that stomachache that I no longer like apples.
- **b.** My first disease was when I was only three weeks old.
- **c.** My brother's temper is probably why I'm so meek.

11. Consider the word *writing* in each of the following sentences. When does it function as a noun? A verb? An adjective?

- **a.** The girl at my left was *writing* a note to her friend.
- **b.** While *writing* to Grandma, I was interrupted by a phone call from her.
- **c.** This is a *writing* desk.
- **d.** The boy *writing* at my right is doing his homework.

12. Consider the words *to write* in each of the following sentences. When do they function as a noun? An adverb?

- **a.** *To write* well is her desire.
- **b.** I want to learn *to write* before I go to college.
- **c.** In kindergarten my sister is learning *to write*.
- **d.** *To write* the report, John had to do research.

13. Take the word *placing* and use it in sentences as many ways as you can. For those of you who remember grammar, think of it as part of a verb, as a noun (gerund), as an adjective (participle). Try to punctuate your sentences correctly.

14. Now take the words *to place*. Use them at the beginning of a sentence, somewhere in the middle, and at the end. With your teacher's help, analyze the sentences to see if you have used *to place* in all the ways it can be used. Try to punctuate your sentences correctly.

More About Commas: Rules 12, 13, and 14

12. Set off long introductory clauses and phrases from the rest of the sentence.

Introductory Prepositional Phrase:

With the help of John and Tom, we finally floated the raft.

Introductory Gerund Phrase:

While studying typing, I mastered the art of punctuation.

Introductory Participial Phrases:

(Present participle):

Seeing the obstacle in front of me, I quickly swerved to the left.

(Past participle):

Having seen that the cellar was quite empty, I no longer believed in ghosts.

(Absolute constructions):

The work done, we packed up and went home.

Introductory Infinitive Phrases:

To season the chicken properly, we need to let it stand overnight in the marinade.

13. Use a comma to set off a group of words which, without punctuation, would give a double meaning to a sentence.

a. After eating, my sister watches television.
b. Smoking, as the doctor says, is injurious to your health.
c. Dieting is necessary for me, to say the least.

14. Use a comma to set off contrasting groups of words at the end of a sentence.

a. He needed love, not pity.
b. I did not try that experiment again, ever.

Verbals: Gerunds, Participles, Absolute Constructions and Infinitives

Gerunds

You will remember from Chapter 2 that the second part of the verb, that ending in "-ing," is a gerund or present participle. As a gerund it functions as both noun and verb; like a noun it may be used, for example, as an object, but it may also have its own object. Note the following examples for this double function of the gerund:

a. The teacher questioned my writing so long a paper.
b. Doing these exercises requires much concentration.
c. Before finishing his homework, John fell asleep.
d. The good pitcher will, before hurling the first pitch, warm up for a while.

Participles

The second part of the verb can also function as an adjective and verb together. We then call it a participle. Find and discuss the functions of the participle in the following examples:

a. The class had a spelling contest.
b. The sounds coming from the room were not melodious.
c. Seeing that he had been trapped, the cat lay down and mewed piteously.
d. The cat, seeing that he had been trapped, lay down and mewed piteously.
e. The cat lay down and mewed piteously, seeing that he had been trapped.

The fourth part of the verb is used also as a verb-adjective and is called the **past participle.** Sometimes it is used singly and at other times in a compound with parts of the verbs "have" and "to be": *seen, having seen, having been seen,* for example. Find and discuss the functions of the past participle in the following examples:

a. Having been caught by the principal, the boy was expelled.
b. The falls, seen from a distance, creates many rainbows.
c. Mary enjoys raw tomatoes sprinkled with sugar and salt.
d. The radio station signed off, having finished its alloted time.

Absolute Constructions

Frequently we give a subject to a participle and make what we call an absolute construction. Find the examples in the following sentences:

a. Our ordeal completed, we sat down to discuss it.

b. The two cronies, their taste for gossip satisfied, sat and smiled.

c. They threw out the dirty water, the windows having been satisfactorily washed.

Infinitives

By adding a "to" to the first part of the verb—and often by implying the "to" but leaving it off—we create an infinitive, a construction that can function as a verb-noun, verb-adjective, or verb-adverb. Discuss the infinitives (with and without "to") in the following sentences and note their functions and punctuation.

a. The President is attempting to correct the rising cost of living.

b. To correct it, he may have to institute price controls.

c. The hardest way to learn to swim is to jump into the water and do your darndest to survive.

d. To produce a clearer jelly, you must not squeeze the jelly bag.

Values and Dangers of the Verbal

By the time we start kindergarten, we are already using verbals constantly in our speaking. We do not, however, always learn to use them properly in our writing. Here are some rules to remember about using them.

1. Make a conscious effort to use verbals more often. Note especially the absolute construction. Good writers need verbal construction to add variety and action to their sentence structure.

2. Learn to punctuate them properly. Generally speaking, if verbals introduce or interrupt the main flow of a sentence, they are set off by commas.

3. Do not let your verbals dangle. That is, do not construct a silly sentence by following your verbal with something it does not modify. Note and correct these examples:

a. Their work completed, hot lunches were provided for the gang.

b. Mary enjoys raw tomatoes when sprinkled with sugar and salt.

c. Having completed my assignment, the radio was my next interest.

d. Before hurling the first pitch, a warm-up is absolutely required.

4. Be careful about using a gerund after a form of the verb "to be." Such usages create double meanings.

wrong: My biggest fear was falling out of bed.

right: Falling out of bed was my biggest fear.
My biggest fear was that of falling out of bed.
My biggest fear was that I'd fall out of bed.

5. Nouns and pronouns before gerunds should be in possessive case. As this is generally an awkward construction, the best rule is to avoid it whenever possible.

weak: Because of John being my brother, I had to humor him.
right: Because of John's being my brother, I had to humor him.
best: Because John was my brother, I had to humor him.
weak: It all started with me having the whooping cough.
right: It all started with my having the whooping cough.
best: It all started when I had the whooping cough.

Two Warnings About "To Be" and its Changes

The verb *to be* has many forms: am, is, are, was, were, will be, can be, should be, would be, has been, have been, will have been—and others.

1. In Standard Written English, avoid the use of the words *when, where,* or *because* directly after any part of the verb *to be.* Notice ways of avoiding this in examples.

wrong: This was when I was three years old.
right: This happened when I was three years old.

wrong: One memory was when I was still a baby.

right: I remember a time when I was still a baby.

wrong: On Maple Street was where I was born.

right: I was born on Maple Street.

wrong: Here was where we moved in Phoenix.

right: We moved to this house in Phoenix.

wrong: It was because I was sick so often that I wore so many clothes.

right: I wore so many clothes because I was sick so often.

2. After forms of the verb *to be,* be certain that your predicate noun means the same as your subject. Remember that this verb and its forms are much the same as equal signs. Notice what the writers of these bloopers are actually saying:

unclear: My greatest childhood fear was the furnace was the devil.

clear: My greatest childhood fear was that the furnace was the devil.

unclear: The picture is a baby boy of four years.

clear: The picture is of a baby boy of four years.

unclear: My earliest memories are a movie house and an opera.

clear: My earliest memories are of a movie house and an opera.

unclear: Mother prophesied that the first time would be a baby boy.

clear: Mother prophesied that she would first have a baby boy.

ASSIGNMENT 4

Write Chapter 3 of your autobiography. It will deal with the events and feelings you had before going to school. You may need some help from others in bringing back memories, but don't neglect the storehouse of your brain. Remember to outline, write a first draft rapidly, and revise meticulously before submitting your final copy.

A 15th century transcriber at work. New York Public Library Picture Collection.

PRACTICE TEST IV

This test covers only those errors noted on the Check Sheets for Chapters 1, 2, 3, and 4. Review the Check Sheets and then, without looking back, do the test. The teacher may want to check your work OR to give you another test of the same sort. Each error will count as 2½ points, if anybody's counting.

I. Each of the following sentences has a word in it with several letters missing. Fill in the letters so that the word will be spelled correctly. Write only the word on your paper.

1. Over the sink hung two wash-cl_______s and a towel.

2. First we l_______ the horses to the trough, and then we watered them.

3. I was hit so hard I thought I had br_______ my last.

4. My sister was then a wh_______ing child, but her disposition has improved.

5. I haven't played on a w_______ing team since that year in Little League.

6. The dictionary ref_______ me to another page.

7. D_______ my little accidents, I came to no real harm until I was seven.

8. Whenever I did wrong, my brother ba______d me out before my father spanked me.

9. Whenever my brother and I qua______d, my oldest sister tried to make peace between us.

10. Because I ate a big p______ of pizza whenever I could get it, I was nicknamed Pizza Babe.

II. Punctuate the following sentences. Three sentences need no further punctuation. Rewrite the other seven correctly.

1. For three weeks we were supposed to read *David Copperfield*.

2. Because I love to travel whenever I can I eagerly seized upon my chance to go to Maine last summer.

3. Being only seven I couldn't be expected to know my right hand from my left.

4. I sat in the corner and cried before turning to my dog and swearing at him.

5. While I eat my lessons must wait.

6. Having eaten twice as much as most babies I weighed twice as much as I should have.

7. There on his wheel lay my lifeless gerbil his exercise having been too much for him.

8. Getting rid of all that I have collected is what I must do if I'm ever to keep my room clean.

9. Mother came to see me every day in the hospital and each time she would bring me a new toy.

10. Whenever I think of Canada I remember the hot springs at Radium there we would lie in the pool which was used even during the coldest days and pretend we were in the South Seas.

III. Each of the following sentences has an error. Write the error on your paper and make the proper correction after it.

1. Independence, Mo., was the place where I discovered girls.

2. It was when I was two that I discovered there was no Eastern bunny.

3. My idea of a good time is fishing for a week.

4. Hearing the noise, the house was thoroughly aroused.

5. The reason I suffered so was because I knew I was wrong.

6. I had only 50 cents with me, and I didn't know what to do.

7. My ideal is having no homework in school.

8. Greece will be where I end my days if I have my way.

9. Because of me singing so loudly so early, we were asked to move to a different motel.

10. I always liked Uncle Elmer more than I do Aunt Fanny.

IV. Put five apostrophes in their proper places in the following short paragraph. Write only the apostrophized words on your paper.

Two thieves work was interrupted last night when Patrolman Jack Jones flashlight revealed them climbing into a residence on Eighth Street. Only an hours time elapsed before they were in Nashvilles jail. Mr. Smiths drug store had also been robbed by these vandals.

V. Follow the directions and rewrite each of these sentences:

1. *Change the clause in commas to an appositive:*

My brother, who was awkward and clumsy when younger, is now a star athlete.

2. *Begin your revision with "Having finished. . . .":*

When they had finished spreading the soft tar on the road, the workmen drove away and left me prey to temptation.

3. *Begin your revision with "To see. . . .":*

If you want to see how fishing is really done by experts, you should watch my Uncle Ed.

4. *Begin your revision with "When. . . .":*

The trio, their mission accomplished, marched triumphantly home.

5. *Write a single sentence beginning with "When. . . .":*

I was seven. I was very covetous. I wanted everything I saw.

5

School Days—How Influential Is Education?

Think of this chapter as one of two which will probably cover your educational experiences from approximately the age of five until the present. During this time you have been influenced by two kinds of education, the formal experience of school and organized classes and the less formal summer experiences of play, camp, travel, work, and your general use of leisure. You might begin by trying to decide which has been more important in creating the you of today. Such a decision could decide the general organization of both this chapter and the next. If, as for some of you, school seems to be the predominant interest, your fifth chapter might center upon this thesis: Since I entered kindergarten, school has been of vital importance in my life. Or, . . . has been of minor importance.

Woody Allen, self-portrait.

A hazard facing the writer of this chapter is verbosity. Most of us could easily follow an outline with each paragraph beginning, "In Grade ______ my teacher was ______." What follows this sort of organization is generally a disaster. Such chapters are liable to recall in tedious detail a sort of chronological report of the year. Try to avoid this sort of organization by thinking in terms of "mosts" and "leasts," "bests" and "worsts," "firsts."

Getting Started

Form a group and start out your session by doing some very rough drawing. Each member in the group might begin by drawing an arrangement of the best classroom he or she ever had in school. Then, each member might show the sketch and explain its meaning. Some of these sketches might find their way into your completed books.

Using the same procedure, draw the classroom you have liked least. Now try your hand at caricature. Draw a sketch of the person you've liked most in your school days; try to show in your sketch the qualities you have liked. Do the same for a peer you have found particularly dangerous, odious, or snobbish; for a teacher you have liked and for one you have disliked. As you talk about these sketches, try to recall incidents and character traits that will be of use to you as you write.

1. What was your first school experience? Was it nursery school or kindergarten? Who was the teacher? How did you react when Father or Mother left you? What first interested you? Did you make any mistakes? What was your first punishment?

2. What have you liked best about school? Was it a continuing interest? If not, what replaced it? Why?

3. What has given you the hardest time in school? Have you mastered it yet? Are you still trying? If not, why not?

4. What teachers have you especially admired? What did you learn from them? What techniques of theirs earned your approval?

5. What friendships have grown out of school experience? What was the experience? Have the friendships continued? If not, why not?

6. What has been the event you have enjoyed most in your years of school? What made it so interesting? What was your part in it?

7. Was there someone who impressed you to act or not to act in a certain way? What did that person do to impress you? Has the lesson you learned been one you follow today?

8. What different educational theories have you been exposed to? Formal classroom? Open classroom? Montessori? Did any one of these theories stand out as especially worthwhile or worthless?

9. Think of specific traits that you consider to be a part of yourself today. Do any of them derive from school experiences? What were they?

10. Think of ideas you once held and now have dropped. What made you drop them? If school influenced these changes, you have at least one paragraph.

11. Are there words you particularly like or dislike today? Write a list of such words. Do your feelings about them in any way derive from school experiences?

An Opening Section from **"Called on the Carpet"**

Thirty seconds after I had been introduced to my kindergarten teacher, a very attractive little girl—who now looks like one of the hippos in *Fantasia*—came up to me and introduced herself. For the sake of preventing a scandal, we will call her Thadie. Right after school was out, she had me escort her home to meet her parents. She introduced me by saying, "Mother, this is my boy friend, Andrew Williams."

Her parents must have drugged her on the subject of romance, but I had never heard of the thing. During recess I would swing her by the hour. All I wanted to be was an average kindergarten boy, but this driving force wouldn't let me. As we walked by, all the other little kindergarteners would shake their heads and look at me as if I were the third sex.

A Third Grade Reminiscence from **"The Academic and Sports"**

Chick Carter was a young detective who, with his friends, was taking an extended trip on a Mississippi River showboat tracking down a band of counterfeiters. The leader of the counterfeiters was named Whisper. Chick Carter's chase of Whisper lasted over six months. The boys of Mrs. Foote's third grade were giving this adventure their fullest attention. We made up two gangs. One of them was the Chick Carter gang, and the other was the Whisper gang. The activities were generally limited to making counterfeit bills whose denominations usually contained twenty-odd digits. We also did a little sinister plotting against each other. The whole conspiracy ended finally in a fight between the two gangs. The Whisper gang eventually joined the Chick Carter gang, and then came summer vacation and we all forgot about the whole thing.

An Opening Paragraph from **"The Canvas"**

The great day had come! Now I—a great, big, strong he-man—could go to school. "School must be a peculiar place," thought I. The theory behind this astounding presumption was that the little kids, my friends, all thought it was lots of fun. The bigger fellows, my ideals, were almost unanimous in their opinion of the place. Joe Rogers was always grumbling about some unknown thing called Latin. Neil Maloney growled about solid geometry, and Lou Hermanson cursed civics in every way known to man. Therefore, as Mother and I walked the long road to school, my little brain must have sounded like a Geiger counter as it buzzed with mixed emotions. We walked to the door—my heart was doing gymnastics—and went down a corridor to a room which had KINDERGARTEN written over the door in big letters. I heard the boisterous voice of gentle, little Al Evans ring out in glowing tones. "Ahh! Shaddup!" it said.

A Reminiscence on Behavior from **"Peck's Bad Boy"**

My school behavior was fine until we moved to Westchester at the end of my third grade in Brooklyn. Here I presented a dead rabbit to Mrs. Stone. It was during recess, and I gently walked up to her, the dead rabbit behind my back. I asked her if she had ever wanted a fur coat. She replied, "Yes!" and I threw the dead animal on her shoulder. Mother heard about this, and I was ashamed to face Mrs. Stone the next day. Two years later I was in sixth grade and in trouble again, this time with Miss Oliphant. She caught me selling bubble gum at a five hundred percent profit. But all this was before seventh grade when trouble became my middle name.

Three Paragraphs from a War Refugee's **"One, Two, Three, and School Is Over"**

After that, things happened very fast. Bombs fell, sirens howled, houses burned; we spent nights and nights in cellars. Then trains rolled, rolled, rolled and things suddenly became quiet again. I was in Silesia. Goodness, was I glad! Mommy had taken me there because it had become too dangerous in Essen. Then the

Russians came. We ran away again. We tramped all over and across Germany, and I had hardly any school until we came to America.

Were these heavenly palaces really schools? They had swings! Oh, how I loved swings; I hadn't swung on one since—since—since Glatz. In the classes the kids grew flowers, and there were real, live turtles. I had never even seen a turtle. Now I have two of my own. The classes had great big windows and shiny floors, and everyone had a whole desk of her own. Oh these beautiful, beautiful schools!

Then after I had seen everything, touched everything, pinched myself a few times, I slowly got around to observing myself. When I had first come here, I had on long, green, woolen stockings with purple stripes around them. I had long, blond braids and was very thin and tall. Even my dresses were different. I felt very strange, but everyone humored me and I liked it. I cut off my braids and put on socks; I got different clothes and tried hard to say words other than "Yes" and "No" and "Thank you." It worked.

Exclusive Interview

When interviewed about his first school experiences, Peter Breslau answered by saying, "I began my schooling at Bronxville Nursery School in 1963. Their report to my parents sums up my activity there: 'It was hard at first for him to express himself and to hold his own in an argument. But he has made great progress in this direction and has become a part of the group play, offering many good suggestions and having them accepted with interest. This group approval does much for Pete, and he needs this encouragement. He is liked and respected by all the children for his fairness, his cooperativeness, and his capabilities.' "

"Where did you go from there?" was the next question.

Peter replied, "I was enrolled in kindergarten in P. S. 5 in Yonkers, New York. Kindergarten and first and second grade slipped by; and before I could catch my breath, I was enrolled in Mrs. Foote's third grade class in Greenacres school."

"Will you pick out a highlight of your first years?" was the next question.

"In third grade," Peter responded, "I embarked on my literary career. To the delight of our third grade class, I wrote a supposedly humorous story about a mouse named Georgie. Feeling very proud of myself, I needed no encouragement to send my story to the magazine, *Calling All Kids*. My effort was to no avail, however, as I soon received my first rejection slip.

"The editor had this to say about my masterpiece. 'The boy certainly has a vivid imagination. *Calling All Kids* could not use the story because there is far too much war, terror, and sadism. But the story flows very smoothly, and there is a minimum of confusion in the presentation of one so young. I think the author should be encouraged, since he has a definite flair for writing.' "

To the next question—How did your schooling continue?—Peter answered,

"I stayed at Greenacres and had Miss Bowman for fourth grade and Mrs. Merrihew for fifth and sixth."

"Over that time, can you pick out any punishment that you remember?"

Pete replied, "Well, frankly, I guess I can. One spring night, a friend and I went over to the playground, looking for something to do. Finding nothing, we turned to mischief. Six new poles had just been set in cement a few hours earlier, and were not yet solid. Within a period of about five minutes, six new poles were resting on the grass.

"We seemed to think it was pretty funny, but the feeling was not general. Over the grapevine the principal found out that we were the guilty ones. We were promptly hauled into the office for discipline. Besides getting it from our parents, we were made to watch the poles being reset from two thirty until eight-thirty the next day. Our job was to see that nobody tampered with them."

When asked what he thought of high school, Pete answered, "At first it was a strange, mysterious place; but after its intricate halls and rooms had been mastered, it was just like the palm of your hand. I think the teachers are good, although I despise school itself."

The last question asked was, "Of your many teachers, which do you think was the best?"

Without any hesitation, Peter responded, "Mrs. Merrihew, by a long shot. She developed traits and habits which have already proven of great value to me. I am sure that as I go through high school, college, and later life I will continue to remember and benefit from the guidance and inspiration she gave me."

CHECK SHEET FOR CHAPTER 5

Analysis of Samples

1. The final paragraph of "Exclusive Interview" is pretty flat. How could the writer have made it more interesting?

2. Pick out the sample that you find most effective. In explaining your choice to the group, point out ways that make it effective.

3. How does the third sample demonstrate that its writer was aware of the need for all paragraphs to cohere?

4. What style of writing is being used by the writer of "Exclusive Interview"? What probably was the general scheme of his entire book?

5. Which of the samples has made its point by using specific references? How do specific references enliven a paragraph?

Spelling

1. already, adv. (What homonym would you use to denote that everyone was ready?)
2. basketball, football, softball
3. everyday, adj. (What is its homonym and when is it used?)
4. fascinate
5. incessant
6. lanyard
7. lay, laying, laid (This means to *place* or *put* and always has an object)
8. nursery, nursery school
9. outside
10. permanent

11. predominant (How do you spell the verb form?)
12. twelfth
13. unique (Why should we not say something is "more" or "most" unique?)
14. weigh, weight

Questions for Group Consideration

1. Each of the following sentences needs a semicolon somewhere. Rewrite the sentence, adding the semicolon where needed and giving your reason for doing so. Add any other punctuation marks which may be needed.

a. I've always had a lot of trouble with math I think it all began in second grade.
b. One secret I have always kept in fact I'm not even mentioning it in this book.
c. Because I was so small I was never chosen for anyone's team but after big Tom became my friend people rushed to choose me.
d. As I recall these were the officers president Tom vice president my sister mascot me.

2. On your paper make the sign for a colon. A dash. A hyphen. Parentheses.

3. Each of the following sentences needs one of the four marks mentioned in No. 2. Write the sentences with the appropriate mark. Include any other necessary punctuation.

a. Camp Tickbite is located in a far out spot in Maine.
b. Miss Anthropus told me my work was 1 hastily done 2 untidily done and 3 totally unsatisfactory.
c. No boy who calls to see my sister today and a lot of them do call would possibly have been interested in her two years ago.
d. The subjects we study in the morning are three solid geometry English and American history.

4. Study the following sentences carefully and decide in what two ways the sentence patterns are alike.

a. Good horsemanship can be learned by anyone willing to learn.
b. The writing of Jim's paper has been done by someone else.
c. An analysis of slime mold was made by our group in biology.

5. Rewrite each of the above sentences in a shorter form:

Begin sentence "a" with *anyone.*
Begin sentence "b" with *someone else.*
Begin sentence "c" with *our group.*

6. Which of the following sentences have direct objects?

a. My typing has been done by my mother.
b. Dad laid his pipe on the table and looked at me.
c. The ball flew through the air and into a swamp.
d. I saw Jennie talking to my best friend and panicked.
e. Mother put the hot dish in front of me.
f. I have been an expert fly fisherman since I was fourteen.

7. Give the past participle for each of the following verbs:

a. to be	**d.** hang (a person)
b. have	**e.** lie (to recline)
c. ride	**f.** sink

8. What information has been omitted from each of the following sentences?

a. My book has been stolen.
b. It is said that the man hanged himself.
c. Much disagreement among the members has been reported.
d. An inconsistency is definitely seen throughout the book.
e. Woof-Woof Dog Food is universally recommended.
f. This locket was really given to me; I didn't snatch it.

More About Punctuation

1. The semicolon (;)

Here is a new rule concerning the semicolon. **In long, involved sentences, use the semicolon between the two main clauses.** This lets readers know when one main thought has ended and another begins; otherwise, they often have to read back to find out what the writer is driving at.

Examples:

When I was only nine, we went to France for a year; but, as I experienced an amazing number of illnesses there, I do not remember the land with much pleasure.

The rest of the family, seeing what was happening, abandoned their confused guest; and finally the five of them got the turkey leg away from me.

Semicolon Review:

a. Use a semicolon to join two independent clauses when the coordinate conjunction is omitted.

My father is head of the house; that is, he thinks he is.

I have two sisters; I also have two brothers.

b. Use a semicolon before a conjunctive adverb—however, moreover, therefore, otherwise, then, thus, indeed—and other joining expressions of the same type.

I lived happily for five years; then I was sent to school.

I enjoy school; however, I enjoy vacations more.

c. Use a semicolon to separate a confusing series of words.

John Jones is president; Tom Spade, vice president; Bill Lux, secretary; and Marty Nekko, treasurer.

Actors and their parts follow: Jim Ghysels, Oberon; Sally Smith, Titania; Robby Ralph, Puck; Jane Rae, Hermia; and Jill Till, Helena.

2. The Colon (:)

Use the colon to separate a list of items. It is often used after some form of the verb, follow.

In seventh grade I took the following subjects: geography, English, arithmetic, and French.

Members of the cast follow: George Inksip, Herman Cuttydorf; Julie Inksip, Theresa Bowie; Melvin, Frank Kronk.

Avoid the colon after any form of the verb to be.

3. The dash (—)

Use the dash sparingly. It is often used to separate an element of the sentence that would cause the reader confusion if other marks were used.

a. Now I—a great, big, strong he-man—could go to school.

b. We walked to the door—my heart was doing gymnastics—and went down the corridor to a room which had KINDERGARTEN written over the door in big letters.

4. Parentheses ( )

Avoid parentheses. Although they do have a legitimate use—to set off completely extraneous material within a long, involved sentence—most of the things you will want to put inside parentheses are better set off by commas.

wrong: I loved this toy (which was a teddy bear) for four years.
right: I loved this toy, which was a teddy bear, for four years.
best: I loved my toy teddy bear for four years.

wrong: All the time I grew smarter. (That is, I thought so.)
right: All the time I grew smarter; that is, I thought so.

5. The Hyphen (-)

Use the hyphen for compound adjectives. You may often want to join two words to make one adjective. When you do this, put a hyphen (-) between the words.

It was my four-year-old cousin.
This had a two-inch edge.
I had then an old, broken-down scooter.

A Further Matter of Style: Capitalization

1. Names of immediate relatives (mother, father, brother, sister, grandpa, etc.) are capitalized when no adjective precedes them. In those cases you can always insert a proper name without ruining the sense of the sentence.

wrong: It was my Mother who was calling. (We could not say: It was my Mrs. Smith . . .)
right: It was Mother who was calling. OR: It was my mother . . .

wrong:
We stayed with my Grandfather Jones.

right: We stayed with my grandfather Jones. OR: We stayed with Grandfather Jones.

2. Capitalize schools, camps, and other names only when they are part of a special title.

DO capitalize: Greenacres School, Hardrock High School, Camp Mohawk or Higby Camp, Lake Mahopac or Green Lake, Rio Grande or Grand River, White Mountains or Mount Rainier. Notice that all of these are specific titles of specific things.

DO NOT capitalize *high school, junior high school, elementary school, camp, lake, river,* or *mountain* unless they are used with a specific title preceding them.

3. Capitalize adjectives, including your classes in school, that derive from the names of countries: American, British, French.

But DO NOT capitalize classes without such derivation, thus: American studies, world civilization, science, British literature.

More About Verbs: Active and Passive Voice

Normally we use verbs in what we call the active voice. We start with a subject, add a verb and—if the verb can be followed by an object—we add the object, thus: Billy hit me. My mother recommends this product.

However, any verb that can take an object can also be put into what we call the passive voice. We form the passive voice by taking the past participle (*hit, recommended*) and placing before it as a helper-verb an appropriate tense of the verb *to be: am* hit, *was* hit, *will be* hit, *has been* recommended, *had been* recommended, *will have been* recommended.

We then begin our sentence with what was the object and put what was once the subject into a *by*-phrase: I was hit *by Billy.* This product is recommended *by my mother.* We can also omit the *by*-phrase completely and still have a complete sentence: I was hit. This product is recommended.

Because we can omit the *by*-phrase, using the passive voice enables us to make less than specific statements, avoiding the responsibility of naming the subject. In communicating with us, others can also make unproved generalizations by not saying WHO recommends or proves something.

The overuse of the passive voice also leads to wordiness. Notice that it takes two more words to say "I was hit by Billy" than it does for "Billy hit me."

Use of the passive voice is necessary in our writing and speaking, if only for sentence variety or for emphasis, but it should not be used excessively or as an excuse for being specific. When you are editing your chapters, seek out sentences using the passive voice. If you can say them more directly, change the passive to active and be a less wordy, more specific, and clearer writer. Here are some rules to remember.

1. Avoid the passive voice as an excuse for being specific.

2. Avoid the passive voice if you gain nothing but more words from its use.

3. Avoid the passive voice if it leads to what we call a subject shift within a sentence.

wrong: I took a paint brush and blobbed the canvas, and on it was drawn a lion.
right: I took a paint brush, blobbed the canvas, and drew a lion.

wrong: We came home late, and a good time was had by all.
right: We came home late after having had a good time.

Two Problem Verbs

Use the forms of *lie* and *lay* correctly.

Forms of Lie: lie, lying, lay, lain.

This word means "to rest on" and NEVER is followed by an object.

right: The rug was lying crooked on the floor.
She has lain down for a nap.
The cat had to lie down for a minute.
Yesterday she lay down for a minute and slept for two hours.

This verb can NEVER be used in the passive voice.

Forms of Lay: lay, laying, laid, laid

This word means *to place* and ALWAYS is followed by an object in the active voice.

right: Shelley is laying dinner on the table.
Dad has laid down the law.
Just lay it on the table, please.
He laid bricks for a living.

This verb CAN be used in the passive voice.

The law was laid down.
The bricks have been laid.

ASSIGNMENT 5

Write Chapter 4 of your autobiography. It will cover part or all of your school days to the present. Remember that your next chapter will also deal with education and that you must have some idea of how to continue your story in that assignment. Don't forget the necessary preliminaries to writing and the careful revision of the rough draft.

PRACTICE TEST V

This test covers only the errors discussed in the first five chapters. Review the Check Sheets and then, without looking back, do the test. The teacher may want to check your work or to give you another test of the same sort. Each error will count as 2½ points, if anybody's counting.

I. The capitalized words in the following sentences have certain letters omitted. Fill in the correct letter to make the word appear in its correct spelling. Write only the word on your paper.

1. At first, school was a FA______ATING experience.

2. My brother is already in TWEL_____ grade.

3. The men were L______NG bricks outside the classroom.

4. By now going to school is an EV______AY experience.

5. What I have learned is now a PERM______T part of me.

II. Punctuate the following sentences properly. Each sentence will need at least one semicolon. On your paper write only the two words to be separated and place the semicolon between them.

1. I had always loved to sit quietly looking at a book thus my parents were not surprised when I began reading before I went to school.

2. For some moments the cat watched the nibbling mouse then it sprang and caught the hapless cretature in its greedy paws.

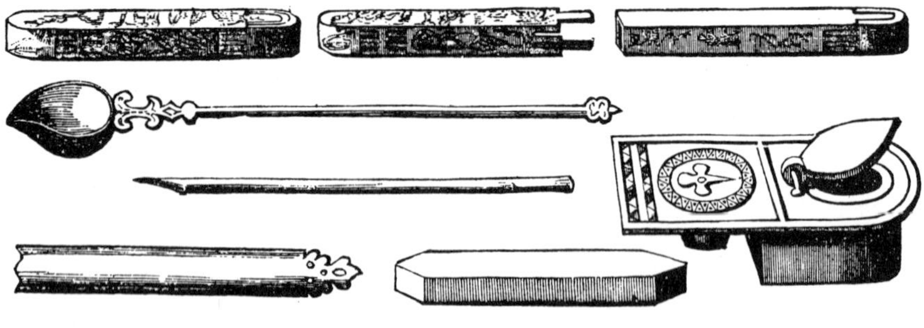

Persian writing instruments. New York Public Library Picture Collection.

3. Jim is the new president Tom the vice president Bill the secretary and I the reporter.

4. Donald is my only brother he is also my best friend.

5. Though it was still raining fiercely I insisted on going to the station and finally my mother who was sick of hearing me whine gave me permission to go.

III. Rewrite the following sentences with correct punctuation.

1. That summer I received A's in the following categories duck waddling pea shooting reading readiness and basic kindness.

2. When I think back to kindergarten I often wonder what we really did I'm certain that we did no work.

3. My mother had seen me get off the bus therefore she was sure that I would be home in a minute.

4. My mother had seen me get off the bus and she was sure that I would be home in a minute.

5. As my mother had seen me get off the bus she was sure that I would be home in a minute.

IV. Rewrite each of the following sentences so that the verbs will all be in the active voice.

1. After the plane had been sighted by my father, he called everyone's attention to it.

2. The walls were painted yellow by the man after a heated argument between him and my mother.

3. I yelled that my sister was being beaten up by the bully of the class.

4. The quotation was first written by Shakespeare.

5. Today the quotation has been memorized by almost everyone in England and America.

V. Properly capitalize five more words in the following short paragraph. On your paper, write only the word to be capitalized.

In junior high school, band followed english class. I had learned to play the saxophone at camp liberty, and I looked forward to music and band each day. Mr. Dribble, the principal, knew that I preferred band to french class. As a result, he would discipline me when I misbehaved in foreign language class by making me miss bandmaster Williams' lessons.

VI. Each of the following sentences has one error or poor choice of words. Write on your paper the correction or improvement after the word or words which need changing.

1. The dog had lain its head in my lap.

2. Swamp Hollow Day Camp was where I was sent to learn how to adjust.

3. The dog was being ornery again, which always made Mom angry.

4. Uncle is one of those men which just don't listen to advice.

5. A lesson which meant a lot to me then and which I shall always try to remember.

6. Jim couldn't remember where he had layed the book.

7. We walked a long way down the road before we see the school.

8. After writing "I'm sorry" 150 times on the blackboard, the teacher sent me home.

9. I have read only one play by Shakespeare, but the benefit that has been done to me by reading it is great.

10. Chapter 4 dealt with my preschool days; this one is my life in school.

11. I told the baby sitter I'd lay down and be quiet.

12. The Burns's have a house just the color of ours.

13. Here is a drawing showing the mountains around our home in Vermont made when I was five.

14. We had toiled up the hill, but the panorama that was seen was worth the effort and made us gasp with ecstasy.

15. When I walked into the house, my first impression was the wrong place had been entered.

Further Lessons

The pieces that follow deal mostly with the kind of lessons we learn from experience. The opening poem looks optimistically at experience. The following piece relates an experience of a fairly cantankerous girl at a Midwestern summer camp. The next relates the poignant experiences of a Winnebago Indian girl who loved school but had to leave it. The section closes in a Boston black ghetto, where Malcolm X began to come to terms with his complex self.

JONI MITCHELL (1943–) was born and raised in western Canada, where she was known as Joan Anderson. Before she was nineteen, she was on her way to becoming a top singer of the 70's. She hit the superstar category of songwriter and guitarist with her 1969 recording of "Woodstock." Of her lyrics Joni has said, "The most important thing is to write in your own blood." Before you read the lyrics to her song, ask yourself what kind of circle games you have played.

The Circle Game

JONI MITCHELL

Yesterday a child came out to wonder.
Caught a dragon fly inside a jar.
Fearful when the sky was full of thunder,
And tearful at the falling of a star.

And the seasons, they go 'round and 'round
And the painted ponies go up and down.
We're captive on the carousel of time.
We can't return, we can only look behind
From where we came and go 'round
And 'round and 'round in the circle game.

Then the child moved ten times
'Round the seasons,
Skated over ten clear frozen streams,
Words like, when you're older
Must appease him, and promises of
Someday make his dreams.

Sixteen springs and sixteen summers
Gone now, cartwheels turn to car wheels
Thru the town, And they tell him,
Take your time, it won't be long now,
Till you drag your feet to
Slow the circles down.

So the years spin by
And now the boy is twenty
Dreams have lost some grandeur
Coming true, There'll be new dreams,
Maybe better dreams, and plenty
Before the last revolving year is through. ♉

". . . and so I was, for the teacher's purpose, the perfect guinea pig."

RUTH McKENNY (1911–   ) published in 1938 a group of adventures centered on herself and her sister Eileen as they matured in Ohio and advanced on New York City. The book was adapted to become eventually the successful Broadway play of the same name, *My Sister, Eileen,* and the Leonard Bernstein musical, *Wonderful Town*. The guinea pig in the selection is the author herself. As you enjoy the piece, ask yourself whether or not you have ever discovered that you were being used. If you have, you probably have a good incident to retell.

Guinea Pig: My Frightful Adventures with the Red Cross

RUTH McKENNY

I was nearly drowned, in my youth, by a Red Cross Lifesaving Examiner, and I once suffered, in the noble cause of saving human life from a watery grave, a black eye which was a perfect daisy and embarrassed me for days. Looking back on my agonies, I feel that none of my sacrifices, especially the black eye, were in the least worth while. Indeed, to be brutally frank about it, I feel that the whole modern school of scientific lifesaving is a lot of hogwash.

Of course, I've had rather bad luck with lifesavers, right from the beginning. Long before I ever had any dealings with professional lifesavers my sister nearly drowned me, quite by mistake. My father once took us to a northern Michigan fishing camp, where we found the life very dull. He used to go trolling for bass on our little lake all day long, and at night come home to our lodge, dead-beat and minus any bass. In the meantime Eileen and I, who were nine and ten at the time, used to take an old rowboat out to a shallow section of the lake and, sitting in the hot sun, feed worms to an unexciting variety of small, undernourished fish called gillies. We hated the whole business.

Father, however, loved to fish, even if he didn't catch a single fish in three weeks, which on this trip he didn't. One night, however, he carried his enthusiasm beyond a decent pitch. He decided to go bass fishing after dark, and rather than leave us alone in the lodge and up to [heaven] knows what, he ordered us to take our boat and row along after him.

Eileen and I were very bored rowing around in the dark, and finally, in desperation, we began to stand up and rock the boat, which resulted, at last, in my falling into the lake with a mighty splash.

When I came up, choking and mad as anything, Eileen saw me struggling, and, as she always says with a catch in her voice, she only meant to help me. Good intentions, however, are of little importance in a situation like that. For she grabbed an oar out of the lock, and with an uncertain gesture hit me square on the chin.

I went down with a howl of pain. Eileen, who could not see much in the darkness, was now really frightened. The cold water revived me after the blow and I came to the surface, considerably weakened but still able to swim over to the boat. Whereupon Eileen, in a noble attempt to give me the oar to grab, raised it once again, and socked me square on the top of the head. I went down again, this time without a murmur, and my last thought was a vague wonder that my own sister should want to murder me with a rowboat oar.

As for Eileen, she heard the dull impact of the oar on my head and saw the shadowy figure of her sister disappear. So she jumped in the lake, screeching furiously, and began to flail around in the water, howling for help and looking for me. At this point I came to the surface and swam over to the boat, with the intention of killing Eileen.

Father, rowing hard, arrived just in time to pull us both out of the water and prevent me from attacking Eileen with the rowboat anchor. The worst part about the whole thing, as far as I was concerned, was that Eileen was considered a heroine and Father told everybody in the lake community that she had saved my life. The postmaster put her name in for a medal.

After what I suffered from amateur lifesaving, I should have known enough to avoid even the merest contact with the professional variety of water mercy. I learned too late that being socked with an oar is as nothing compared to what the Red Cross can think up.

From the very beginning of that awful lifesaving course I took the last season I went to a girls' camp, I was a marked woman. The rest of the embryo lifesavers were little, slender maidens, but I am a peasant type, and I was monstrously big for my fourteen years. I approximated, in poundage anyway, the theoretical adult we energetic young lifesavers were scheduled to rescue, and so I was, for the teacher's purpose, the perfect guinea pig.

The first few days of the course were unpleasant for me, but not terribly dangerous. The elementary lifesaving hold, in case you haven't seen some hapless victim being rescued by our brave beach guardians, is a snakelike arrangement for supporting the drowning citizen with one hand while you paddle him in to shore with the other. You are supposed to wrap your arm around his neck and shoulders, and keep his head well above water by resting it on your collarbone.

This is all very well in theory, of course, but the trick that none of Miss Folgil's little pupils could master was keeping the victim's nose and mouth above the waterline. Time and again I was held in a viselike grip by one of the earnest students with my whole face an inch or two under the billowing waves.

"No, no, Betsy," Miss Folgil would scream through her megaphone, as I felt the water rush into my lungs. "No, no, you must keep the head a little higher." At this point I would begin to kick and struggle, and generally the pupil would have to let go while I came up for air. Miss Folgil was always very stern with me.

"Ruth," she would shriek from her boat, "I insist! You must allow Betsy to tow you all the way in. We come to Struggling in Lesson Six."

This was but the mere beginning, however. A few lessons later we came to the section of the course where we learned how to undress under water in forty seconds. Perhaps I should say we came to the point where the *rest* of the pupils learned how to get rid of shoes and such while holding their breaths. I never did.

There was quite a little ceremony connected with this part of the course. Miss Folgil, and some lucky creature named as timekeeper and armed with a stopwatch, rowed the prospective victim out to deep water. The pupil, dressed in high, laced tennis shoes, long stockings, heavy bloomers, and a middy blouse, then stood poised at the end of the boat. When the timekeeper yelled "Go!" the future boon to mankind dived into the water and, while holding her breath under the surface, unlaced her shoes and stripped down to her bathing suit. Miss Folgil never explained what connection, if any, this curious rite had with saving human lives.

I had no middy of my own, so I borrowed one of my sister's. My sister was a slender little thing and I was, as I said, robust, which puts it politely. Eileen had some trouble wedging me into that middy, and once in it I looked like a stuffed sausage. It never occurred to me how

Culver Pictures.

hard it was going to be to get that middy off, especially when it was wet and slippery.

As we rowed out for my ordeal by undressing, Miss Folgil was snappish and bored.

"Hurry up," she said, looking irritated. "Let's get this over with quick. I don't think you're ready to pass the test, anyway."

I was good and mad when I jumped off the boat, and determined to Make Good and show that old Miss Folgil, whom I was beginning to dislike thoroughly. As soon as I was under water, I got my shoes off, and I had no trouble with the bloomers or stockings. I was just beginning to run out of breath when I held up my arms and started to pull off the middy.

Now, the middy, in the event you don't understand the principle of this girl-child garment, is made with a small head opening, long sleeves, and no front opening. You pull it on and off over your head. You do if you are lucky, that is. I got the middy just past my neck so that my face was covered with heavy linen cloth, when it stuck.

I pulled frantically and my lungs started to burst. Finally I thought the heck with the test, the heck with saving other people's lives, anyway. I came to the surface, a curious sight, my head enfolded in a water-soaked middy blouse. I made a brief sound, a desperate glub-glub, a call for help. My arms were stuck in the middy and I couldn't swim. I went down. I breathed in large quantities of water and linen cloth.

I came up again, making final frantic appeals. Four feet away sat a professional lifesaver, paying absolutely no attention to somebody drowning right under her nose. I went down again, struggling with last panic-stricken feverishness, fighting water and a middy blouse for my life. At this point the timekeeper pointed out to Miss Folgil that I had been under water for eighty-five seconds, which was quite a time for anybody. Miss Folgil was very annoyed, as she hated to get her bathing suit wet, but, a thoughtful teacher, she picked up her megaphone, shouted to the rest of the class on the beach to watch, and dived in after me.

If I say so myself, I gave her quite a time rescuing me. I presented a new and different problem, and probably am written up in textbooks now under the heading "What to Do When the Victim Is Entangled in a Tight Middy Blouse." Miss Folgil finally towed my still-breathing body over to the boat, reached for her bowie knife, which she carried on a ring with her whistle, and cut Eileen's middy straight up the front. Then she towed me with Hold No. 2 right in to the shore and delivered me up to the class for artificial respiration. I will never forgive the Red Cross for that terrible trip through the water, when I might have been hoisted into the boat and rowed in except for Miss Folgil's overdeveloped sense of drama and pedagogy.

I tried to quit the lifesaving class after that, but the head counselor at the camp said I must keep on, to show that I was the kind of girl who always finished what she planned to do. Otherwise, she assured me, I would be a weak character and never amount to anything when I grew up.

So I stayed for Lesson 6: "Struggling." After that I didn't care if I never amounted to anything when I grew up. In fact, I hoped I wouldn't. It would serve everybody right, especially Miss Folgil. I came a little late to the class session that day and missed the discussion of theory, always held on the beach before the actual practice in the lake. That was just my hard luck. I was always a child of misfortune. I wonder that I survived my youth at all.

"We were waiting for you, Ruth," Miss Folgil chirped cheerily to me as I arrived, sullen and downcast, at the little group of earnest students sitting on the sand.

"What for?" I said warily. I was determined not to be a guinea pig any more. The last wave had washed over my helpless face.

"You swim out," Miss Folgil went on, ignoring my bad temper, "until you are in deep water—about twelve feet will do. Then you begin to flail around and shout for help. One of the students will swim out to you."

All of this sounded familiar and terrible. I had been doing that for days, and getting water in my nose for my pains.

"But when the student arrives," Miss Folgil went on, "you must not allow her to simply tow you away. You must struggle, just as hard as you can. You must try to clutch her by the head, you must try to twine your legs about her, and otherwise hamper her in trying to save you."

Now, *this* sounded something like. I was foolishly fired by the attractive thought of getting back at some of the fiends who had been ducking me in the name of science for the past two weeks. Unfortunately, I hadn't studied Chapter 9, entitled "How to Break Holds the Drowning Swimmer Uses." Worse, I hadn't heard Miss Folgil's lecture on "Be Firm with the Panic-Stricken Swimmer—Better a Few Bruises Than a Watery Grave." This last was Miss Folgil's own opinion, of course.

So I swam out to my doom, happy as a lark. Maybelle Anne Pettijohn, a tall, lean girl who ordinarily wore horn-rimmed spectacles, was Miss Folgil's choice to rescue Exhibit A, the panic-stricken swimmer.

I laughed when I saw her coming. I thought I could clean up Maybelle Anne easily enough, but alas, I hadn't counted on Maybelle Anne's methodical approach to life. She had read Chapter 9 in our textbook, and she had listened carefully to Miss Folgil's inspiring words. Besides, Maybelle Anne was just naturally the kind of girl who ran around doing people dirty for their own good. "This may hurt your feelings," she used to say mournfully, "but I feel I have to tell you . . ."

When Maybelle Anne got near me, I enthusiastically lunged for her neck and hung on with both hands while getting her around her waist with my legs. Maybelle Anne thereupon dug her fingernails into my hands with ferocious force, and I let go and swam away, hurt and surprised. This was distinctly not playing fair.

"What's the idea?" I called out.

"It says to do that in the book," Maybelle Anne replied, treading water.

"Well, you lay off of that stuff," I said, angered, book or no book. Maybelle Anne was a Girl Scout, too, and I was shocked to think she'd go around using her fingernails in a fair fight.

"Come on, struggle," Maybelle Anne said, getting winded from treading water. I swam over, pretty reluctant and much more wary. Believe it or not, this time Maybelle Anne, who was two medals from being a Beaver or whatever it is Girl Scouts with a lot of medals get to be, bit me.

In addition to biting me, Maybelle Anne swung her arm around my neck, with the intention of towing me in to the shore. But I still had plenty of fight left and I had never been so mad in my life. I got Maybelle Anne under water two or three times, and I almost thought I had her when suddenly, to my earnest surprise, she hauled off and hit me as hard as she could, right in the eye. Then she towed me in, triumphant as anything.

Maybelle Anne afterward claimed it was all in the book, and she wouldn't even apologize for my black eye. Eileen and I fixed her, though. We put a little garter snake in her bed and scared the daylights out of her. Maybelle Anne was easy to scare anyway, and really a very disagreeable girl. I used to hope that she would come to a bad end, which, from my point of view, at least, she did. Maybelle Anne grew up to be a Regional Red Cross Lifesaving examiner.

I'll bet she just loves her work.

Vocabulary

So she jumped in the lake, screeching furiously, and began to *flail* around in the water, howling for help . . . . (125:27); in case you haven't seen some *hapless* victim being rescued by our brave beach guardians . . . . (126:7); I swam over, pretty reluctant and much more *wary*. . . . (129:39)

Study Questions and Activities

1. Many pieces of exposition, like this one, manage in their first paragraph to set the tone of the essay and precisely foreshadow most of what is to be discussed. After finishing this excerpt, reread the first three sentences and demonstrate how they establish both the tone and much of what follows.

2. Paragraphs 2 through 7 appear to have little to do with either the title or the Red Cross course. How does the author manage to make the incident with her father and sister a part of the unified whole? Look for words and phrases that make this incident cohere to the rest of the essay. Does the tone of the incident add to the coherence?

3. Now look carefully at paragraph 8, which we can label a transition paragraph. What words and phrases smoothly aid the transition in time and place? What ones are used to maintain the tone?

4. Have you ever known an adult similar to Miss Folgil? What generalization can you make that would link the two in comparison? You might begin your sentence with "Both Miss Folgil and. . . ." Be sure to generalize the characteristic that the two have in common.

5. Humorists frequently depend upon final lines to release the laughter they have been building up within the reader or viewer. How many such final lines can you find in this passage?

6. Which of the principals in the cast has been most vividly characterized? Be able to argue your case.

7. Read again paragraph 11, page 126. In it you will find several vivid epithets: "*hapless* victim," "*brave beach* guardians," "*snakelike* arrangement," for examples. By noting their usage, how would you define an epithet? Check your definition with that in a dictionary. With a group of classmates select five nouns and see how many epithets you can find for each. Read the most colorful epithets to the class.

"Alas, I was enjoying school so much, and they made me stop. . . . I was going to be married. . . . What would my crying avail me?"

MOUNTAIN WOLF WOMAN (1884–1959) was a Winnebago Indian born on a reservation in Wisconsin. In this part of her autobiography she recalls her growth, schooling, and marriage in a culture that was by then resigned to the white man's dominance. She also presents a picture of woman's secondary role in her tribe, as well as one of her own emerging independent spirit. NANCY OESTREICH LURIE (1924–), who translated the writing, is a well-known anthropologist.

The culture of the Winnebagos was in many ways different from that with which most of us are familiar. Reading this selection may help you realize the vitality of certain customs followed by much of humanity.

"Growing Up and Marriage"

From *Mountain Wolf Woman*

NANCY OESTREICH LURIE, editor

At the place where they hunted, father and older brother killed as many deer as they would need for a feast. They set aside ten deer on a high, narrow rack made for storing meat. They cut down crotched poles and set them up in a rectangle with poles across the crotches and other poles forming a platform, similar to the open-sided square shelters used as sun shades, but narrower and higher. They put the deer on it and covered them with the hides.

Once there was a lot of snow on the ground when we went back home. We had come in wagons and when we went back the wagon wheels made a loud noise rolling over the snow. We always returned to our home at Black River Falls where we ordinarily lived. Other Winnebago also did this. They too went away some place, wherever they chose to go to hunt, and then they would give a feast. Father and all the Indians used to give feasts. Father used to hold big feasts, ten fireplaces they said. The row of fireplaces used to stretch off into the distance. Many Indians attended and father used to feed a wigwam full of people. There we would dance all night. Sometimes children were named at feasts. This is what they used to do time and again. Sometimes, those who had been fasting would then eat at the feast.

That is what my older brother Hágaga did, he alone fasted. Hénaga did not have any patience with such things, but brother Hágaga fasted in the woods. My father built a shelter for them to live in and they slept there four nights. But my older brother Hénaga did not do that. Hénaga came home during that time. Mother wept. "Why did you do that? Why did you do that?" she said. "Oh," he said, "I am sick of it so I stopped." But brother Hágaga stayed there. He was trying to remain until feast time. When it was about time for the feast, father and his nephews built the lodge and made all the preparations for it. All these kinsmen that father would invite to the feast he could make work for him. That is what they did. Brother was allowed to return at the time of the feast since at that time one who fasts for a vision may eat.

When he was about to return they went around the lodge with a deer hide. They took a deer hide around the morning he was going to come back. Brother Hágaga must have been a little boy at the time they were taking this white deer hide around. They used it when dancing, taking the deer hide and dancing with it. It seemed to be a very pleasant time. There brother cried to the Thunders. Our aunts and older sisters heard my older brother crying and they cried too, they said. Today they do not do that any more.

My older sister Hínakega and I also used to fast. They used to make us do this. We would blacken our cheeks and would not eat all day. That was at the time of the hunting I have told about, before we returned from hunting. We used to blacken our cheeks with charcoal at the time father left in the morning to go hunting. We used coals from the fire to blacken our cheeks and we did not eat all day. I used to play outside but my older sister used to sit indoors and weave yarn belts. When father returned from hunting in the evening he used to say to us, "Go cry to the Thunders." When father was ready to eat he would give us tobacco and say to us, "Here, go cry to the Thunders." Just as it was getting dark my sister and I used to go off a certain distance and she would say to me, "Go stand by a tree and I am going to go farther on." We used to stand there and look at the stars and cry to the Thunders. This is what we used to sing:

"Oh, Good Spirits
Will they pity me? Here am I, pleading."

We used to sing and scatter tobacco, standing there and watching the stars and the moon. We used to cry because, after all, we were hungry. We used to think we were pitied. We really wanted to mean what we were saying.

When we finished with our song we scattered tobacco at the foot of the tree and returned home. When we got back home father ate and we ate too. We did not eat all day, only at night and when we had finished eating we put the dishes away. Then father used to say, "All right, prepare your bedding and go to bed and I will tell you some stories." I really enjoyed listening to my father tell stories. Everybody, the entire household, was very quiet and in this atmosphere my father used to tell stories. He used to tell myths, the sacred stories, and that is why I also know some myths. I do not know all of them any more, I just remember parts of stories.

Again we went hunting and returned to Black River Falls and had our feast there. I was a little girl. The people followed the same cycle, winter, spring, summer, and when it was almost fall my oldest brother said, "My little sister should go to school." I was nine years old. He said, "I like to hear women speak English so I would like my little sister to learn how to speak English." They let me go to school at Tomah, Wisconsin, and I attended school there for two years. Then I did not go to school again for a long time. Well, whatever the reason, that is the way with Indians. The Indians do not stay home so that their children can attend school. That is what they have done through the years, but at present they can no longer act in this way.

Then I lived at home and the family went on a short hunting trip. After that they went off to find cranberries and on our return we stopped at the home of grandfather Náqi-Johnga. . . .

Spring arrived, and again deer-hunting time, and winter back at Black River Falls when my father gave feasts, and then it was spring again. Once more we moved to the Mississippi River. When the muskrat season was over we returned to our home. The people engaged in their usual activities, but that time when we returned, after a while, mother and father said that they were not going to put in any garden.—Father must have had word from his uncles, although I did not hear about it. Father's uncles at Wittenberg, Wisconsin, were old men. They lived there at Wittenberg for many years. Father pitied his uncles because they were old and could not help themselves. My parents said that was where we were going to move. My older sister also accompanied us and we moved there. We used big wagons drawn by horses.

North of the town of Marshfield there was a settlement of Indians and we slept there. Some lived in frame houses and some lived in

Culver Pictures.

bark-sided gabled cabins with earth-covered roofs. They built these cabins themselves and these were scattered throughout the settlement. They were Potawatomi Indians and mother had relatives there. They were called Chippewa Woman and Hínuga, her daughter. They spoke Winnebago very fluently. Mother knew them and knew that they were living there so we stopped at that place. We must have slept there twice in order to rest the horses. There was a tall frame house where we stayed and the name of the person who lived there was Crotched

Tree. He had a wife. It would seem that father was also part Potawatomi because she was his relative. They invited us to eat and so we ate. At that place there was a dance area. It was a sacred place. They invited us to eat there that evening and so we went there to eat. . . .

We left that place and arrived at Wittenberg. We had a grandfather there whose name was High Snake and he lived in a big log cabin. We stopped there and my father went off to get those two dear little old men. They were very old men. It was their son who lived at the place where we stopped. The old men lived at another place and my father went there for them. One was called Good Snake and the other was called Fear the Snake Den. He soon brought them and they began to make preparations at grandfather High Snake's place. They cut trees for lodge poles and hauled them back in a big horse-drawn wagon. There they set up a long lodge. They built a Medicine Lodge. On the east side where the sun rises they completed it and sang upon reaching that end. My older sister White Thunder and my older brother Hénaga were initiated into the lodge and I imagine that is why we went there. Evidently father's uncles told us to come there, and because they were old men we went there. They had the paraphernalia for a Medicine Dance so the Medicine Dance was held there. They held the Medicine Dance as soon as we arrived. During that time Indians came there to Wittenberg from various places. The Indians were real Indians! Some of them brought wagons and some of them let the horses back-pack their belongings. Some of them arrived riding horseback. There were many Indians and they held a Medicine Dance. We were gathered there in a big group. . . .

It must have been fall by that time and my sisters went back to Black River Falls. Father, mother, my brothers and my older sister Hínakega did not go back. We remained there for a while. One of my grandfathers who was called Rattlesnake had land next to the highway and told us that we should live there. My father made a big round wigwam of bark and there we lived. That fall I did not go to school at all. We moved to another place where my father trapped. He was still with my grandfathers. We went to a place where there is a lake, Grass Lake it is called. My grandfathers were acquainted with some white people where they used to trap. Father trapped there along with the grandfathers and they went to some other places as well. That was during the fall and when the cold weather was about to set in we went back to Wittenberg. They should have put me in school that fall. Not until we returned did they put me in school. I went to the Lutheran Mission School at Wittenberg. I had attended school at Tomah and finally I want to school again. I was a teen-age girl and I went to school there every year. . . .

At the school there was an Oneida woman who was the girls' matron. She was called Nancy Smith. Whenever the Indians were going to have a dance, Nancy Smith and I would ride there on our bicycles. Once when the Indians were going to hold a dance Nancy said, "It would be more fun if we went on horseback." In town they used to have ponies at the place where they sold wagons. They used to be tough. She asked me to hire some of those ponies. There were many horse stalls at the livery stable where I went for the ponies. They put saddles on the horses and I sat on one and went outside. I had a terribly hard time getting on as it was skittish. Leading the other one, I started back. The horse I was riding tried to run, so I held back on the reins. I had to fight that horse all the way, but I finally got back. I used to think horseback riding was a lot of fun. I was like a boy riding horses. When I got back, Nancy also had a hard time getting in the saddle. We started off immediately, letting the horses run. After a while we held the reins in on the horses so they would walk. We continued on our way letting the horses alternately run and walk. We finally arrived where the Indians were dancing. We dismounted and sat and watched the people dance. We sat on a big log, watching them dance. The horses were standing nearby and we were sitting there holding the reins. They had been having a war dance and then they had a "squaw dance." Four women came over and asked me to dance. Nancy told me to go ahead and dance, and so I did. I was dressed in "citizens' clothing," and I really danced! When they used to ask me to dance I would do so. They said that they really liked it for me. When I watched the horse races they used to tell me that they liked it when I enjoyed myself dancing. Whenever something of that sort was taking place I was never embarrassed, no matter the circumstances. I always used to be there. Eventually we started back. We arrived at town and returned the horses. I do not know how much Nancy paid for their hire. When we got to town we walked back to the school. . . .

Then I stopped attending school. They took me out of school. Alas, I was enjoying school so much, and they made me stop. They took me back home. They had let me go to school and now they made me quit. It was then that they told me I was going to be married. I cried but it did not do any good. What would my crying avail me? They had already arranged it. As they were telling me about it my mother said, "My little daughter, I prize you highly. You alone are my youngest child. I prize you highly but nothing can be done about this matter. It is your brothers' doing. You must do whatever your brothers say. If you do not do so, you are going to embarrass them. They have been drinking again, but if you do not do this they will be disgraced. They might even experience something unfortunate." Thus mother spoke to me, she rather frightened me.

My father said, "My little daughter, you do not have very many things to wear, but you will go riding on your little pony. You do not have anything, but you will not walk there." I had a little horse, a dapple-gray kind of pony that was about three years old. Father brought it for me and there the pony stood. They dressed me. I wore a ribbon embroidery skirt and I wore one as a shawl. I wore a heavily beaded binding for the braid of hair down my back, and I had on earrings. It looked as if I were going to a dance. That man was sitting nearby. He started out leading the pony and I followed after. When we reached a road that had high banks on the side he mounted the horse and I got on behind him. That is the way he brought me home. We rode together. That is how I became a daughter-in-law.

As a daughter-in-law I arrived. When I arrived he had me go in the wigwam and I went in and sat down. They told me to sit on the bed and I sat there. I took off all the clothing that I was wearing when I got there. I took it all off. I laid down a shawl and whatever I had, all the finery, I put on it; beads, the necklaces, clothing, even the blouse that I was wearing. Finally, the man's mother came in. Outside the wigwam there were canvas-covered wigwams standing here and there. The woman took the things and left. There were women sitting all about outside. They were his female relatives. They divided the things among themselves. As they distributed the things around, everybody contributed something in return. Two or three days from the time of my arrival they took me back with four horses and a double shawl so full of things they could barely tie the corners together. They took me home and later I received two more horses, so they gave me six horses in all. That is how they used to arrange things for young women in the past. They made the girls marry into whatever family they decided upon. They made the arrangements. That is the way they used to do.

At the time that my mother was combing my hair and I was weeping at the prospect of becoming a daughter-in-law she told me, "Daughter, I prize you very much, but this matter cannot be helped. When you are older and know better, you can marry whomever you yourself think that you want to marry." Mother said that to me and I did not forget it!

In the first place, before they made me get married, my older brother had been drinking and was asleep. I guess he slept there all day and when he awoke that man they made me marry, who was not a drinker, was there. He sat there using his hat to fan away the mosquitoes from my brother's face. That is why they made me marry that man. My brother awoke and he surmised, "He is doing this for me because I have sisters. That is what he is thinking to himself." So they made me marry that man. That is what the Indians used to do in the past.

That man was very easily aroused to jealousy of other men. He used to accuse me of being with other men. That made me angry. I hated him. He used to watch me too. So, I said to him one time, "No matter how closely you watch me, if I am going to leave you, I am going to leave you! There are a lot of things right now that I do not like." That is what I did to him. I left him taking the two children with me. . . .

Vocabulary

father and his nephews built the lodge. . . . All these *kinsmen* that father would invite to the feast he could make work for him . . . . (132:16); They had the *paraphernalia* for a Medicine Dance . . . . (135:20); They put saddles on the horses. . . . I had a terribly hard time getting on as it was *skittish* . . . . (136:10); My brother awoke and he *surmised,* "He is doing this for me because I have sisters. That is what he is thinking . . . ." (138:1)

Study Questions and Activities

1. This selection has been edited from the writings of an Indian woman with very little formal education. How many evidences can you offer to show that the narrator writes and organizes differently from many of the other authors?

2. If we concede that the writer's style and organization suffer from flaws, why might many people consider this an important addition to the autobiographies of the world?

3. The untutored writer frequently charms the reader by compressing into a short phrase or sentence ideas that many of us would take more words to express. Such a sentence, one capturing time, is this writer's: "Spring arrived, and again deer-hunting time, and winter back at Black River Falls when my father gave feasts, and then it was spring again." How much time has passed in this sentence? How many seasons can you identify? How would you account for the omission of one season?

4. What similarities and differences can you discover in the religious training of Mountain Wolf Woman and that you are familiar with?

5. Was the culture Mountain Wolf Woman knew dominated by men or by women? Give your reasons.

6. Of her education, Mountain Wolf Woman writes, "They had let me go to school and now they made me quit." How does the writer's choice of verbs exactly mirror her feelings? Try rewriting the sentence to agree with your own mood of the moment. In both your sentence and in the original, who are meant by "they"?

7. How many years of schooling would you guess that the writer had before her marriage? Why do you suppose that her only detailed writing about it concerned an out-of-school dance?

8. From what we read in the selection, what seem to have been the Winnebago customs of marriage and divorce?

9. Choose a committee or a classmate to look up in the library a history of the United States and its treaties with the Winnebago Indians up to the present. In discussing the report, the class may want to ponder this question: "Why does Mountain Wolf Woman, who was alive during the Nebraska migration, make no mention of the politics of her times?"

"How ridiculous I was! Stupid enough to stand there simply lost in admiration of my hair now looking 'white'. . . ."

Boston in 1940, when MALCOLM X (1925–1965) came to that city to live with a half-sister, was hardly the city Henry Adams had known, especially the Roxbury area, which was now a black ghetto. Describing his life there, Malcolm X recalls both his first attempts to rise in the world and the origins of his awareness that blacks should not lose their identity by becoming imitators of whites.

The incident is Chapter 3 of *The Autobiography of Malcolm X,* the first-person account of a great black leader. Much of the book was written by ALEX HALEY, the author of the selection from *Roots* in Chapter 1. He constructed it from remembrances that Malcolm X wrote on scraps of paper or recounted during the two men's close association from 1960 until 1965, the year of Malcolm X's murder.

In the selection the older Malcolm X recalls youthful experiences of which he is no longer proud. What similar denials of once proud experiments can you recall in your own life?

Homeboy

MALCOLM X

I looked like Li'l Abner. Mason, Michigan, was written all over me. My kinky, reddish hair was cut hick style, and I didn't even use grease in it. My green suit's coat sleeves stopped above my wrists, the pants legs showed three inches of socks. Just a shade lighter green than the suit was my narrow-collared, three-quarter length Lansing department store topcoat. My appearance was too much for even Ella. But she told me later she had seen countrified members of the Little family come up from Georgia in even worse shape than I was.

Ella had fixed up a nice little upstairs room for me. And she was truly a Georgia Negro woman when she got into the kitchen with her pots and pans. She was the kind of cook who would heap up your plate with such as ham hock, greens, black-eyed peas, fried fish, cabbage, sweet potatoes, grits and gravy, and cornbread. And the more you put away, the better she felt. I worked out at Ella's kitchen table like there was no tomorrow.

Ella still seemed to be as big, black, outspoken and impressive a woman as she had been in Mason and Lansing. Only about two weeks before I arrived, she had split up with her second husband—the soldier, Frank, whom I had met there the previous summer; but she was taking it right in stride. I could see, though I didn't say, how any average man would find it almost impossible to live for very long with a woman whose every instinct was to run everything and everybody she had anything to do with—including me. About my second day there in Roxbury, Ella told me that she didn't want me to start hunting for a job right away, like most newcomer Negroes did. She said that she had told all those she'd brought North to take their time, to walk around, to travel the buses and the subway, and get the feel of Boston, before they tied themselves down working somewhere, because they would never again have the time to really see and get to know anything about the city they were living in. Ella said she'd help me find a job when it was time for me to go to work.

So I went gawking around the neighborhood—the Waumbeck and Humboldt Avenue Hill section of Roxbury, which is something like Harlem's Sugar Hill, where I'd later live. I saw those Roxbury Negroes acting and living differently from any black people I'd ever dreamed of in my life. This was the snooty-black neighborhood; they called themselves the "Four Hundred," and looked down their noses at the Negroes of the black ghetto, or so-called "town" section where Mary, my other half-sister, lived.

What I thought I was seeing there in Roxbury were high-class, educated, important Negroes, living well, working in big jobs and positions. Their quiet homes sat back in their mowed yards. These Negroes walked along the sidewalks looking haughty and dignified, on their way to work, to shop, to visit, to church. I know now, of course, that what I was really seeing was only a big-city version of those "successful" Negro bootblacks and janitors back in Lansing. The only difference was that the ones in Boston had been brainwashed even more thoroughly. They prided themselves on being incomparably more "cultured," "cultivated," "dignified," and better off than their black brethren down in the ghetto, which was no further away than you could throw a rock. Under the pitiful misapprehension that it would make them "better," these Hill Negroes were breaking their backs trying to imitate white people.

Any black family that had been around Boston long enough to own the home they lived in was considered among the Hill elite. It didn't make any difference that they had to rent out rooms to make ends meet. Then the native-born New Englanders among them looked down upon recently migrated Southern home-owners who lived next door, like Ella. And a big percentage of the Hill dwellers were in Ella's category—Southern strivers and scramblers, and West Indian Negroes, whom both the New Englanders and the Southerners called "Black Jews." Usually it was the Southerners and the West Indians who not only managed to own the places where they lived, but also at least one other house which they rented as income property. The snooty New Englanders usually owned less than they.

In those days on the Hill, any who could claim "professional" status—teachers, preachers, practical nurses—also considered themselves superior. Foreign diplomats could have modeled their conduct on the way the Negro postmen, Pullman porters, and dining car waiters of Roxbury acted, striding around as if they were wearing top hats and cutaways.

I'd guess that eight out of ten of the Hill Negroes of Roxbury, despite the impressive-sounding job titles they affected, actually worked as menials and servants. "He's in banking," or "He's in securities." It sounded as though they were discussing a Rockefeller or a Mellon—and not some gray-headed, dignity-posturing bank janitor, or bond-house messenger. "I'm with an old family" was the euphemism used to dignify the professions of white folks' cooks and maids who talked so affectedly among their own kind in Roxbury that you couldn't even understand them. I don't know how many forty- and fifty-year-old errand boys went down the Hill dressed like ambassadors in black suits and white collars, to downtown jobs "in government," "in finance," or "in law." It has never ceased to amaze me how so many Negroes, then and now, could stand the indignity of that kind of self-delusion.

Soon I ranged out of Roxbury and began to explore Boston proper. Historic buildings everywhere I turned, and plaques and markers and statues for famous events and men. One statue in the Boston Commons astonished me: a Negro named Crispus Attucks, who had been the first man to fall in the Boston Massacre. I had never known anything like that.

I roamed everywhere. In one direction, I walked as far as Boston University. Another day, I took my first subway ride. When most of the people got off, I followed. It was Cambridge, and I circled all around in the Harvard University campus. Somewhere, I had already heard of Harvard—though I didn't know much more about it. Nobody that day could have told me I would give an address before the Harvard Law School Forum some twenty years later. . . .

Ella began to grow concerned, because even when I had finally had enough sight-seeing, I didn't stick around very much on the Hill. She kept dropping hints that I ought to mingle with the "nice young people my age" who were to be seen in the Townsend Drugstore two blocks from her house, and a couple of other places. . . .

I didn't want to disappoint or upset Ella, but despite her advice, I began going down into the town ghetto section. That world of grocery stores, walk-up flats, cheap restaurants, poolrooms, bars, storefront churches, and pawnshops seemed to hold a natural lure for me.

Not only was this part of Roxbury much more exciting, but I felt more relaxed among Negroes who were being their natural selves and not putting on airs. Even though I did live on the Hill, my instincts were never—and still aren't—to feel myself any better than any other Negro. . . .

I wanted to find a job myself, to surprise Ella. One afternoon, something told me to go inside a poolroom whose window I was looking through. I had looked through that window many times. I wasn't yearning to play pool; in fact, I had never held a cue stick. But I was drawn by the sight of the cool-looking "cats" standing around inside, bending over the big, green, felt-topped tables, making bets and shooting the bright-colored balls into the holes. As I stared through the window this particular afternoon, something made me decide to venture inside and talk to a dark, stubby, conk-headed fellow who racked up balls for the pool-players, whom I'd heard called "Shorty." One day he had come outside and seen me standing there and said "Hi, Red," so that made me figure he was friendly.

As inconspicuously as I could, I slipped inside the door and around the side of the poolroom, avoiding people, and on to the back, where Shorty was filling an aluminum can with the powder that pool players dust on their hands. He looked up at me. Later on, Shorty would enjoy teasing me about how with that first glance he knew my whole story. "Man, that cat still *smelled* country!" he'd say, laughing. "Cat's legs was so long and his pants so short his knees showed—an' his head looked like a briar patch!"

But that afternoon Shorty didn't let it show in his face how "country" I appeared when I told him I'd appreciate it if he'd tell me how could somebody go about getting a job like his.

Malcolm X. John Launois, Black Star.

"If you mean racking up balls," said Shorty, "I don't know of no pool joints around here needing anybody. You mean you just want any slave you can find?" A "slave" meant work, a job.

He asked what kind of work I had done. I told him that I'd washed restaurant dishes in Mason, Michigan. He nearly dropped the powder can. "My homeboy! Man, gimme some skin! I'm from Lansing!"

I never told Shorty—and he never suspected—that he was about ten years older than I. He took us to be about the same age. At first I would have been embarrassed to tell him, later I just never bothered. Shorty had dropped out of first-year high school in Lansing, lived a while with an uncle and aunt in Detroit, and had spent the last six years living with his cousin in Roxbury. But when I mentioned the names of Lansing people and places, he remembered many, and pretty soon we sounded as if we had been raised in the same block. I could sense Shorty's genuine gladness, and I don't have to say how lucky I felt to find a friend as hip as he obviously was.

"Man, this is a swinging town if you dig it," Shorty said. "You're my homeboy—I'm going to school you to the happenings." I stood there and grinned like a fool. "You got to go anywhere now? Well, stick around until I get off."

One thing I liked immediately about Shorty was his frankness. When I told him where I lived, he said what I already knew—that nobody in town could stand the Hill Negroes. But he thought a sister who gave me a "pad," not charging me rent, not even running me out to find "some slave," couldn't be all bad. Shorty's slave in the poolroom, he said, was just to keep ends together while he learned his horn. A couple of years before, he'd hit the numbers and bought a saxophone. "Got it right in there in the closet now, for my lesson tonight." Shorty was taking lessons "with some other studs," and he intended one day to organize his own small band. "There's a lot of bread to be made gigging right around here in Roxbury," Shorty explained to me. "I don't dig joining some big band, one-nighting all over just to say I played with Count or Duke or somebody." I thought that was smart. I wished I had studied a horn; but I never had been exposed to one. . . .

At seven o'clock, when the night ball-racker came on, Shorty told me he had to hurry to his saxophone lesson. But before he left, he held out to me the six or seven dollars he had collected that day in nickel and dime tips. "You got enough bread, homeboy?"

I was okay, I told him—I had two dollars. But Shorty made me take three more. "Little fattening for your pocket," he said. Before we went out, he opened his saxophone case and showed me the horn. It was gleaming brass against the green velvet, an alto sax. He said, "Keep cool, homeboy, and come back tomorrow. Some of the cats will turn you up a slave."

When I got home, Ella said there had been a telephone call from somebody named Shorty. He had left a message that over at the Roseland State Ballroom, the shoeshine boy was quitting that night, and Shorty had told him to hold the job for me.

"Malcolm, you haven't had any experience shining shoes," Ella said. Her expression and tone of voice told me she wasn't happy about my taking that job. I didn't particularly care, because I was already speechless thinking about being somewhere close to the greatest bands in the world. I didn't even wait to eat any dinner.

The ballroom was all lighted when I got there. A man at the front door was letting in members of Benny Goodman's band. I told him I wanted to see the shoeshine boy, Freddie.

"You're going to be the new one?" he asked. I said I thought I was, and he laughed, "Well, maybe you'll hit the numbers and get a Cadillac, too." He told me that I'd find Freddie upstairs in the men's room on the second floor.

But downstairs before I went up, I stepped over and snatched a glimpse inside the ballroom. I just couldn't believe the size of that waxed floor! At the far end, under the soft, rose-colored lights, was the bandstand with the Benny Goodman musicians moving around, laughing and talking, arranging their horns and stands.

A wiry, brown-skinned, conked fellow upstairs in the men's room greeted me. "You Shorty's homeboy?" I said I was, and he said he was Freddie. "Good old boy," he said. "He called me, he just heard I hit the big number, and he figured right I'd be quitting." I told Freddie what the man at the front door had said about a Cadillac. He laughed and said, "Burns them white cats up when you get yourself something. Yeah, I told them I was going to get me one—just to bug them."

Freddie then said for me to pay close attention, that he was going to be busy and for me to watch but not get in the way, and he'd try to get me ready to take over at the next dance, a couple of nights later.

As Freddie busied himself setting up the shoeshine stand, he told me, "Get here early . . . your shoeshine rags and brushes by this foot-stand . . . your polish bottles, paste wax, suede brushes over here . . . everything in place, you get rushed, you never need to waste motion. . . ."

While you shined shoes, I learned, you also kept watch on customers inside, leaving the urinals. You darted over and offered a small white hand towel. "A lot of cats who ain't planning to wash their hands, sometimes you can run up with a towel and shame them. Your towels are really your best hustle in here. Cost you a penny apiece to launder—you always get at least a nickel tip."

The shoeshine customers, and any from the inside rest room who took a towel, you whiskbroomed a couple of licks. "A nickel or a dime tip, just give 'em that," Freddie said. "But for two bits, Uncle Tom a little—white cats especially like that. I've had them to come back two, three times a dance."

From down below, the sound of the music had begun floating up. I guess I stood transfixed. "You never seen a big dance?" asked Freddie. "Run on awhile, and watch." . . .

"It knocked me out, too, when I first broke in here," Freddie said, grinning, when I went back in there. "But, look, you ever shined any shoes?" He laughed when I said I hadn't, excepting my own. "Well, let's get to work. I never had neither." Freddie got on the stand and went to work on his own shoes. Brush, liquid polish, brush, paste wax, shine rag, lacquer sole dressing . . . step by step, Freddie showed me what to do.

"But you got a get a whole lot faster. You can't waste time!" Freddie showed me how fast on my own shoes. Then, because business was tapering off, he had time to give me a demonstration of how to make the shine rag pop like a firecracker. "Dig the action?" he asked. He did it in slow motion. I got down and tried it on his shoes. I had the principle of it. "Just got to do it faster," Freddie said. "It's a jive noise, that's all. Cats tip better, they figure you're knocking yourself out!"

By the end of the dance, Freddie had let me shine the shoes of three or four stray drunks he talked into having shines, and I had practiced picking up my speed on Freddie's shoes until they looked like mirrors. After we had helped the janitors to clean up the ballroom after the dance, throwing out all the paper and cigarette butts and empty liquor bottles, Freddie was nice enough to drive me all the way home to Ella's on the Hill in the second-hand maroon Buick he said he was going to trade in on his Cadillac. . . . I started hanging out at night with Shorty and his friends. Shorty's jokes about how country I had been made us all laugh. I still was country, I know now, but it all felt so great because I was accepted. . . .

Everybody understood that my head had to stay kinky a while longer, to grow long enough for Shorty to conk it for me. One of these nights, I remarked that I had saved about half enough to get a zoot.

"*Save?*" Shorty couldn't believe it. "Homeboy, you never heard of credit?" He told me he'd call a neighborhood clothing store the first thing in the morning, and that I should be there early.

A salesman, a young Jew, met me when I came in. "You're Shorty's friend?" I said I was; it amazed me—all of Shorty's contacts. The salesman wrote my name on a form, and the Lakeland as where I worked, and Ella's address as where I lived. Shorty's name was put down as recommending me. The salesman said, "Shorty's one of our best customers."

I was measured, and the young salesman picked off a rack a zoot suit that was just wild: sky-blue pants thirty inches in the knee and angle-narrowed down to twelve inches at the bottom, and a long coat that pinched my waist and flared out below my knees.

As a gift, the salesman said, the store would give me a narrow leather belt with my initial "L" on it. Then he said I ought to also buy a hat, and I did—blue, with a feather in the four-inch brim. Then the store gave me another present: a long, thick-linked, gold-plated chain that swung down lower than my coat hem. I was sold forever on credit.

When I modeled the zoot for Ella, she took a long look and said, "Well, I guess it had to happen." I took three of those twenty-five-cent sepia-toned, while-you-wait pictures of myself, posed the way "hipsters" wearing their zoots would "cool it"—hat dangled, knees drawn close together, feet wide apart, both index fingers jabbed toward the floor. The long coat and swinging chain and the Punjab pants were much more dramatic if you stood that way. One picture, I autographed and airmailed to my brothers and sisters in Lansing, to let them see how well I was doing. I gave another one to Ella, and the third to Shorty, who was really moved: I could tell by the way he said, "Thanks, homeboy." It was part of our "hip" code not to show that kind of affection.

Shorty soon decided that my hair was finally long enough to be conked. He had promised to school me in how to beat the barbershops' three- and four-dollar price by making up congolene, and then conking ourselves.

I took the little list of ingredients he had printed out for me, and went to a grocery store, where I got a can of Red Devil lye, two eggs, and two medium-sized white potatoes. Then at a drugstore near the poolroom, I asked for a large jar of vaseline, a large bar of soap, a large-toothed comb and a fine-toothed comb, one of those rubber hoses with a metal spray-head, a rubber apron and a pair of gloves.

"Going to lay on that first conk?" the drugstore man asked me. I proudly told him, grinning, "Right!"

Shorty paid six dollars a week for a room in his cousin's shabby apartment. His cousin wasn't at home. "It's like the pad's mine, he spends so much time with his woman," Shorty said. "Now, you watch me—"

He peeled the potatoes and thin-sliced them into a quart-sized Mason fruit jar, then started stirring them with a wooden spoon as he gradually poured in a little over half the can of lye. "Never use a metal spoon; the lye will turn it black," he told me.

A jelly-like, starchy-looking glop resulted from the lye and potatoes, and Shorty broke in the two eggs, stirring real fast—his own conk and dark face bent down close. The congolene turned pale-yellowish. "Feel the jar," Shorty said. I cupped my hand against the outside, and snatched it away. "Damn right, it's hot, that's the lye," he said. "So you know it's going to burn when I comb it in—it burns *bad*. But the longer you can stand it, the straighter the hair."

He made me sit down, and he tied the string of the new rubber apron tightly around my neck, and combed up my bush of hair. Then, from the big vaseline jar, he took a handful and massaged it hard all through my hair and into the scalp. He also thickly vaselined my neck, ears and forehead. "When I get to washing out your head, be sure to tell me anywhere you feel any little stinging," Shorty warned me, washing his hands, then pulling on the rubber gloves, and tying on his own rubber apron. "You always got to remember that any congolene left in burns a sore into your head."

The congolene just felt warm when Shorty started combing it in. But then my head caught fire.

I gritted my teeth and tried to pull the sides of the kitchen table together. The comb felt as if it was raking my skin off.

My eyes watered, my nose was running. I couldn't stand it any longer; I bolted to the washbasin. I was cursing Shorty with every name I could think of when he got the spray going and started soap-lathering my head.

He lathered and spray-rinsed, lathered and spray-rinsed, maybe ten or twelve times, each time gradually closing the hot-water faucet, until the rinse was cold, and that helped some.

"You feel any stinging spots?"

"No," I managed to say. My knees were trembling.

"Sit back down, then. I think we got it all out okay."

The flame came back as Shorty, with a thick towel, started drying my head, rubbing hard. *"Easy, man, easy!"* I kept shouting.

"The first time's always worst. You get used to it better before long. You took it real good, homeboy. You got a good conk."

When Shorty let me stand up and see in the mirror, my hair hung down in limp, damp strings. My scalp still flamed, but not as badly; I could bear it. He draped the towel around my shoulders, over my rubber apron, and began again vaselining my hair.

I could feel him combing, straight back, first the big comb, then the fine-tooth one.

Then, he was using a razor, very delicately, on the back of my neck. Then, finally, shaping the sideburns.

My first view in the mirror blotted out the hurting. I'd seen some pretty conks, but when it's the first time, on your *own* head, the transformation, after the lifetime of kinks, is staggering.

The mirror reflected Shorty behind me. We both were grinning and sweating. And on top of my head was this thick, smooth sheen of shining red hair—real red—as straight as any white man's.

How ridiculous I was! Stupid enough to stand there simply lost in admiration of my hair now looking "white," reflected in the mirror in Shorty's room. I vowed that I'd never again be without a conk, and I never was for many years.

This was my first really big step toward self-degradation: when I endured all of that pain, literally burning my flesh to have it look like a white man's hair. I had joined that multitude of Negro men and women in America who are brainwashed into believing that the black people are "inferior"—and white people "superior"—that they will even violate and multilate their God-created bodies to try to look "pretty" by white standards.

Look around today, in every small town and big city, from two-bit catfish and soda-pop joints into the "integrated" lobby of the Waldorf-Astoria, and you'll see conks on black men. And you'll see black women wearing these green and pink and purple and red and platinum-blonde wigs. They're all more ridiculous than a slapstick comedy. It makes you wonder if the Negro has completely lost his sense of identity, lost touch with himself.

You'll see the conk worn by many, many so-called "upper class" Negroes, and, as much as I hate to say it about them, on all too many Negro entertainers. One of the reasons that I've especially admired some of them, like Lionel Hampton and Sidney Poitier, among others, is that they have kept their natural hair and fought to the top. I admire any Negro man who has never had himself conked, or who has had the sense to get rid of it—as I finally did.

I don't know which kind of self-defacing conk is the greater shame—the one you'll see on the heads of the black so-called "middle class" and "upper class," who ought to know better, or the one you'll see on the heads of the poorest, most downtrodden, ignorant black men. I mean the legal-minimum-wage ghetto-dwelling kind of Negro, as I was when I got my first one. It's generally among these poor fools that you'll see a black kerchief over the man's head, like Aunt

Jemima; he's trying to make his conk last longer, between trips to the barbershop. Only for special occasions is this kerchief-protected conk exposed—to show off how "sharp" and "hip" its owner is. The ironic thing is that I have never heard any woman, white or black, express any admiration for a conk. . . . I don't see how on earth a black woman with any race pride could walk down the street with any black man wearing a conk—the emblem of his shame that he is black.

To my own shame, when I say all of this I'm talking first of all about myself—because you can't show me any Negro who ever conked more faithfully than I did. I'm speaking from personal experience when I say of any black man who conks today, or any white-wigged black woman, that if they gave the brains in their heads just half as much attention as they do their hair, they would be a thousand times better off. ❦

Vocabulary

Under the pitiful *misapprehension* that it would make them "better", these Hill Negroes were breaking their backs trying to imitate white people . . . . (141:1); Any black family that had been around long enough to own the home they lived in was considered among the Hill *elite* . . . . (141:5); despite the impressive job titles they affected, they actually worked as *menials* and servants . . . . (141:24); "I'm with an old family" was the *euphemism* used to dignify the professions of white folks' cooks and maids . . . . (141:27); the sound of the music had begun floating up. I guess I stood *transfixed* . . . . (146:10); My first view in the mirror blotted out the hurting. . . . the *transformation,* after a lifetime of kinks, is staggering . . . . (149:7); I vowed that I'd never again be without a conk. . . . This was my first really big step toward self-*degradation*. . . . (149:16)

Study Questions and Activities

1. As she is depicted by her half-brother, what is Ella's outstanding characteristic? How does the young man react to her?

2. What do you suppose was the particular astonishment Malcolm X felt when he discovered the statue of Crispus Attucks? Did his discovery in any way astonish you? If so, how?

3. Under what single generalization could we label Malcolm X's attacks upon the "Hill Negroes" and the "Conked Negroes"?

4. At the end of the incident detailing the purchase of his first zoot suit, Malcolm X declares, "I was sold forever on credit." What is the tone of that sentence?

5. Pay close attention to the last sentence of the passage and demonstrate how the writer uses contrast to make an effective, powerful sentence.

6. How do you explain the meaning of the title of this chapter? What other implications does the title have which could be related to the theme running throughout the chapter?

7. Primarily, Malcolm X's chapter traces a young man's degradation stemming from his lack of "race pride." What lesson beyond race pride and concerning self-image can be learned by anyone reading about Malcolm X's experience?

8. The writer pokes fun at the euphemisms the "Hill Negroes" used to describe their often menial jobs. What euphemisms are common today among people trying to make a low-status job sound like a profession?

9. The author uses many words current in the language of the blacks at the time he was fifteen in Roxbury. Many of these words eventually entered the vocabulary of most Americans. How many such words can you find? Do they have the same meanings today? What expressions did not become generally known?

10. In one sense Malcolm X's first conk was an initiation into a world he wanted to join but one he later found woefully wanting. The initiation included the pain of ordeal, the joy of joining, and subsequent disillusion. Can you recall your own or another's initiation rite with a similar pattern?

11. When he arrived in Boston from Michigan, Malcolm X had just finished eighth grade and was little older than Roberto Sanchez and Henry Adams of the previous selections. How does his outlook on life differ from these two boys? Is there any way—or ways—in which the three are similar?

VOCABULARY: ANALOGIES

Study the vocabulary words in the previous selections and then try your hand at an exercise in analogies. The two capitalized words will indicate some kind of relationship: for example, MISER:SPENDTHRIFT indicates opposites; PEN:INK indicates usage. In the choices find the pair of words that indicates a similar relationship AND a correct use of both words. Number your paper and list the correct letter.

1. HAPLESS:UNLUCKY:: (**a**) frigid:cold

A monk copying a manuscript. New York Public Library Picture Collection.

(**b**) happen:mishap (**c**) useless:usury (**d**) friendless:friendly

2. SKITTISH:HORSE:: (**a**) stolid:conservative (**b**) miser:money (**c**) mule:stubborn (**d**) nervous:person

3. MENIALS:ELITE:: (**a**) slaves:underprivileged (**b**) taskmasters:aristocracy (**c**) drudges:fortunate (**d**) middlemen:bourgeoisie

4. FLAIL:FLAGELLANT:: (**a**) post:postulate (**b**) knife:butcher (**c**) sling:slingshot (**d**) scourge:penitent

5. EXCESS:WASTE:: (**a**) dissipation: degradation (**b**) guess:surmise (**c**) anarchy: riot (**d**) poison:suicide

6. FEMININE:BLOOMERS:: (**a**) girls: buds (**b**) feline:cats (**c**) masculine:pantaloons (**d**) neuter:unisex

6

School Days—Summer Is for Learning, Too

What informal education has been important in your life? Many of us would agree that we learn more from what happens to us outside of school than from what happens within. After all, we learned the most difficult discipline of all—how to speak our native language—long before we even entered nursery school.

This chapter is the place for you to begin writing about places other than schools which have influenced you. You might think of it, roughly, as dealing with the time intervals between classroom experiences, summers for most of us. During these times we have time to travel, to play at what we like, to read, to pursue our hobbies, to go to camp. Some of us may merely move to another location for the summer with our families or with close relatives and spend the summer months by a lake, in the woods, on a farm, or in a larger city. Others may have worked—for fun, for profit, or for both.

Nor should you neglect thinking about those wonderful long recesses when school closed for a week or two and you had time to progress from your interests in holidays and gift-giving. One thing seems certain. From these experiences you have learned a lot not only about sports, hobbies, and vacations but about how to deal with new ideas, other people, and yourself.

Getting Started

Form a group. Have your teacher or the leader of your group assign to each of you a real character—Henry Adams, a President of the United States, a prominent figure in sports, Napoleon, Socrates, a character in a novel or short story you have read, Malcolm X, a character in the outside reading you are doing now—to name but a few possibilities. Spend an evening doing some further reading about the name assigned you. Then return to the group and have the character you have studied, speaking through you, discuss the question, "I scarcely needed to go to school for the good it did me in my profession." Don't forget that you may argue against as well as for this premise.

Think of your vacation periods and what you did during those times. Quickly list the various activities. Then try to think of generalized headings for several of them. Sports, for example, might include swimming, softball, tennis, soccer, skiing, and many others. List these activities, then, under sports. Do the same with other general headings. Some examples of possible headings follow.

HOBBIES: How many have you pursued and for how long? What made you drop or stay with them? Did any of them ever pay off in some way or another?

SPECIAL PLACES: Think of descriptions here. How does a summer place look as you remember it on your arrival? Your departure? At various times of the day? In light and in darkness?

SPECIAL PLEASURES: Was there a summer game that intrigued you? A group you were once deeply involved in? An activity you now enjoy, such as cooking, that began with a simple experiment?

SPECIAL EDUCATION: What camps have you gone to? Were all the experiences pleasurable? How enlightening were the family trips? Did you ever enroll in vacation schools?

POSSESSIONS: Again think of descriptions: of caves, play places, something you constructed by yourself or with others, projects you at least started and may have completed to be later adored or abominated.

ORGANIZATIONS: Are you now or have you been a Scout? A member of a church group? A Little League player? A solicitor or helper for a charitable organization?

WORK: What jobs have you done for pay? Or just for fun? How did you enjoy the paper route or the volunteer work in a hospital? Have you learned anything from baby-sitting? Are you working at something now that seems closely allied with your future goals?

THE OPPOSITE SEX: Have you always been aware there was such a thing? If not, when and how did you make the discovery? Get hold of and read Thomas Sancton's "Young Man with a Horn," an essay about camp and the first intimations of love.

LESSONS LEARNED: Try to draw conclusions from your experiences. What have your punishments taught you? Your rewards? Has what happened to someone else's behavior in a certain situation influenced you? How have you learned to tell what is accepted and not accepted by your group? By your parents? By your neighbors? By society?

Jules Feiffer, self-portrait.

A Quick Review

Are you following good organizational practice in planning? How many of the following questions can you answer with *yes*?

1. Am I making a list of things I remember so that I can check those I wish to leave out and categorize those I wish to include?

2. Am I making a rough outline using Roman numbers to indicate paragraphs?

3. Am I writing a rough draft and then checking it against the Check Sheets as I carefully edit it?

4. Am I making a conscientious effort to remember all the rules I am learning on the Check Sheets?

5. Am I being neat and careful as I compose my final copy?

6. Am I planning far enough ahead so that I am not pressed for time the night I must make my final copy?

A Camp Experience from "**Odds and Ends**"

One experience I believe I will never forget occurred during my second season at Camp Lilliput. One rainy morning my cabin mates and I were busily making our beds when we discovered that the foundation of the cabin was on fire. We managed to put the fire out, and for the next week the main topic of conversation was our cabin and how it had happened to catch fire. One afternoon, about a week or so after the fire, the director informed us that she knew it was one of the girls in our cabin who had set the fire. She said that, if this girl would come to her and admit what she had done, the whole incident would be forgotten. If none reported to her, she said, she would have to call in a state trooper who would question each girl in the cabin. The trooper was called in, and I felt very excited when it came time for my interview. I expected to be cross-questioned by a dashing Tyrone Power; but alas, I was questioned by a likeness of Walter Huston, homely and rugged. The girl who had set the fire was discovered and sent home.

A Summer Place Description from "**Chatham**"

The part of Chatham I liked best was the sand bar where we went for picnics. It was an all-day trip. We put on the outboard motor, and all five of us got into the boat. The tides had to be just right so that we could cross the long shoals beween Monornoy Point and the town. If we were late coming or going, the water was too shallow for the motor. Then the whole family would have to get out and wade, pulling the boat about a mile until we reached the Outer Chatham harbor. Sometimes the tide was very fast as we crossed to a sand bar which was some distance off the shore. We would anchor and climb over the dunes to the ocean side. The white sand stretched for miles, uninhabited except for sea gulls and sand pipers. The dunes were covered with waving beach grass and an occasional piece of wreckage. There was always surf which broke in long rolls for miles up the beach. It was so barren and lonely out there that, when we left, we felt we were coming back into civilization from another world.

About Hobbies from "**Summers, Scouts and Hobbies**"

Many boys have hobbies, and I'm no exception. Well, maybe I am an exception. A hobby with me lasts for a short while. A few years back, a radio program offered a hundred excellent stamps for a dime. Being a sucker, I sent in for mine, and with that started my hobby. For a year the stamp companies made money. I dropped stamp collecting when a relative brought me some foreign coins. I soon dropped this when I discovered something strange and exciting, the art of prestidigitation, which at one time or another has thrilled many a boy. Wholeheartedly I swung into this new hobby, and it lasted for two years. At the end of two years I dropped magic because it was making my money run like water. Last year model cars and airplanes were the new fad with me. But with a younger brother and an even younger sister destroying my work, I was soon discouraged. Right now I'm a man without a hobby.

About a Scout Camp from **"A Good Scout"**

For the past two summers I have gone to Sage Hill Camp, owned by Troop Four. Mr. Smith is, of course, the head of it. He has an assistant and is helped by the older boys. Sage Hill nestles in the wonderful woodsy section of the Green Mountains, about forty-five minutes from Brattleboro, Vermont. A rumbling, rock ridden river surrounds the mountain on which the camp is located. The camp has no electricity and only a one-wire telephone system which seldom works. Through the years that Troop Four has owned the camp, it has been building it. We have built the swimming pool, the playing fields, a well and, last summer, a chapel. In the course of building these various projects, we learn a lot about all sorts of crafts and skills—all, of course, part of the Boy Scout aim. Since the place is so wild and rustic, we also have lots of opportunity for nature study. Last year we had a Cooper's hawk in camp with us. The year before, we had a pet crow.

About Summer Travel from **"Swiss School Days"**

The first thing we liked about France was the food. There wasn't too much of it, but everything was cooked just right. And even if you don't have butter, one of those narrow, flaky "baguettes," just out of the oven, can taste pretty fine. We stayed in Paris at Le Royal in the Montparnasse section, where Mother had lived when she studied at the Sorbonne. We did a lot of sightseeing into her past, and we did see just about everything there is in Paris: The Arc de Triomphe, Napoleon's Tomb, the Eiffel Tower, Louvre, Tuilleries, Latin Quarter. I have skipped something here, but, believe me, we didn't miss a thing over there. Then we discovered the movies—v.o. Do you know what v.o. means? Just *version originale*, my friend. That means, if you see a Roy Rogers picture, that the cowboys and Mexicans all talk English. Those first weeks in France, it was very important for my brother and me to find movies in English. We studied the *Semaine de Paris* and then planned our trips by subway. The metro system in Paris is pretty complicated, but when you get it figured out, there is no place in Paris that is out of reach. Mother was so proud of the way Jim and I found our way around Paris alone that she let us see lots of extra movies while she and Margot went shopping.

About Horses from "**In Days Gone By**"

I have always been very fortunate with my hobby, horses, because, for as long as I can remember, there was always a horse of some description around our summer place. My first horse we bought from Winnemont, where she had been the stable plug. However, I wasn't bothered in the least. Anything with four legs and a tail was all that mattered to me. A piebald mare, Dolly was as smart as a whip. She taught me many lessons as well as all of the tricks of the horse. For, although she was very patient, Dolly had a mind of her own. After Dolly I had two other horses: Nuggett, a small strawberry roan; and Tommy Tucker, a large hunter. I was spending most of my days in the saddle.

I'm a Stranger Here Myself

While I was still staggering under the realization that Purity and Obedience may be cardinal virtues but do not necessarily insure popularity in the younger set, I went to Central High School. To my horrified seventh grade eyes it looked as big and as complicated as the Pentagon in Washington.

I would scuttle down the long corridors with the conviction that some day I'd get lost from my group and burst in upon the wrong class. One of the teachers mentioned regretfully that I never volunteered any comment in class. Volunteered, indeed! I would as soon have given a speech in Congress. My sheltered youth and the stern ways of the world were coming in conflict at that turbulent time known to our elders as "adolescence"—a loathsome word. I felt as if everything I did or said or thought was wrong.

Furthermore, at Central there were Big Boys. They were not the familiar creatures with whom I played baseball every night after school; I'd learned how to handle them. But these big boys looked smooth and superior and grinned when they saw the new little kids fresh out of grade school. Every time they looked at me with that tolerant grin, I felt convinced that I had a smudge of soot on my shin or a hole in my sock. One horrible day one of my baseball pals whacked me playfully on the back, just as we were entering English class. He no doubt meant it for a friendly tap, but I was totally unprepared for it, and the results were embarrassing. I leaped through the door and fell flat on my face, with all my books and papers flying ahead of me.

About that time my sister and I, who had affectionately shared a bedroom and everything else from the time she was born, suddenly grew years apart. Throughout one whole year we battled grimly and loudly over everything from how far to open the window at night to which clothes were whose. Then my mother separated us as completely as only a big house will allow.

Meanwhile, I spent summers at the farm, learning first-hand that turkeys don't have sense enough to come in out of the rain, that you never turn your back on a ram or a gander, the reason why people say "growing like a weed," and the fact that pigs are smart—so smart that no pen on earth will hold them unless they want to be penned. My father put us on alternating schedules, a week at a time. The pigs *always* broke out on *my* week. Oh, the many gray dawns that I've been awakened by the smug little grunt a pig makes when it's going somewhere it should not. Then I had to hustle into jeans and rush out to head off those pigs before they reached our neighbor's corn field. After all the stock had been fed and watered and put to bed, we went fishing, rode horseback—or read.

I find that I have not mentioned before one of the things that I like most to do. Probably I have not because, in our family, reading is like eating or breathing. We take it for granted.

When I went into the ninth grade, my parents transferred us all to East Grand Rapids. I liked the school. But again I felt uncomfortably strange. Not a single girl I knew was in my division that first term. Before I found my bearings, I was ill and absent for a month. Then I had my tonsils out. That is a horrid procedure which always brings much discomfort and little sympathy. Christmas holidays I spent having an appendectomy. Eventually I returned to school, and spent the rest of the year getting acquainted and trying desperately to catch up in my studies. Altogether, it was the kind of year anybody would take pleasure in forgetting.

But this year—that's different. Though I am certainly not the teachers' joy scholastically, I begin to feel at home, to feel loyalty for the school, and to have fun. My father says no one can write intelligently about the present; we can only live it. That's what I aim to do right now.

CHECK SHEET FOR CHAPTER 6

Analysis of Samples

1. In the last sentence of sample 1, point out the use of passive voice. Does the sentence benefit by its use?

2. In sentence 7 of sample 2, change "a sand bar which" to "the sand bar, which." How is the meaning of the sentence now different from the writer's version?

3. Give a reason for each of the commas used in sample 3.

4. In sample 4 what would have happened to the final sentence if the writer had omitted the comma?

5. Discover the incomplete sentence in sample 5. Why is this fragment not in error here? When can we properly use such fragments?

6. The complete chapter sample seems to deal partly with school experiences. How is it, really, a fulfillment of the assignment for Chapter 6?

Spelling

1. altogether, adv. (How would you spell it if everyone were together in one group?)
2. boulder, meaning large rock (What is its homonym?)

3. congratulate
4. embarrass
5. horrible (Write its adverb form)
6. incidental (Write its adverb form and discuss its difference from that in No. 5)
7. intramural (If you don't know its meaning, look it up)
8. intrigue
9. muscle (What is the homonym for this spelling? Which denotes a sinew of your body?)
10. notice, noticeable
11. shepherd
12. salivate
13. temperature
14. yacht

Questions for Group Consideration: Figurative Language

Are you writing as vigorously as you are able? One way to write vigorously is to exercise care in the choice of appropriate nouns and verbs, the words that are the very sinews of the language. Hazards to this choice, in verbs, are the verbs *be, get,* and *have* in their various forms. What verbs can you find to replace more exactly the imprecise verbs underlined in the following sentences? (You should see, as you revise, that your new sentence becomes less wordy.)

1. There are many things that I get in the mail and throw away.
2. It was in South Dakota that I got the measles.
3. Ms. Dennis was kind and gentle, and she was able to get us to confide in her.
4. I had a feeling that I was a bad prophet and would be wrong again.
5. It is my belief that teachers can be wrong, too.

Another way to write vigorously is to avoid comparisons and figurative language that we all use in speech but which, in writing, become clichés that demean our own powers of imagination. What clichés do you find in the following sentences? (If you don't know the meaning of *cliché,* look it up.) How can you eliminate them?

1. John was white as a sheet after his initiation.
2. Scouting has played a major role in my life.
3. One aspect of my life has always bothered me, the other sex.
4. I do not worry much about the material factors of life.
5. That night Dad slept like a log.

Consider now some ways of sharpening your use of words and substituting better expressions for worn-out ones. One such method is by considering sounds. A repetition of sounds often makes for felicitous phrasing. One such device, alliteration, places side by side two or more words beginning with the same sound. The repetition should not be noticeable enough, unless you are using the device for humor, to make the reader say, "Oh, look, Bob's using alliteration." It should, instead, please only the writer; others should just be impressed by your style.

1. How many uses of alliteration can you find in the preceding paragraph?
2. Write a sentence containing alliteration. Read the sentences aloud and have the group decide whether or not the alliteration is too obtrusive.

Another sound device we call internal rhyme. Notice, for example, in the sample chapter how the phrase, "smug little grunt," repeats the sound of short vowel "u" in its first and last word. Often, in editing work, if we come to a word we know is not particularly good in that spot, we can, by thinking a minute, come up with one that is not only more exact but one that contains some repetition of initial or internal sound.

1. Make groups containing the words "bad," "said," "fits," "spotty," and "rough," and in each group have some example of internal rhyme. As you read them aloud for group criticism, decide whether anyone has come up with another kind of sound device that has not been defined.
2. Make an original sentence containing internal rhyme. Read it and see if everyone in the group can spot it. Decide whether the rhyme is too obtrusive.

Don't neglect figures of speech, even though you may have thought of these as devices reserved for poetry. They are not. Let's review three figures by spotting and naming them in the following sentences.

1. She uttered a strangled shriek. Alexander, the biggest alligator, lay . . . hissing evilly at her.
2. I had wings, a halo, and a heart of gold; but they often were entangled with my imagination.
3. This attractive little girl looks like one of the hippos in *Fantasia* now.
4. Her parents had drugged her on the subject of romance.
5. The other boys would look at me as if I were the third sex.

Now that you have identified the figures and refreshed your own definitions, try your hands at

1. writing a sentence using a *metaphor.*
2. writing a sentence using a *simile.*
3. writing a sentence containing *onomatopoeia.*

Learn to play with words, but don't overuse any figurative device. Our language often permits us to use the same word as a noun, a verb, an adjective, and an adverb, such use depending upon where the word comes in the sentence. Note the following changes in one word by its placement and, sometimes, by shifts in its final letters.

1. At six I thought I was casting a long *shadow.*
2. The elm *shadowed* my room until it was cut down.
3. We had imagined Forest Lawn to be a place filled with *shadowy* dells.
4. My little brother always followed me—*shadowily,* creepily, persistently.

Try your hand at taking a word and using it as at least two parts of speech. As you or a group of classmates judge your efforts, test whether or not each usage seems sane or logical. Start with the following words and add others if you wish.

1. ooze
2. snug
3. turtle
4. hornet
5. frog

More About Punctuation: Avoiding Its Overuse

1. The semicolon (;)—except when it is used to separate a series of double appositives as in "Mary Jones, treasurer; Bill Smith, secretary;"—must separate only independent clauses. Never use it to set a phrase off from the rest of the sentence. Never use it to set off a dependent clause.

wrong: We ran quickly to the road; having seen the fire from our room. (Change the ; to a ,)

wrong: I would like to be an actress; although I know it takes talent. (Omit all marks of punctuation.)

2. Do not separate any part of the sentence framework with commas unless phrases or clauses come in between.

a. Don't separate subject from predicate.

wrong: Father, and Mother were in the front seat. (Omit the ,)

b. Don't separate verb from object or complement.

wrong: I had been reading, *Swiss Family Robinson.* (Omit the ,)

wrong: My favorite subjects are: math and science. (Omit the :)

c. Don't separate preposition from its object.

wrong: Before we knew it, we were in, the house. (Omit the , after *in*)

d. Don't set off introductory phrases unless each phrase is unreasonably long or unless leaving out the comma would change the sense of the sentence.

wrong: In the summer, we go to Cape Cod.

wrong: During the war, I was in Texas.

right: For sleeping, Beauty wins all prizes.

right: In choosing an occupation for a life's work, it is wise to consider many things.

e. Don't set off only one part of a phrase or clause that needs to have a comma on either side. Where should additional commas go in the following sentences?

The beauty contest which had been open to all six-year-olds, now had a five-year-old in competition.

The wrong thing to do I learned, was to start baking a cake after having read only half the recipe.

Then the table having been cleared, we began a poker game that lasted ten hours.

Mother had told me that if I behaved properly in church, I could have a Carvel on the way home.

We learned after eating all the fruit from the lower branches, that a stomach is not a thing to be cherried with.

Our experience taught us that to reach the proper conclusions, it was necessary to follow the directions in the lab book.

Who has I say once more, the right to tell me what books to read?

Another Way to Avoid Wordiness

Avoid the overuse of sentences beginning with THERE IS, THERE ARE, HERE IS, and HERE ARE. Do not avoid them altogether; they are necessary for sentence variety. Too frequently, though, the neophyte starts with these words while trying to think of something to say. In revising your manuscript, try to gain economy by cutting down on the number of times you use such beginnings. Note how the samples are word-wasters.

1. *There are two reasons why I prefer the city to the country.*

better: I prefer the city to the country for two reasons.
better: I prefer the city to the country because. . . .

2. *Here are pictures of my brothers when they were two and five.*

better: These pictures show my brothers at two and five.

3. *There is a second reason I prefer living in Arizona rather than in Connecticut; Arizona has more sunny weather.*

better: Because Arizona has more sunny weather than Connecticut, I prefer living there.
better: A second reason I prefer living in Arizona rather than in Connecticut is that. . . .

Usage

1. Don't fall, jump, or dive OFF OF something. Just dive OFF.

wrong: When I was seven, I was pushed off of the dock.
right: When I was seven, I was pushed off the dock.

2. Avoid trite use of SURE, as in "it sure was," "I was sure pleased." Instead of *sure,* use *certainly, surely, really, actually,* or some other synonym suitable for your purpose. *Very often the word is just redundant. Omit it entirely then.*

wrong: It was sure a hard year.
right: The year was really hard.

wrong: He was sure pleased.
right: He was certainly pleased.

wrong: It was sure great to be back.
right: It was great to be back.

3. Avoid using the abbreviation etc. Beginners too often use it as a crutch to hide the fact that they are out of words or that they are too lazy to use them. Be specific and you won't have to use it.

wrong: At camp I like best swimming, rowing, riding, etc.
right: At camp I like best swimming, rowing, and riding.
right: At camp I like such activities as swimming, rowing, and riding.

4. The word "use" is present tense. The past tense and participle is spelled and pronounced "used".

wrong: We use to live on Watling Street. We had a use car.
right: We used to live on Watling Street. We had a used car.

A Further Matter of Style

Do not capitalize names of professions.

My father is a lawyer.
I would not care to study teaching.

Agreement of Subject with Verb

If the subject of your sentence or clause is singular in number—that is, if it means only one thing—it will take a verb singu-

lar in number. Review the following conjugation of *to be,* regularly used as helper-verbs and the one which causes the most trouble to the writer.

	Singular			Plural		
	Present	Past	Present Perfect	Present	Past	Present Perfect
1.	I am	was	have been	We are	were	have been
2.	You are	were	have been	You are	were	have been
3.	He She is It	was	has been	They are	were	have been

Other verbs cause less trouble, the only change usually being in the third person singular, when an "s" sound is added. Thus: I have, you have, he *has,* we, you, and they have; I, you, we, and they lose but he *loses.*

Most agreements follow naturally from the way in which we learned to speak: My mother *goes* to the store daily. This bicycle *is* my property.

The other part of this rule states that **subjects plural in number take a plural verb.** Again, familiarity with this pattern causes little trouble. We have no trouble saying or writing: A few people *were* eager to leave. You *know* the rules, *do*n't you?

Yet some pitfalls lie in wait to trap the hapless beginner. Study the following rules.

1. Subjects joined by "and" take a plural verb because the "and" has joined one with one (or another number) to make more than one.

- **a.** Jack and Bobby Mickleheimer were not my favorite neighbors.
- **b.** My sister and I were inseparable until we were twelve.

2. Subjects joined by "or" or "nor" take the number of the verb that agrees with the final one of the multiple subjects.

- **a.** Neither my sister nor her friend is going to the fair.
- **b.** Either the tube or the record player has my vote of confidence.
- **c.** Neither my sister nor her friends are going to the fair.
- **d.** Neither Babe nor her kittens were anywhere to be found.

3. The subject still governs the number of the verb even if phrases intervene between subject and verb.

- **a.** Not one of my friends is going.
- **b.** Each of the two boys was willing.

Be especially careful of phrases beginning with any of the following: *of, with, together with, as well as, including.*

- **a.** Then Huck together with Jim proceeds down the river.
- **b.** Mother as well as my two Puritanical aunts agrees that dating is not for sophomores.

4. Sentences beginning with "there" and "here" have subjects that normally follow the verb, but the agreement rule still applies.

- **a.** There are (V) many things (S) to be said for my parents' position.
- **b.** Here are (V) two examples (S) to prove my point.

5. In questions, the subject normally follows the verb, but the agreement rule still applies.

- **a.** Where are John and Mary going?
- **b.** Have Loretta and Jane forgotten their homework?

6. Although this rule is changing rapidly in spoken English, **the following pronouns are usually considered singular in number in Standard Written English: each, either, neither, one, no one, nobody, anyone, anybody, someone, somebody, everyone, everybody.**

- **a.** Has everyone seen the exhibit of Van Gogh prints?
- **b.** Each of us has to make a five-minute speech tomorrow.
- **c.** Not one of those books appeals to me.

d. Anyway, one of our swimmers is bound to win.

7. When using a third person singular subject, be sure to change present tense of the verb "do" to its third person form "does."

a. My dog doesn't like thunderstorms.
b. She doesn't want to go with us.

8. Sometimes a form of the verb "to be" joins a subject and a complement of different number. When this happens, remember that the subject, not the complement, governs the number of the verb.

right: The loot (**S**) the gang collected was (**V**) mostly bottle caps and nails (**complement**).
wrong: The loot the gang collected were mostly bottle caps and nails.

ASSIGNMENT 6

Write Chapter 5 of your autobiography. Like the previous one, it will deal with recollections of education, in all seasons. Reserve the next chapter for telling about people and happenings that have influenced you.

Have you noticed a decrease in the errors you make while writing? If you have, your study is beginning to pay off.

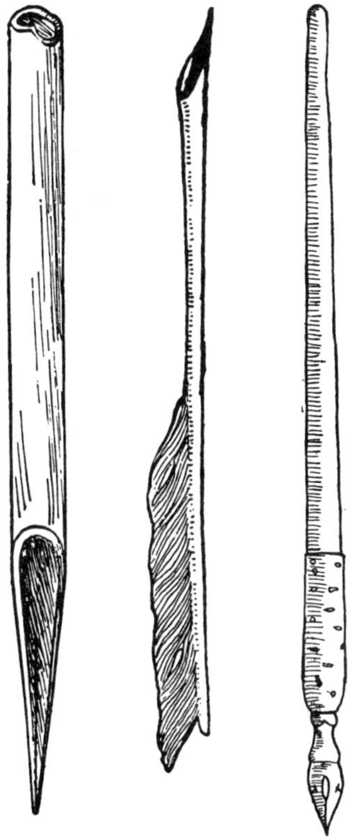

Early pens. New York Public Library Picture Collection.

PRACTICE TEST VI

This test covers only the errors discussed in the first six chapters. Study the Check Sheets and then, without looking back, do the test. The teacher may want to check your work OR to give you another test of the same sort. Each error will count as 2½ points, if anybody's counting.

I. In each of the following groups, only ONE of the words is misspelled. Spell the word correctly on your paper.

1. decent	ancesters	feud	genealogy
2. alot	separate	fourth	neighborhood
3. despite	breaths	passtime	catastrophe
4. facinate	permanent	lanyard	incessant
5. embarrass	temperature	yacht	congradulate
6. traveling	paternal	quarrells	grandfather
7. kindergarten	fourth	occured	nearby
8. picnicking	lead	whined	carring
9. nurcery	twelfth	laid	everyday
10. incidently	embarrass	shepherd	horribly

II. Rewrite these sentences, putting in commas where they are needed. Take out commas where they are not needed. Each sentence has a problem.

1. My brother Sammie, didn't learn to talk until he was three.

2. I'm reading a good autobiography called, *Boy on Horseback.*

3. Before we knew it we were in, the water, over our heads.

4. For leisure reading, many boys prefer sports magazines, and comic books.

5. After being shamed by his best friend, my brother picked up his knitting, and walked sulkily from the room.

6. No one, but Chester and me wanted to go, but we persuaded the rest to join us.

7. Loon Lake which takes its name from the looniest sort of bird, has become my favorite spot.

8. We should try instead, to do our best right now.

9. Carmen told me that if no one else asked her before Wednesday, she'd go to the movies with me.

10. The wind having spent its force, subsided, and left us to repair the damage.

11. Our dog, a real coward last year has suddenly become the terror of the block.

12. We discovered from skating that winter, that it was best to have a fire to return to.

13. Everyone but me I am sure, once believed in Santa Claus.

14. The book said that if I exercised dutifully daily for five minutes, I would be rewarded with biceps the size of coconuts.

15. He has had to leave school early, because he has a doctor's appointment.

III. Each of the following sentences has one error or poor choice of words. Rewrite the sentences correctly on your paper.

1. One thing I remember was when I belched in church.

2. I have four grandparents, of which Grandpa Jones is the nicest.

3. She was planning to leap right off of the high slide.

4. As I dream of the plan, I realize that someone probably had dreamed of it before me.

5. Uncle Bob didn't graduate high school until he was thirty.

6. Not one of these books appeal to me.

7. Everybody in here have to report to the principal.

8. Why does the teacher and the class disagree with me so often?

9. At this camp there is swimming, canoeing and many other water sports.

10. Neither Fred nor Joanne have seen the movie.

11. Here's your papers back.

12. Beth was sure startled when I put the frog down her back.

13. Stories about crime and violence fascinates many of my peers.

14. Neither John nor my other cousins has discovered the hiding place yet.

15. Where's the ruler and the protractor?

An early type of pen. New York Public Library Picture Collection.

7

All Experience Is an Arch—People, Places, Events, Discoveries

All of us have been influenced by more things than we can ever account for. We learn to like something because a friend or parent likes it. We admire an action and unconsciously copy it. We see an action that we do not like, and we try to avoid both the action and the type of person who admires it. In such ways we are unconsciously influenced. However, all of us also can trace certain of our actions, our likes and dislikes—even the way we dress—to the influence of someone. It may have been a parent, a teacher, a friend, a movie star, a book, even someone we don't like. It may also have been a place—one where we have felt beautifully at home or one we have read or heard a great deal about.

But people and places do not contribute entirely to what we are. Unpleasant things happen to us; we are baffled and try to understand why they happened. We try something for the first time and discover a latent talent or interest. Other things we try we find we cannot begin to master, and we are frustrated. We daydream and from our dreams often find solutions. All sorts of things have contributed to the you who are writing this autobiography.

This chapter asks you, first, to think of yourself as you are today and, then, to write about the environmental influences which have contributed to that you. People and places will rate high on your list as you think back, but do not neglect other influences. Refer now to the Then and Now chart you made for Chapter 4. Try to analyze the changes you find in yourself between then and now. It is those changes that you will want to write about in this chapter. Keep the chart handy also for work in the following two chapters; it should help you with those as well as with this one.

Getting Started

Read through the headings that follow. Form a group and have each member pick one of those headings and then relate an anecdote or a happening that has or could have been personally significant. A variation of this activity is for the student to relate the anecdote and then ask the group to guess its possible influences.

Follow the same procedure for organizing that you used in the previous chapter. Those influences which present the most answers will be the ones you will wish to use in writing this chapter.

PEOPLE: What in particular have I learned from parents, siblings, and other relatives? What other adults have influenced me? What have I learned from friends? What person has influenced me more than any other? What people do I want to know and why? What pets have I known that have influenced me as much as people have?

PLACES: What are the most interesting places I have ever seen? Read about? Why did I like certain places I feel have influenced me? Why do I want to go to certain places I have yet to visit?

HEROES AND VILLAINS: Who have been my heroes and how have I copied them? Have I maintained my interest in them? If not, why not? What have I learned from people I have detested? Did I detest them because of something I knew they had done or because of things I had heard about them? Have I ever changed my opinions of them? If so, why?

BOOKS: How has reading helped to shape your life? Does the same sort of reading interest you now as it once did? What sort of books do you like? Do you read to escape from life or to learn about it?

EVENTS: How have I reacted to certain crises such as being hospitalized, away from home, in new and frightening situations? How have I reacted to such events as births and deaths in my immediate family?

ACTIVITIES: Have you preferred organized or unorganized physical activities? Do you remember moments of tense experience centered on psychological conflicts—hate, rivalry, fair play, approval of others, conflicts with others of your own team? Do you remember moments of experience when you enjoyed handling a good rifle, using sharp tools, hearing and seeing powerful machinery? Do you remember moments of tense experience centered on more physical achievement in sports? What work have you tried and enjoyed, or hated? Factory work, typing, digging ditches, farming, making model planes or furniture, cleaning house, cooking, designing clothes? Did any of these labor processes have psychological importance because you discovered tastes and interests, achieved something, or wished to please another person?

DISCOVERIES: Have you ever discovered from specific experience that friends change? That the home town doesn't stay the same? That time ceases when you wait between two worlds, the past and the future? Have you ever known a fear that troubled you for days or weeks? Thought you had an incurable disease or a social stigma that you could never live down? Known insecurity? Economic or social insecurity? Loss of personal relationships? Loss of belief in civilization or in religion? Discovered that you were inadequate when you wished to be adequate? Tried to appear self-reliant and sophisticated when you did not feel so? Enjoyed giving your best to a cause or an undertaking? Discovered an undesirable character trait in yourself? Discovered an undesirable trait in another person whom you valued?

FRUSTRATIONS: Have you ever felt helpless because you couldn't make another person understand a moral or social principle which you had taken for granted or your reason for having another as a friend? Suffered because of a wound or some physical condition which made you conspicuous? Discovered that you can never understand another person completely? Suffered because you were misunderstood? Suffered because you misunderstood a situation or another person, or because you were too sensitive? Watched a sensitive person suffer when you could do nothing?

ATTITUDES: Have you ever discovered a racial prejudice or some other prejudice which you felt against another person? Discovered another's prejudice toward you? Recognized your own gain in maturity—when you assumed leadership, kept yourself under control, learned to understand parental feelings, began to think of giving rather than getting on holidays? Harmed yourself by your own stubbornness? Changed your attitude toward death, toward immortality, or toward some religious belief? Realized the smallness of the individual in contrast to eternity, infinity, perfect beauty? Tried to understand the feelings of an old man or an old woman? Found satisfaction because you dared to be yourself instead of following custom, convention?

Thought for the Day

Are you continuing to find suitable and adequate illustrations for your book? This chapter presents a peculiar challenge for illustration. What can you think of besides photographs of places and people?

An Opening Section from "**My Brother Convinces Me**"

My brother has helped me to grow up, sometimes not in a very gentle way.

"Why are you so crazy about the Yankees?" asked my father when we visited the Stadium this summer.

"I can't help it," I replied. "Johnny brought me up that way!"

I became a firm Yankee fan at the age of five when, to tease my brother, I spoke disrespectfully of DiMaggio. After I had picked myself up from the bottom of the stairs, I was a completely converted Yankee fan.

An End Section from "**My Directors**"

[This follows an opening that dealt with the writer's infatuation for the movie *National Velvet* and its star, Elizabeth Taylor.]

I'll never forget the year I had my gland trouble and was in the hospital for almost three weeks. When I returned home, I became Nurse Hernandez. My poor dolls had needles stuck in them all day long, and my desk became an operating table. The little shoe closet in the corner of my room was the supply closet. It contained bottles filled with water, cotton, and many other things. Every day afer school I would bring home a new friend, some girl I had hooked into being a nurse because I was a doctor. My little closet grew with supplies, and my beds were made six times a day. I had six helpless dolls who had operations every day.

My imagination was full of life and made my life more fun. Seeing *National Velvet* filled up a gap for only six or seven months. My operation may have decided a future for me.

A Paragraph of Discovery from "**The Large and the Small**"

I lived in New England for twelve years, and always I dreamed of the day when I should see someone important. I was under the impression that, when I saw such a person, he would be different. Yet, when I saw Vice President Agnew presiding over the Senate in Washington, I realized that he was the same as anyone else, except that he had claimed a larger share of recognition. I no longer yearn to see a movie star or famous singer. The people whom I know are as great to me as any actors or actresses who are allowed no privacy from their admiring public.

A Paragraph About the Influence of Books from "**At Anchor**"

I found out that one can make mutual friends through books. One spring day at anchor up the Connecticut River, I saw a girl sailing in a little dinghy named *Amazons*. That name and her little skull and cross-bones pennant led me to believe she had read some of Ransom's books which I had read. When I asked her if she had, she was enormously pleased that I knew about the Ransom sailing books. We became good friends, all because we had read the same exciting books.

Two Paragraphs on Influences from "**What Makes Me Me**"

As with most children, the people who have influenced me the most were and are my parents. From them I have learned what is right and what is wrong, what young boys should do and what they should not. Seeing my mother lock herself out of the house and have to call a neighbor to bring a ladder and climb into the house through the porch door has taught me always to carry my key. Hearing my father tell how smoking ruined his health and how hard it was for him to stop has made me resolve never to smoke.

Sometimes I neglect to listen to what my parents tell me. I learned that I shouldn't play ball in the house by breaking my nose trying to catch a ball. I received a terrible shock by sticking my foot in an uncovered wall socket. I found that it is best not to fight with older girls. One such vixen broke my toe. I learned to put my toys away by stepping on a lead airplane in the middle of the night; it cut my foot open, and it was infected for a long time afterward.

A Paragraph on a Best Friend from "**Gretchen**"

After thinking over all my travels through Germany, I have come to the conclusion that one person and one place have especially made deep and lasting impressions on me. The one person is my cousin Gretchen. Gretchen is seven years older than I, and I adored her. In my eyes Gretchen was superior and big and always seemed to do everything right. I would imitate her whenever I could. I especially loved to do the things she was scolded for—because I admired her courage. Even now, hardly a day passes that I do not think of her; I just have to. When I eat, I mash my food with my fork—just like Gretchen. Then I mix my food—just like Gretchen. And then I eat just like Gretchen. When I go to sleep at night, I puff up my pillow—just like Gretchen; and, still, when I talk to smaller children, I try to make my voice sound just like Gretchen's. To Mommy's disgust I also laugh like her; I roar. I dress like her, preferring her colors and styles. I even try to be as sloppy as she was. I should be ashamed of myself, but I'm not—yet. Of course, I realize now that her ways of doing things were far from perfect, but that's why I still love her and can't help imitating her. And besides, who wants to be perfect? Not me!

A Paragraph About a Teacher from "**Equal Rights for All**"

My third grade teacher was named Miss Gelis. She was a beautiful woman, who later became a radio and television actress. She made not only me, but the whole class, feel a sense of responsibility for our personal neatness and our school work. In an effort to make her students neat, Miss Gelis started a contest. The symbol was a bird's nest. If one had his hands and face clean and his hair and his teeth brushed for a week, he could cut a bird's nest from paper and color it. As each week passed, he could add eggs, grass, and a bird, providing that he was continuously neat and clean. The nests, each bearing a student's name, were placed all around the room to tell of the class's progress. My nest never really filled, but at least I was conscious of the fact that I was expected to keep clean.

My One and Only Influence

When I was two I spent a frigid winter in Alabama. The following summer, my parents wanted to find some change of scenery from that of the small town where we had been living. My aunt and uncle had built a house in the mountains of western North Carolina, where the summers were quiet and peaceful, yet not at all dull. There my parents went, with us traipsing along behind them. They were so sold on the place that they bought a cottage next door to that of our relatives. Since then we have been going back there nearly every summer. There are many ice-cold mountain streams in which we built dams; there was a frigid lake in which we took our quotidian swim; that is to say, we the younger generation took our quotidian swim. Our parents could never be convinced that they wouldn't get frozen in the middle, like the Ancient Mariner in the silent sea. This never happened, but I often expected it to happen when I first entered the water.

Montreat, the settlement where we lived, was in the heart of the rattlesnake country. Once, after our family had returned to Scarsdale, my uncle shot a rattlesnake which was sleeping on the steps of our house. It was very unusual to see them so far down the mountain, but one had to be on constant look-out for them. Once a group of my cousins and I were walking along a mountain trail when one boy found in the road what he thought was a dead milk snake. Just as he was bending over to pick it up, it started agitating its tail violently; it was a diamond-backed rattler. We at once started agitating our tails violently. We didn't stop until we were a long way from there. From then on, my cousin was careful not to pick up any "dead milk snakes."

There were a boys' club and a girls' club in the vicinity. One night we took a hike up a mountain; as we had heard that there was going to be a big meteor fall that night, we were all very excited. After cooking supper, we laid out our beds in a fairly open spot from which we could see a large percentage of the stars; then we settled down to watch, expecting to see shooting stars wherever we looked. Although we sat up until way in the night, we never saw a single shooting star. On other nights we were luckier; sometimes I saw as many as ten shooting stars. It was always fun watching, whether we saw any of them or not.

Yes, Montreat was lots of fun; our families used to sit on the porch of our house and sing spirituals after supper was finished. We often cooked our dinners over fires out in the woods, near some stream. I have many pleasant memories of toasting marshmallows and feet over a warm fire after the sun had set.

Then I remember the famous Montreat rains. When it rains there, it doesn't just drizzle, as it often does in Scarsdale; it doesn't pour, as it sometimes does in Scarsdale. When it rains, it rains so hard that it seems as if all of the valley is going to float away. The mountain streams, usually not much more than small trickles, become huge rivers of swirling, gushing water; they move like lava, letting nothing stop them or even deflect them from their courses. Roads become streams; streams become wide rivers, and rivers become huge lakes, spreading wherever the terrain will allow, and sometimes farther. Lightning and thunder growl and crack continuously, like the roll of drums on a parade grounds. The water and electricity supplies are cut off; we are like babes in the arms of nature, isolated completely from the outside world, like Robinson Crusoe on his island.

These storms usually break about twice a summer; they are among the most thrilling and exciting, yet frightening, experiences that are to be found in our wide world. In Montreat, no matter how often these inundations occur, they always seem to take on new vigor, new excitement. I will never forget them.

Montreat was a wonderful place for anyone; if you wanted to be a loafer, you could just sit on the front porch and watch the clouds drift by; if, on the other hand, you had ants in your pants, you could always find plenty of interesting things to do to keep you occupied. It was an ideal spot for hunting, swimming, or just being.

CHECK SHEET FOR CHAPTER 7

Analysis of Samples

1. In sample 1, what occupation do you think the writer has in mind for her future?

2. Look closely at the first paragraph of "What Makes Me Me" and explain how the writer has used gerunds in his sentence.

3. In sample 2, give reasons for each of the commas the writer uses.

4. The writer of "Gretchen" uses a great many dashes to punctuate her paragraph. What purpose do these dashes serve?

5. What seems to have been the biggest contribution of Miss Gelis in "Equal Rights for All" to the writer's growth?

6. How many figures of speech can you find in the complete chapter? Try to identify them by name. How effective do you find them?

7. The title of the complete chapter is probably an example of a figure we call hyperbole. Discuss the meaning of hyperbole and give some examples of your own.

Spelling

1. accident (Write its adjective and adverb forms. What other words can you think of that change the same way?)
2. aeronautics (Consult a dictionary and account for this difficult spelling.)
3. architect (How many other forms of this word can you spell properly?)
4. canyon
5. executive

6. gauge
7. lightning (What is its homonym?)
8. marshmallow
9. memento (How does it form its plural?)
10. missile
11. precede (Why do we mix this word up with "proceed"?)
12. terrific, terrible
13. tremendous
14. until

Problems for Group Consideration

For the last chapter you discussed ways of making your writing style more personal, more imaginative. However, some figurative writing does little more than betray the writer's imagination. If we write, for exemple, "That politician's pockets are lined with the sweat of honest working people," we have made a laughable example of what we call a mixed metaphor; for sweat would hardly make a pocket-lining. One trouble with inept and mixed metaphors is that they convey little or no meaning. Printed below are eight sentences that demonstrate sparse or shoddy thinking and, therefore, are almost without meaning or laughable—or both. Try to rephrase each sentence in a way that at least will clarify what the writer intended to say.

1. The very crux of the tragedy is that Oedipus falls from his pillar of success.

2. Jim's environment again threw him a curve when the Patna came a cropper and sank.

3. Gauguin, an escapist of the first water, finally found the end of the rainbow in the South Seas.

4. Its good points notwithstanding, the essence of communism is so full of loopholes that it can never speak to free men.

5. Our tax structure hangs like an albatross around the neck of our economy and is in dire need of repair.

6. No new doors to wisdom are opened, and everyone dies on the vine.

7. I had been literally wrapped up in a bubble made stronger by the dirt in its walls.

8. A teenager is no more than a crumb on the bread of life.

Toward Better Sentence Construction

1. Avoid "freight-car" sentences. These occur when you try to load everything you want in one sentence and couple your clauses with many coordinate conjunctions —*for, and, nor, but, or, yet.*

poor: I wanted to go and my sister did too, but we didn't for my mother wanted us to stay home so we could do our homework so we did.

better: Although my sister and I wanted to go, we were not able to because our mother wanted us to stay with her and do homework.

or: Both my sister and I wanted to go, but we weren't able to. Mother thought we should stay in and do our homework. We did.

2. Avoid beginning a lot of sentences with the following: so, but, and, also, for. Such beginnings are often justified for the sake of variety, but do not make a habit of it. Many times these words may be omitted, and the sentence sense will stay the same; sometimes the clauses may be joined.

poor: I had planned for weeks to go to the dance. But Fate had something else in store for me.

better: Though I had planned for weeks to go to the dance, Fate had something else in store for me.

3. Learn to substitute other transitions for the following: so, but, and, also, for.

SO—thus, in this way, likewise, therefore.

BUT—however, nevertheless.

AND—furthermore, moreover (often you can omit this word).

ALSO—in addition, too (*Also* will often be better used within a sentence rather than as the first word).

Three Ways of Gaining Variety in Sentences

1. *Subordination by use of adverb clauses*

These clauses begin with what we call subordinate conjunctions. Twelve of the most frequently used ones follow: *after, although, as, because, before, if, since, until, when, whenever, where, while.* What others can you add?

Now try making one sentence, each time using one of these conjunctions, from the two that follow in each example. Remember that long introductory adverb clauses are set off by commas.

a. That day we visited the haunted house. For weeks afterwards I had bad dreams.

b. I may not live to be ninety. I hope I will then see roads without billboards.

2. *Subordination by use of verbal phrases*

Review the use of these phrases in Chapter 4. Now try to make better sense of the following two sentences by the use of such phrases in your revision. Remember not to let your verbals dangle and to punctuate properly.

a. I had heard the expression before, and I did not know what it really meant. To have egg on your face. But I found out. One day I came in from lunch with egg yolk on my face. And everybody laughed at me.

b. I had seen the sunset many times, but I never really appreciated it. Then one day at camp the sun went down with the force and color of a bomb exploding.

3. *Subordination by use of noun clauses*

These clauses begin with the word *that,* either expressed or implied. Use them instead of an awkward piece of direct speech.

awkward: My father said no, I may not go. (*that* implied)

better: My father said that I may not go. (*that* expressed)

Experiment with them as the subject of your sentence, as in the following transformations.

a. It is taken for granted that fire burns and ice freezes.
That fire burns and ice freezes is taken for granted.

b. I had accepted it as a fact that Thadie's feelings could not be hurt.
That Thadie's feelings could not be hurt I had accepted as fact.

Agreement of Pronoun with Its Antecedent

If the antecedent of a pronoun—the word replaced by the pronoun—is singular, the pronoun is singular; if the antecedent is plural, the pronoun is plural.

ante. **pro.**

1. Each of the boys tried his hardest.

2. One of the girls has broken her wrist.

Note that, in the two preceding sentences, the sex of the antecedent is clearly known. A rule that has consistently been followed in Standard Written English is that, if the sex of the antecedent is unknown, we use a masculine pronoun, thus:

Anyone finding the ring may claim *his* reward at the office. Today, in an attempt to reflect the equality of the two sexes, this rule is changing. You may want to ask your teacher which of the following is preferred:

a. Anyone finding the ring may claim his reward at the office.

b. Anyone finding the ring may claim his or her reward at the office.

c. Anyone finding the ring may claim their reward at the office.

d. Anyone finding the ring may claim a reward at the office.

Review in Chapter 6 the pitfalls attendant upon the agreement of subject and verb, consider them as governing the agreement of pronoun with antecedent, and discuss why each of the following sentences is written as it is in Standard Written English.

1. One of the girls asked if we were on the right street for the movie, but we told her we were lost, too.

2. Every man is liable for the errors he makes.

3. Neither the cat nor the dogs were giving us their usual attention.

4. Mr. Harsch told Jack and Joan, when he caught them talking, that they would have to serve detention.

5. Here are three words, each with its own esoteric origin.

6. My dog doesn't want to have its ears clipped.

7. If you see people in Paris we know, give them my regards.

Usage

1. Learn the distinction between the following words:

a. BETWEEN—used only between two objects or groups of objects
AMONG—used for three or more objects or groups

Between my sister and me . . .
Among my friends . . .

b. IN—used when one is within something
INTO—denotes action of entering

I went *into* the garage and found the thief *in* it.

c. MOST—is a pronoun or adjective, denotes number
ALMOST—adverb or adjective meaning nearly.

Most of us went. *Almost* all of us went. NOT: Most all of us went.

2. Avoid the following common written errors.

a. Where is he at? (Drop the *at*)

b. Where is he going to? (Drop the *to*)

c. I could of done it. (Change *of* to *have*. *Of* is never a helper-verb.)

d. What would you of done in my place? (Change *of* to *have*)

e. *I* had ought to do this. (Drop *had*.) Parts of the verb *have* are not used with the verb *ought*.)

ASSIGNMENT 7

Write Chapter 6 of your autobiography. In it consider what you are today, your likes and dislikes, what you have learned from your mistakes and those of others. Then write about the people and things that have helped you to your present position. Reserve the next chapter for assessing your abilities. But demonstrate ability in this one by making fewer writing errors than ever.

PRACTICE TEST VII

Review the Check Sheets for the first seven chapters and then, without looking back, do the test. The teacher may want to check your work OR to give you another test of the same sort. Each error will count as 2½ points, if anybody's counting.

I. In each of the following groups, only ONE of the words is misspelled. Spell the word correctly on your paper.

1.	ancestors	a lot	pastime	fassinate
2.	congradulate	quarreling	occurring	carrying
3.	nursery	incidentally	seperated	grandfather's
4.	executive	gauge	marshmellow	preceded
5.	tremendious	muscle	picnicking	until

II. Answer the following questions.

1. Write the past participle of *procrastinate*.

2. Write the gerund form of *adhere*.

3. Write the adverb form of *accident*.

4. Write the adjective form of *notice*.

5. Write the past tense form of *hurry*.

III. We use commas to separate and/or set off

a. appositives
b. interrupting expressions, phrases, and clauses
c. independent clauses joined by the FANBOY conjunctions
d. long introductory clauses and phrases
e. nonrestrictive clauses and phrases

Number your paper. Study the following sentences and, beside the corresponding number, put the reason for the comma(s), using one of the five listed above.

1. Possessing no real interest in classical music, I dropped that teacher at once.

2. My brother, one of the most influential people I've known, taught me in the school of hard knocks.

3. People should early in life strive to do their best, for much knowledge grows with much application.

4. Being far beyond my years at the age of ten, I was already reading Salinger and Mailer.

5. The kitten finally caught his tail, having chased it for exactly eight minutes.

6. How can my mother, who is thirty years older than I, remember what it was like to be in love?

7. His long struggle over, Santiago climbed wearily up the hill.

8. I have never been much of a reader and, to tell the truth, am not likely to be.

9. Before Greta could stop talking, the teacher had given both her and Jean dirty looks.

10. My oldest sister, who was already in college then, tried to teach me to dance.

IV. Make transformations in each of the following sentences by taking the suggested new beginning for your transformation.

1. *Begin with "My father told . . .":*
"You have done the right thing," Father told me.

2. *Begin with "My mother asked me . . .":*
"Where are you going?" my mother asked.

3. *Begin with "Having . . .":*
I had slid down the hill twenty times, and I was tired.

4. *Begin a single sentence with "If I . . .":*
I was too young to know better. Otherwise I wouldn't have written those four letters on the sidewalk.

5. *Begin with "Because . . .":*
It was Sunday and a day of rest and I was supposed to be reading quietly.

6. *Begin with "That the knack . . .":*
It must be true that the knack of writing is necessary in college because everyone tells me so.

7. *Begin with "Since . . .":*
I began to draw recognizable objects at three and I have continued to this day.

8. *Begin with "As . . .":*
I was five and I was graduating from kindergarten and I was ready to lick the world.

9. *Begin with "Because . . .":*
The clock had struck twelve, and we knew it was Christmas morning, and we set out to see what Santa had left.

10. *Begin with "The rope having . . .":*
The rope slipped from our grasp, and we hung helpless where we were—five hundred feet above the gorge.

V. Each of the following sentences has an error. On your paper write the error and its correction.

1. Although most everyone likes dogs, I find them disgusting.

2. Abraham Lincoln was born in a log cabin he had built with his own hands.

3. It's a secret between us three girls.

4. Neither of the three occupations interest me any longer.

5. He found he couldn't get off of the trestle before the train caught up with him.

6. There's only two states I haven't yet visited, Hawaii and Alaska.

7. What could you of been thinking about?

8. When I came to, I didn't know where I was at.

9. Their engagement was supposed to be a secret, but most everyone knew about it.

10. Because Dad had laid quietly for so long, we felt we should call the doctor.

Looking Ahead

The remainder of your autobiography will be concerned with the present and your plans for the future. Two of the selections that follow deal with college. The initial poem provides an introduction in that it is written by an adult assessing her past—and finding it good. Your past, too, has been your subject so far. The first prose piece relates a trying college experience of a former football superstar for the New York Giants. The final one is the reminiscence of a real scholastic discovery by a man who went on to fame as a writer. If college is your goal—in order to be a star athlete, a crack student, a big wheel on campus, or a person in training for a good job—you are no doubt wondering about some of the experience ahead of you. What you read here may begin to inform you.

NIKKI GIOVANNI (1943–   ), who describes herself as twice a college dropout, has published in various magazines and a collection, *Black Feeling.*

Her poem puts an unusual focus on what some consider a hard childhood and makes a universal conclusion about what does make childhood happy. The lack of conventional punctuation and capitalization may give you trouble at first. Be sure you hear the poem several times. You'll find it remarkably easy to understand and like.

Nikki-Rosa

NIKKI GIOVANNI

childhood remembrances are always a drag
if you're Black
you always remember things like living in Woodlawn
with no inside toilet
and if you become famous or something
they never talk about how happy you were to have your mother
all to yourself and
how good the water felt when you got your bath from one of those
big tubs that folk in chicago barbecue in
and somehow when you talk about home
it never gets across how much you
understood their feelings
as the whole family attended meetings about Hollydale
and even though you remember
your biographers never understand
your father's pain as he sells his stock
and another dream goes
and though you're poor it isn't poverty that
concerns you
and though they fought a lot
it isn't your father's drinking that makes any difference
but only that everybody is together and you
and your sister have happy birthdays and very good christmases
and I really hope no white person ever has cause to write about me
because they never understand Black love is Black wealth and they'll
probably talk about my hard childhood and never understand that
all the while I was quite happy

"Recruiting in those days was
a case of every coach for himself."

Y. A. TITTLE (1926–) told his amanuensis, Don Smith, that any male Texan growing up in the town of Marshall in the late 1930's "came by football naturally." Yet Tittle, who eventually became star quarterback for the New York Giants and for three years was voted the most valuable player in the National Football League, did not begin as a superstar. In this incident he recalls his indecision and lack of finesse in leaving one college scholarship for another.

Barefoot in Austin

Y. A. TITTLE

A number of colleges in the southwest were interested in me when I graduated from Marshall High School in June of 1944. This interest was based on two factors. One, I was a 185-pound tailback who could throw . . . the ball. Two, as an asthma sufferer (I still had not completely outgrown the condition), I was likely to be a 4-F in the draft. With World War II in full swing and manpower scarce in the college ranks, my draft status was understandably more important to the college recruiters than my passing records. What impressed them most, I believe, was the prospect that, good or bad, I would at least be around for the full four years.

I received grant-in-aid scholarship offers from all the Texas schools—T.C.U., Texas A & M, University of Texas, Rice, Southern Methodist; and from Tulsa, Louisiana State and Tulane, where my brother Jack had played. Many of these offers took the form of letters or phone calls from the coaches. But often the schools delegated the direct recruiting to prominent alumni who lived in or near Marshall.

Myron Blaylock, presently a prominent attorney in Marshall, was a Texas alumnus, and he gave me a pretty strong pitch during my last semester in high school.

There were others, too. They visited the high school, and they came out to the house for dinner, armed with pamphlets and other propaganda material. It was a steady parade of scouts and coaches.

My parents were impressed by all this. They thought it was quite wonderful that so many important colleges and universities were interested in their boy Y. A. They really enjoyed entertaining the scouts at dinner. As for me, well, I really was not that interested. I wanted to play football in college but up until the time I graduated, I did not think much about which school I would like to go to.

College football recruiting in the southwest in 1944 was a free-wheeling affair, completely lacking the strict regulations that exist today. It was perfectly legal to have a prospective scholarship player visit the campus. I spent considerable time on trips to schools in Texas and Louisiana. I visited the Louisiana State campus at Baton Rouge several times and got to know Bernie Moore, the head coach, quite well. He struck me as being the kind of man I would like to play for. When the time arrived to make a decision, I chose L. S. U.

I must admit my decision was influenced by more than just my regard for Bernie Moore. L. S. U. was one of the few all-civilian schools in the southwest in those war years. Most of the colleges had service programs, such as the Navy's V-12, and this meant that the guys playing football were older and more experienced. My chances of playing were better at L. S. U. where my competition would come from other 17-year-olds plus some 4-Fs. At a place like Texas, I might have to compete against fellows two and three years older who had played varsity ball at, say Georgia Tech, Notre Dame or Ohio State, before entering the officer training programs.

Bernie Moore sent me the grant-in-aid papers and I signed them around the middle of May, a few weeks before I was to graduate from Marshall High School. My scholarship would entitle me to tuition, room and board, and books. It was the standard type of scholarship being offered at the time. I was happy to be going to Louisiana State because I liked Moore and I knew a little about the school. L. S. U. and Tulane were great rivals, and I had seen several games when Jack was a blocking back for Tulane.

Right, here, though, I must tell a story of which I am not overly proud. Still, it deserves telling.

Even though I had committed myself to L. S. U., the University of Texas people did not abandon their efforts to make me change my mind. Myron Blaylock was constantly talking to me. And if I remember correctly, Blair Cherry, one of the Texas coaches, might have been on the scene. They did a terrific selling job, and eventually they convinced me that my real football future was with the University of Texas.

Two days after by graduation, and three days before I was to enroll at L. S. U., I was on my way to Austin.

Everything happened so fast that to this day I do not know what made me change my mind. The shame of violating my written and spoken agreement with Bernie Moore has been with me ever since. It happened a long time ago but it still weighs heavily on my conscience. As a plea in my behalf I can only offer that I was immature and probably not too smart.

Anyway, there I was in a car with a couple of assistant coaches from Texas heading for Austin on a scorching hot June afternoon. I was not yet fully aware what was hapepning. But apparently everything had been laid out very nicely. The plan was to enroll me in summer school, get me a part-time job and keep me hidden from the L. S. U. counterspies until fall practice got under way.

We arrived in Austin that evening and the car stopped in front of a large frame building on the fringe of the Texas campus. A large sign over the door read: "Mrs. Poole's Boarding House."

Mrs. Poole was not unused to having all-state football players deposited on her doorstep. She quickly ushered me into the front room, had me sign the register, and then showed me upstairs to my room.

"It's nice and quiet here," she said. "You'll like it at the university."

I wish I had been as sure of this as she seemed to be.

The door to the room next to mine was open. After unpacking, I stuck my head in and said, "Hiya, my name is Y. A. Title."

The fellow lying on the bed was husky and blond. He rolled over on his side, looked at me for a second out of half-closed eyes and said, "Glad to meet you. My name is Layne . . . Bobby Layne."

Layne had never heard of me. But I knew all about him. He had played at Highland Park High School in Dallas. He had been the first team All-State quarterback. They said he was the hottest . . . schoolboy player in the whole state of Texas.

"They got you too, huh?" said Bobby. "Man, they don't miss anybody." And then he chuckled.

Layne was my age, or close to it. But he seemed much older, more confident. I liked him from the first, but he made me uneasy in a way that I could not explain.

That night I took stock of my situation. With Bobby Layne on the scene it would not be easy to make the Texas ball club. His reputation made him the top freshman in the school. Obviously the rest of us would be at a disadvantage. I was concerned, but I was not going to be scared off. Layne would still have to prove he could

Y. A. Tittle. Courtesy of the New York Giants.

throw the ball better than me. I was sure he couldn't. I was not cocky. It's just that I had confidence in my ability as a passer. I was not about to be psyched out by Bobby Layne or anyone else.

The next morning, Blair Cherry came and got me at Mrs. Poole's and took me across the street to the C. and S. Sporting Goods store, which was run by a great little guy called Rooster Andrews, who today is one of my closest friends. They had a job for me there that would keep me busy until summer school started. I was to work two or three hours a day stacking boxes, sweeping and running errands.

Other football players from all over the state were similarly employed around the campus. They were big and tough and there were a lot of them. Layne had been right; the Texas scouts had done their job extremely well.

As might have been expected, Bobby Layne was not involved in any of the menial tasks that befell the rest of us at Austin the summer of 1944. Bobby was a great baseball pitcher, and he had hooked up with a well-paying semi-pro outfit that had a franchise in Austin. While the rest of us were sweeping and stacking, Layne was sleeping so he would be rested for the game that night. I kind of envied Bobby. He sure was a lot smarter than the others, including Y. A. Tittle.

At first, Layne and I were together a lot. But later on he was off playing ball most of the time and I was left with nothing to do after I finished my job at Rooster Andrews' store across from Mrs. Poole's. I had not made friends with anyone else on the campus, so there was not much to do until Bobby came back. I do not know why we hit it off so well. Bobby was a city-slicker from Dallas; I was a green-eared kid from Marshall. We did not have much in common except for football. But we did respect each other and got along fine.

In the evening when Bobby was not pitching baseball, we often got out in the street in front of Mrs. Poole's and ran races. We ran in our bare feet because we thought we could run faster that way. We ran right down the middle of the street with everybody looking at us like we were crazy. Maybe we were, at that. But at least it was competition, and Bobby and I thrived on competition of any kind. We just had to be competing.

Whenever I run across Layne today, which is not as often as it used to be since he retired after the 1962 season, we sit down to have a few beers and the conversation always gets around to our days at Mrs. Poole's.

"I can still outrun you, Tittle," he says in that gravel voice of his. . . .

I think Bobby really believes he used to beat me in our races. But actually I whipped him most of the time. Neither of us ever amounted to anything as runners in pro ball, so I guess it does not matter too much who won the barefoot races in Austin.

After a few weeks, I was ready to leave the University of Texas. I was sorry I had gone there in the first place. The rest of the high school players on campus seemed much older and more experienced. They were different than the kids I had played with in Marshall. Then too, I noticed a lot of officer training fellows signing up for football.

"Y. A.," I said, "you will never get a chance to play in this kind of company."

About this time back in Marshall, my mother put in a telephone call to Bernie Moore at Baton Rouge.

"Y. A. is down at Austin," she told Moore. "But I am not so sure he likes it there."

"Do you think he still wants to come to Louisiana State?" asked Bernie.

"Yes. He won't admit it of course, but I believe he would."

Moore thanked my mother for calling and said he would do whatever he could. Mom did not realize it, of course, but what Bernie meant was that he was going to recruit me right back off the Texas campus. In his opinion, turnabout was fair play. Texas had grabbed me away from the L. S. U. camp, so Bernie was prepared to resort to the same thing. Recruiting in those days was a case of every coach for himself.

Bernie called in his line coach, Red Swanson, and told him, "Go to Austin and find Tittle. Don't come back without him."

Swanson showed up in Austin on a Sunday morning and called me at Mrs. Poole's. He said he wanted to talk to me. I was so lonely that I was happy to have anyone to talk to. I told him I would meet him at the hotel for breakfast. It did not even occur to me to wonder why Red had suddenly appeared in Austin or how he had found me so easily.

At breakfast, Swanson was tactful enough not to pressure me on why I had wound up at Texas instead of going to Baton Rouge as I had agreed. I was glad he did not bring up the subject of my defection. I was still embarrassed by the whole incident. I appreciated his thoughtfulness in not mentioning it over coffee and toast that morning.

"You like it here, Y. A.?" he asked me point-blank.

"I thought I would, Red," I replied. "Now I am not so sure."

"Why?"

"To begin with, I do not think I will get a chance to play much here. It seems like every high school kid in the state is here. It's like an Army camp."

Swanson could see I was unhappy at Austin, so he made his pitch right away.

"Do you want to reconsider and come to Louisiana State?" he asked.

"Would they still want me back there, Red?"

"Why do you think I am here?" he said. "Bernie Moore wants you to play tailback for us."

"That's great," I said. "I'll go back to Mrs. Poole's and pack my bag right away."

"Whoa, hold on there. Not so fast, boy. There's something you have to do first."

"What's that?"

"You've got to call Mr. Bible and tell him you are leaving. It's the right thing to do. You just can't walk out of here. I'm not taking you back until you tell him you changed your mind about playing at Texas."

Dana X. Bible was the head football coach at Texas, one of the most respected men in his profession, and I was certain he would not be happy to learn I was pulling out. The thought of calling him scared me to death. I tried to wiggle out of it.

"He won't be in his office, Red," I stammered. "It's Sunday, you know."

"I thought of that too," said Swanson, "so I took the trouble of looking up Mr. Bible's home phone number. You can reach him there."

I was trapped. I took the slip of paper with Mr. Bible's number on it and walked over to a phone booth. My heart was pounding. I did not have the slightest idea what I would say to him. I dialed the number and waited. It rang once. It rang twice. Then two or three more times. Happy days, no one was home! Or maybe they were alseep. At any rate, I had tried. My intentions had been good. I felt as if a heavy weight had been lifted from my shoulders.

Later, there was considerable bitterness between D. X. Bible and Bernie Moore over my return to L. S. U., even though this sort of thing happened all the time during that period. To put the record straight, though, I did try to call Bible that morning. And it was Red Swanson, the L. S. U. line coach, who insisted that I make the call. That's more than the Texas people did when they talked me out of going to L. S. U.

Swanson took me back to Mrs. Poole's. I packed my suitcase and we left. Layne and the others did not even know I had gone.

We drove all the way to Baton Rouge, a distance of 450 miles, stopping in Houston briefly to take on another passenger, a kid by the name of Jim Cason. He was from Victoria, Texas, and though we did not realize it at the time, we were to become fast friends in the years ahead. Jim and I played together for four seasons at L. S. U. and later with the San Francisco Forty-Niners. I guess our friendship began that first day on the ride from Houston to Baton Rouge. Jim was only sixteen and we were both frightened. For most of the trip we sat in silence and stared out the window as Swanson pushed the car eastward.

I have often stopped to wonder what might have happened had I stayed at the University of Texas that summer of 1944. Maybe pro football never would have heard of Yelberton Abraham Tittle, or perhaps Bobby Layne's career would have been different. We were both quarterbacks and we might have eliminated each other entirely. It is odd how fate steps in and changes the course of a man's life. In my case, fate was called Red Swanson. Bobby Layne went his way with Texas and I went to Louisiana State. Our paths were to cross many times over the next twenty years, but in 1944 we headed our separate ways.

Vocabulary

They visited the high school, and they came out to the house for dinner, armed with pamphlets and other *propaganda* material . . . . . (179:2); Swanson was *tactful* enough not to pressure me on why I had wound up at Texas instead of going to Baton Rouge as I had agreed. I was glad he did not bring up the subject of my *defection* . . . . (183:34)

Study Questions and Activities

1. In the world of 1944, when Y. A. Tittle was graduated from high school, what more serious competition than football was holding the headlines of the world's newspapers? How did this world event influence favorably the young quarterback's future and college? How did it become a major consideration in his defection from the Texas team? Do only college athletes allow such practical considerations to affect their choice of university?

2. In what ways did Tittle's early meeting with Bobby Layne at Austin affect both his present and his future? How common is it in life for a person to meet, like, and consciously avoid a confrontation with a major rival?

3. What possible meanings for the chapter are contained in the title, "Barefoot in Austin"?

4. What evidence of Tittle's immaturity do you find in his disenchantment with Austin, in his decision to leave, and in his departure?

5. Why does Tittle equate Red Swanson with fate?

6. The writer states that, at the time of his graduation, football recruiting in the Southwest was "completely lacking the strict regulations that apply today." Research what sort of regulations govern football recruiting today? How are they enforced? What evidence does Title offer to show that in 1944 recruiting "was a completely free-wheeling affair"?

"There was something for Youth to do;
those superior old men had not done anything, finally."

LINCOLN STEFFENS (1866–1936) grew up in a middle-class American family near San Francisco, leading the life of Huck Finn in an exceedingly well-bred way. He lived to be a leading muckraker at the turn of the century and a famous journalist and autobiographer. In this incident he discusses his change from a young man in attendance at the University of California to the probing scholar he felt he had become in his adulthood.

I Become a Student

LINCOLN STEFFENS

It is possible to get an education at a university. It has been done; not often, but the fact that a proportion, however small, of college students do get a start in interested, methodical study, proves my thesis, and the two personal experiences I have to offer illustrate it and show how to circumvent the faculty, the other students, and the whole college system of mind-fixing. My method might lose a boy his degree, but a degree is not worth so much as the capacity and the drive to learn, and the undergraduate desire for an empty baccalaureate is one of the holds the educational system has on students. Wise students some day will refuse to take degrees, as the best men (in England, for instance) give, but do not themselves accept, titles.

My method was hit on by accident and some instinct. I specialized. With several courses prescribed, I concentrated on the one or two that interested me most, and letting the others go, I worked intensively on my favorites. In my first two years, for example, I worked at English and political economy and read philosophy. At the beginning of my junior year I had several cinches in history. Now I liked history; I had neglected it partly because I rebelled at the way it was taught, as positive knowledge unrelated to politics, art, life, or any-

Lincoln Steffens, Culver Pictures.

thing else. The professors gave us chapters out of a few books to read, con, and be quizzed on. Blessed as I was with a "bad memory," I could not commit to it anything that I did not understand and intellectually need. The bare record of the story of man, with names, dates, and irrelative events, bored me. But I had discovered in my readings of literature, philosophy, and political economy that history had light to throw upon unhistorical questions. So I proposed in my junior and senior years to specialize in history, taking all the courses required and those also that I had flunked in. With this in mind I listened attentively to the first introductory talk of Professor William Cary Jones on American constitutional history. He was a dull lecturer, but I noticed that, after telling us what pages of what books we must be prepared in, he mumbled off some other references "for those that may care to dig deeper."

When the rest of the class rushed out into the sunshine, I went up to the professor and, to his surprise, asked for this memorandum. He gave it me. Up in the library I ran through the required chapters in the two different books, and they differed on several points. Turning to the other authorities, I saw that they disagreed on the same facts and also on others. The librarian, appealed to, helped me search the bookshelves till the library closed, and then I called on Professor Jones for more references. He was astonished, invited me in, and began to approve my industry, which astonished me. I was not trying to be a good boy; I was better than that: I was a curious boy. He lent me a couple of his books, and I went off to my club to read them. They only deepened the mystery, clearing up the historical question, but leaving the answer to be dug for and written.

The historians did not know! History was not a science, but a field for research, a field for me, for any young man, to explore, to make discoveries in and write a scientific report about. I was fascinated. As I went on from chapter to chapter, day after day, finding frequently essential differences of opinion and of fact, I saw more and more work to do. In this course, American constitutional history, I hunted far enough to suspect that the Fathers of the Republic who wrote our sacred Constitution of the United States not only did not, but did not want to, establish a democratic government, and I dreamed for a while—as I used as a child to play I was Napoleon or a trapper—I promised myself to write a true history of the making of the American Constitution. I found other events, men, and epochs waiting for students. In all my other courses, in ancient, in European, and in modern history, the disagreeing authorities carried me back to the need of a fresh search for (or of) the original documents or other clinching testimony. Of course I did well in my classes. The history professors soon knew me as a student and seldom put a question to me except when the class had flunked it. Then Professor Jones would say, "Well, Steffens, tell them about it."

Fine. But vanity wasn't my ruling passion then. What I had was a quickening sense that I was learning a method of studying history and that every chapter of it, from the beginning of the world to the end, is crying out to be rewritten. There was something for Youth to do; these superior old men had not done anything, finally.

Nothing is done. Everything in the world remains to be done or done over. "The greatest picture is not yet painted, the greatest play isn't written (not even by Shakespeare), the greatest poem is unsung. There isn't in all the world a perfect railroad, nor a good government, nor a sound law." Physics, mathematics, and especially the most advanced and exact of the sciences, are being fundamentally revised. Chemistry is just becoming a science; psychology, economics, and sociology are awaiting a Darwin, whose work in turn is awaiting an Einstein. If the rah-rah boys in our colleges could be told this, they might not all be such specialists in football . . . and unearned degrees. They are not told it, however; they are told to learn what is known. This is nothing, philosophically speaking.

I read the books over again with a fresh eye, with a real interest, and I could see that, as in history, so in other branches of knowledge, everything was in the air. And I was glad of it. Rebel though I was, I had got the religion of scholarship and science; I was in awe of the authorities in the academic world. It was a release to feel my worship cool and pass. But I could not be sure. I must go elsewhere, see and hear other professors, men these California professors quoted and looked up to as their high priests. I decided to go as a student to Europe when I was through Berkeley, and I would start with the German universities.

My father listened to my plan, and he was disappointed. He had hoped I would succeed him in his business; it was for that that he was staying in it. When I said that, whatever I might do, I would never go into business, he said, rather sadly, that he would sell out his interest and retire. And he did soon after our talk. But he wanted me to stay home and, to keep me, offered to buy an interest in a certain San Francisco daily paper. He had evidently had this in mind for some time. I had always done some writing, verse at the poetical age of puberty, then a novel which my mother alone treasured. Journalism was the business for a boy who liked to write, he thought, and he said I had often spoken of a newspaper as my ambition. No doubt I had in the intervals between my campaigns as Napoleon. But no more. I was now going to be a scientist, a philosopher. He sighed; he thought it over, and with the approval of my mother, who was for every sort of education, he gave his consent.

Vocabulary

the fact that a proportion, however small, of college students do get a start in interested, methodical study, proves my *thesis* .... (186:4); the two personal experiences I have to offer illustrate it [my thesis] and show how to *circumvent* the faculty. (186:5); I promised myself to write a true history of the making of the American Constitution. I found other events, men, and *epochs* waiting for students.. (188:39); the disagreeing authorities carried me back to the need of a fresh search for (or of) the original documents or other *clinching* testimony.... (188:43); The history professors soon knew me as a student and seldom put a question to me except when the class had flunked it. . . . Fine. But *vanity* wasn't my ruling passion then .... (189:3); I was in *awe* of the authorities in the academic world.... (189:23); I had always done some writing, verse at the poetical age of *puberty,* then a novel .... (189:38)

Study Questions

1. Define Mr. Steffens' meaning of the word "student" in his title.

2. What specific charges does the writer make against the university system of his day? Do any of these charges seem to you to be valid today? Do any apply to the education you are or have been receiving? Support your answer with evidence.

3. What was the major discovery Steffens made as he began to study with Professor Jones?

4. How did the young man broaden the discovery he had made about history books to a more universal generalization? Put the final generalization into your own words.

5. What was the effect of Steffens' discovery upon his attitude toward academic life in general?

6. Lincoln Steffens' final fame will probably rest upon his career as a muckraking journalist and an autobiographer. In view of this possibility, what ironies can you find in this chapter?

7. Compare this selection with the one written by Henry Adams. In what ways do they agree? Disagree?

8. In your own studies so far, have you discovered any points upon which the "experts" disagree? How many such points can your class come up with? Can you decide the answers to any of these questions yet in a way that satisfies you?

VOCABULARY: COMPLETIONS

Using the vocabulary words from the previous two selections, try your hand at completing the following phrases under Column A. Six of the words in Column B will correctly fit. Write the correct letters after the corresponding numbers on your paper.

Column A	Column B
1. _______ of time	**a.** puberty
2. the _______ of the traitor	**b.** tactful
3. the age of _______	**c.** thesis
4. in _______ of someone	**d.** epochs
5. _______ a point	**e.** clinching
6. writing a _______	**f.** defection
	g. awe

An early type of pen. New York Public Library Picture Collection.

8

What's Next—What Am I Good For?

Everyone has a goal for the future. Most people, except those rare ones unlucky enough to inherit a life of coupon-clipping luxury, plan to work. Many will marry and support a family as well as themselves.

All of us know that the future holds more than a few years—or months—of added education. Already, most of you have worked for pay, and some may be already self-supporting. A few may have found the work for which they are suited. The majority, though, are thinking of something better, a future that will bring satisfaction, happiness, even fame. This chapter concerns itself with your thoughts about what you hope for in the future. What kind of life do you envision? One like your parents'? One somewhat different? One radically different? Do you favor a married or single existence? What will your job be?

In considering your own possibilities of a profession, take into account your past ambitions, your present interests, the talents you have developed and those you feel can be developed, occupations you abhor and those you have some sympathy for. Such a chapter may well develop into one which carefully explores a single occupation: the traits and skills necessary for it, the education it requires, a description of the duties involved; your findings on range of salary, chances for advancement, the range of possibilities within it, and the probability of being employed once you are prepared. Such a chapter is likely to be lengthy and may easily omit discussion of the future home life you desire, reserving that for Chapter 9.

The samples given for this chapter do not help much for such an organization. They are, instead, geared mainly to one in which you discuss your future in terms of less specific discussion of your plans for the future. Before choosing which plan to use, consult your Then and Now chart for whatever help it can give you, work for a period with a group of classmates, and then get to work.

Getting Started

1. Take a day in which to do little else than spend time with someone who pursues an interesting job. The person may be a friend, a sibling, a parent, or just anyone willing to let you tag along for a time. Observe the planning for the work, the actual work being done, the skill with which the job is performed. Talk with your companion about the training, the openings, the satisfactions and dissatisfactions involved. You may be able to persuade your superiors that you are entitled to a day off from classes to do this research, or you may have to settle for a school holiday or an after-school visit. Report to the class the discoveries you have made.

2. With a group of classmates find out what occupations are of prime interest to each of you. Then assign each member a different occupation to be researched through books and interviews and reported on to the class.

3. Take as a topic "The Ideal Family" and with a group discuss what each member's ideas of such a unit would be.

Here again are some possible headings to consider for organizing separate or related paragraphs.

FIRST AMBITIONS: What were they? Why did you change your mind? How did hobbies aid or discourage your ambitions?

WORK YOU KNOW: What are your parents' occupations? What else have they worked at? What do you feel about such types of work? Have you been influenced by any siblings' work? By your friends'? Who has influenced your present ambition? What have they told you, both bad and good, about it?

WORK YOU HAVE DONE: What are the hardest things that you have ever done? the heaviest physical labor? the most exacting task or skill? the most difficult interview or conversation? the most depressing or discouraging task? the severest effort of your will or perseverance? Were there satisfactions in doing this work?

PRESENT AMBITIONS: What are your ideas about work? Is it merely a means of making a living, a police power to keep people out of trouble, or a chief satisfaction in a good life? Should work be creative? A means of continuing one's education? A contribution to general human life? Do you wish to see something tangible or to believe that something valuable but intangible is growing from your work? Are you pursuing a hobby similar to your ambition? How much do you know about the work you hope to do? What places do you want to see? Will your present ambition enable you to see them?

ASSESSING POTENTIAL: Have you ever defended yourself from an accusation by another person? From an accusation by yourself? Are you able to understand people whose religious, moral, political, or social ideas differ from yours? Whose artistic or intellectual tastes differ from yours? What is the greatest personal problem that you have ever had to decide? What is the greatest one that you foresee in the future?

OTHER QUESTIONS TO PONDER:

a. What feelings have you had when you tried to borrow something, to persuade someone to vote for you, or to ask some other help or support—when you were in conflict about your action? Tried to persuade other people to do something inconvenient for them or against their principles? Won or lost in a physical contest?

b. What moral, ethical, or religious environment are you most familiar with? Is it tolerant or intolerant, social or self-centered?

c. Have you had some contact with an entirely different moral and ethical environment? What was the result of this contact?

d. What social class do you know best? What other social classes do you know well enough to contrast with it? Would you be at home in a class other than your own?

Norman Mailer, self-portrait.

A Reason for Rejecting a Profession from "**Finishing Touches**"

I do not wish to enter my father's work. He is an insurance manager, and I have no desire to go into that kind of work. It may be, however, that I shall inevitably and unwillingly end up following in his footsteps. He has been an insurance man for fifteen years, and he has worked with both the Travelers and the Royal-Liverpool Companies. He may—fortunately for him but not for me—move this summer to a bigger office. We have an idea that it may be to Cleveland, Ohio. That is the way with the insurance business. When one is a field man, traveling is what he is paid for. When he is in higher offices, he may become too good for one office and be moved to another. That is the reason we moved to Grand Rapids from Syracuse. Such moves do, however, give me self-confidence. When we made our first move, I shivered and sweated, feeling the eyes of the boys and girls burning into my back. When we moved to Breton Downs, I was somewhat more at ease, and here at East I quickly fell right into line.

An Early Fantasy About a Profession from "**Command Decision**"

This time I would be the President of the United States of America. Being the first lady president would mean playing a very demanding, yet dramatic, role. My imagination centered around my taking the Oath of Office. I would have dashingly appeared in a magnificent red satin gown, and I would have graciously accepted my grave duties. I would have settled all the world's difficult problems and instituted a lasting bond of friendship among the once hostile nations. Strangely, I pictured myself as a person physically different from me, but spiritually I was myself. At the age of twelve I returned to reality and forgot my spectacular aspiration.

A Career in Writing from "**My Ambitions and Talents**"

I was always very happy when I could find a victim who would patiently listen to one of my tales, and I would thrill to my own stories. When I was around eleven, for the first time I really wrote down some of my stories. The one about the little quartz stone was the first one. He was made into an inkwell and married to a penholder, but unfortunately the inkwell broke and its pieces were swept down the river into the sea. There it was eventually reunited with all his old friends. Then there was the story of little Nelly Nosy. She snooped around in Mommy's closets for Christmas presents and landed in heaven through a secret door. There the angels taught her a lesson for being so nosy. It had a happy ending, though, when she woke up and learned that she had just been dreaming. Then there was the story of the triplet dwarves with but one name, and the story of the twin rain drops, and many more. How good or bad those stories were I have no idea, but I do know that I got a great kick out of them.

A Reason for Rejecting Cities from **"Still Undecided"**

I decided a long time ago that I would not commute on a train if I could possibly avoid it. I saw, and still see, my father awaken every morning, dash through breakfast, and race to catch the train. I have decided that this way of life is out. I want to be a lawyer in a small town in New England. There I won't have to live in a big city where I hardly know anyone. In a small town everyone knows everyone else.

A Consideration of Politics from **"Future Unlimited"**

As for being a lawyer, politics, which is an easy step from the practice of law, has always appealed to me. But politics is no career for a man who wants to make money. Money and corruption frequently go hand in hand in politics. It is all very well to want to go into politics, but how do I know that my mature personality will be of the sort necessary for a successful politician? My interest in politics grew from my interest in history; but from my own observation, I have noticed that there is a great deal of doorbell ringing and tedious jobs to be done before there is any opportunity for campaigning, let alone office-holding. My political views are unformed at the moment. None of the present parties seems perfect to me. I think I am a liberal, but with more education and more experience, I might change.

An Early Ambition from **"Unforgotten Years"**

My first ambition came to me at the ripe old age of five. I was given the gift of drawing. Mother blessed those days as she would give me a pad of paper, a ruler, and a few pencils. That would be the last she heard of me for the rest of the day. Mother was also lucky that she never had the mess of paints or the mess of chalks as I was never given the art of sketching. I was drawing designs. My uncles and aunts often would bring me drawing sets and stenciling sets. As you can gather, I had no choice of my life ambition. Mother and my relatives were so amazed at my work of designing that they would take my masterpieces and show them to professionals. They seemed to like my work, for one day I noticed my aunt wearing a dress she had made with the print designed from one of my drawings. Some people told Mother that some day I would design prints for clothing and become an expert at this, but I laid my foot down and refused to draw designs any more. I am afraid that, when I gave up drawing, I gave up my lifetime work and made a big mistake; for today, when I look at some of my past work, I know I was a fool to give it up. But like most boys I wanted to become a policeman.

Looking to the Future

I wish that I could be as absolutely positive now as I was at the age of five of what vocation I should choose for my life work.

At five my career was planned and already being practiced; for I had received a doctor's kit for my birthday, and whenever the opportunity arose I was only too glad to spend the day tending to my dolls. These poor things were constantly being stricken with some of the worst and most contagious diseases. I would spend hours giving pills, taking pulses and temperatures.

Three years later I had completely abandoned nursing, and I was all set to be an operator in a beauty "saloon," as I referred to it. Mother was my chief victim during this trying period, and I spent many nights twisting mother's tresses into many different and peculiar styles. Dad would become much perturbed at these experiments and would often remark that he couldn't understand why Mother would spend three dollars to have her hair fixed, only to have me rip it all apart. I still enjoy hairdressing; the only difficulty I find is that the results are sometimes unusual and grotesque. Now somewhat older, I know that hairdressing is neither the most profitable nor satisfying job there is.

My next ambition, so far as a career was concerned, started when Mother took me to look at the switchboard of a small telephone company in one of Vermont's little rural communities. I was fascinated by the efficiency and accuracy with which the operators put the plugs in the correct holes on the board. This desire soon disappeared too, and all my talents were bent on becoming an author. To a sixth grader, writing seemed both glamorous and profitable. I started immediately to write a bloodcurdling detective mystery. This novel possessed the unique and original title of "Susie the Detective." After typing the masterpiece, I announced to my family that I was going to take it to one of our neighbors, who was a publisher. Dad, astonished at this idea, crushed all my hopes with one decisive "No, you can't." I thereupon decided not to be an author. There was no encouragement!

Since entering high school, I have given much thought to what I would like to make my life work. I have considered music as a career; but since I have no time to practice, nor quite what it takes to reach the top, I'm afraid this is not for me.

I enjoy people and being with them. For this reason, I am again considering nursing. Nursing is not only a profession on which one can rely for a livelihood, but it is work which is helpful to others besides oneself. It benefits people when they are sick and need help most. For several months now I have been doing service work at Blythedale, a home for crippled children, and at the rehabilitation ward of St. Agnes Hospital. I find this work satisfying in that I feel that I am doing a little to help these poor children, who are either bedridden or hobble around on crooked limbs with the assistance of crutches or braces. I think nursing is a wonderful career and offers any girl a wonderful opportunity to be of service to others.

CHECK SHEET FOR CHAPTER 8

Analysis of Samples

1. Underline all the pronouns in sample 1. Does each of them have a clear antecedent? How does their use make the paragraph easy for the reader to follow?

2. How many illustrations does the writer of sample 3 use? How does she add detail to the illustrations?

3. Study the sample "Still Undecided." What arguments could you offer against the writer's choice?

4. Both "Still Undecided" and "Future Unlimited" deal with arguments stemming from what we call broad generalizations. What is a broad generalization? What is the one made in "Future Unlimited"? How can we narrow a broad generalization?

5. The "Unforgotten Years" chapter is organized toward a climax. As a result of its construction, what surprise awaits the reader?

Spelling

1. despair (What are its adjective and adverb forms?)
2. destroy (Write its noun form)
3. dilemma (What might your teacher criticize if you used the phrase, "on the horns of a dilemma"?)
4. during
5. excel (Write the three other parts of this verb and its adjective form. What general spelling rule does it follow?)
6. fulfill
7. itself
8. laboratory (Learn to pronounce this one properly)
9. marry (Write the three other parts of this verb and its noun form. What problem do you see?)
10. necessary (Write the verb and adverb forms)
11. spectacle (Write its adjective and adverb forms)
12. surgeon
13. thorough (Be sure you pronounce this one correctly)
14. try (Write the three other verb forms and a noun form. What other words in this lesson does it resemble in its spelling changes?)

Case of Pronouns

The one part of speech in our language which probably causes students the most trouble is the pronoun. Like pronouns in the foreign language you may be studying, many are inflected. That is, they change their form when used as a subject, a possessive, or an object. We call these three forms *Nominative, Possessive,* and *Objective.* Review the following chart of pronouns with changes.

Singular

Person	*Nominative*	*Possessive*	*Objective*
1	I	my, mine	me
2	you	your, yours	you
3, masc.	he	his	him
3, fem.	she	her, hers	her
3, neut.	it	its	it
Relative	who	whose	whom
	which	——	which
	that	——	that
	this	——	this

Plural

Person	*Nominative*	*Possessive*	*Objective*
1	we	our, ours	us
2	you	your, yours	you
3	they	their, theirs	them
	who	whose	whom
	which	——	which
	those	——	those
	these	——	these

1. Subjects and predicate nominatives (pronouns used after forms of the verb to be) use nominative case. An exception is "It is me," a form now considered proper by all except the purest Purist.

- **a.** Mary and *she* went to camp together.
- **b.** Aunt Alice and *I* both saw the accident.
- **c.** It was *they* who reported it to the police. (If the "It was they" offends you, try the simpler and better "They reported it.")

2. Object forms, which usually follow the verb or end of a prepositional phrase, use the objective case.

- **a.** Uncle Jack took my father and *me* to his camp. (Direct object)
- **b.** Will you give Mary and *me* some time, please? (Indirect object)
- **c.** He did it especially for John and *us.* (Object of preposition)
- **d.** I waited for Aunt Madge and *her* to come. (Object with verbal)

An Easy Out for This Problem

Almost no one uses a pronoun incorrectly if there is only one word to consider. Who, for example, would say "Her went to camp," unless they were talking infant language? Nor would we say "Me saw the accident," "Them reported it," Uncle Jack took I to camp," "Give I more time," "He did it for we," or "I waited for she to come."

Using what you already have known for years about good pronoun usage, make this test whenever you find a pronoun whose case to you is uncertain because it is part of a pair. Remove the noun from the pair. If the pronoun sounds correct to you without the noun, it is almost certainly used properly. Consider the following examples:

- **a.** When do Dick and (me, I) have to have the project in? (Remove *Dick*)
- **b.** By the time Morgan and (he, him) arrived, the dance was over. (Remove *Morgan*)
- **c.** Let me know when my mother and (I, me) have to be there. (Remove *my mother*)
- **d.** Will (we, us) boys be invited too? (Remove *boys*)
- **e.** Just tell my father or (I, me) what to bring. (Remove *my father*)
- **f.** It was strictly a matter between John and (I, me). (Remove *John*)
- **g.** The teacher made (we, us) boys promise to clean up the mess. (Remove *boys*)

Six Problems with Pronouns

1. BETWEEN and AMONG are prepositions that make little sense when the second element is removed from their phrase. Just remember that they do take the objective case.

2. ITS, without an apostrophe, is the pronoun form. Whenever you write IT'S, you have written a contraction for "it is." Notice, also, that none of the possessive pronouns use apostrophes.

3. The words AS and THAN frequently introduce incomplete clauses: He squanders more money than (I, me). Because the intention is "than I squander," the correct pronoun is "I." With "me," the sentence would mean, "He squanders more money than he squanders me." Solve the following examples.

- **a.** Ramona is not so tall as (I, me).
- **b.** Tom is a month older than (I, me).
- **c.** I like her sister more than (she, her). [Why could either be correct?]
- **d.** Susie is as eager as (I, me) to leave for college.

4. While WHO and WHOM (also WHOEVER and WHOMEVER) follow the same rules as do personal pronouns, common usage today is gradually causing the objective form to disappear from the language. A reasonable general rule to follow is this: Unless a sentence sounds silly with *who,* (Consider "To who shall I give this?" "For who is it intended?"), whenever you are in doubt, choose the *who* form.

5. Because a gerund is a verbal used as a noun, Standard Written English prefers the possessive form preceding it.

- **a.** I object to *your* following me so closely.
- **b.** This dress was not of *my* choosing.
- **c.** We're late because of *his* procrastinating.

6. KIND and SORT are singular and should be preceded by THIS or THAT.

- **a.** He likes *this sort* of books. He likes *these sorts* of books.
- **b.** I always use *that kind* of towels. I always use *those kinds* of towels.

Fuzzy Reference of Pronouns

Written English must be more precise than spoken English. Beware in writing that you use THIS, THESE, THAT, THOSE, and WHICH clearly, generally to refer to a specific one-word antecedent. Avoid using them to refer to ideas presented in groups of words.

weak: Riding and swimming have always been my favorite sports. This has caused me to think of going into physical education in college.

better: Because I have always enjoyed riding and swimming, I am considering physical education as my college major.

weak: I didn't enjoy my flight to Israel. That is why I've never flown since.

better: Because I didn't enjoy my flight to Israel, I haven't flown since.

weak: At five I had food in my mouth almost every waking minute, which is why Mother put me on a strict diet.

better: Mother put me on a strict diet at five because I was constantly eating.

A Warning About "So"

In speaking we commonly use *so* as an intensifier to mean *very:* I was *so* busy. The play was *so* interesting.

Avoid this usage in writing. If you mean *very,* write *very.* Generally you can avoid it altogether. Think of *so,* in writing, as part of a conjunction followed by *that* a few words later: I blew *so* hard *that* the balloon burst. He has *so* much work to do *that* he cannot come.

More About Punctuation

1. Do not underline or put quotes around the title at the top of your composition.

2. Underline the titles of books, plays, movies, TV series, newspapers, and magazines.

3. Put quotes around titles of parts of books, articles in newspapers and magazines, short stories, poems, and episodes in a series.

Correct Usage:

The Sea of Life (Your own title)

I saw in the Times an editorial titled "Do It Now."

The short story, "Misbegotten," is included in the anthology, Greater Short Stories.

The poem, "Little One," first appeared in Nation's Business.

ASSIGNMENT 8

Write Chapter 7 of your autobiography. In this you will want to assess your job preferences. What jobs have interested you? What kinds of work have you done? What do you want to be? If you are still undecided, what possibilities are you considering? Or you may just write about a kind of work you have recently explored and the thinking that followed that exploration.

Only one chapter to go! Your next one will deal with the most important person in the world, yourself today.

PRACTICE TEST VIII

Review all the Check Sheets and then, without looking back, do the test. The teacher may want to check your work OR to give you another test of the same sort. Each error will count as 2½ points, if anybody's counting.

I. Spelling. Have your teacher choose ten words from the Check Sheets and dictate them to you. Spell them correctly.

II. On your paper, copy the following sentences and put in all omitted punctuation marks. Two are correct as they stand.

1. If I saw a ghost I think I should scream.

2. He likes the following things candy cokes popcorn and ice cream.

3. We followed the girls that night because we expected them to have their homework done.

4. Having been seen by the teacher I just sat and awaited my punishment.

5. He likes caddying and golfing and he shoots in the low nineties.

6. John really has two girl friends and sees them as often as possible.

7. Since we were sure of the result we left the game at the half.

8. We quickly turned on the TV having just completed our English assignment.

9. Bruce said goodbye to Joanne then he turned and threw her a kiss.

10. I have often gone to Florida however I had the most fun there last Christmas.

III. Put in eight apostrophes where needed. Write only the apostrophized word on your paper.

He makes his "as" like "os," and nobody can tell whether he writes "and" or "ond." On Mondays work he made so many mistakes he exhausted his teachers patience, and she made him rewrite everything. She believes he shouldnt try so hard, and its her notion that hed do better if he relaxed and tried to copy Freddys cool way of writing or studied as do the Joneses.

IV. On your paper, correct the error or poor choice of words in each of the following sentences. Some sentences may have to be rewritten entirely.

1. I have tried all the following sports: riding, Ping-Pong, hockey, basketball, golf, etc.

2. For two days before the party Mother had scrubbed floors, washed windows, curried the cat, and the dog was bathed daily.

3. In the sixth grade I thought I would become an Anthropologist.

4. I do not like algebra so I seldom study but that isn't a good habit for I always fail and then Dad bawls me out.

5. She was the footsie champion of her grade. But she didn't care for her title.

6. Mary says that, if Donald and him go to the dance, she will stay home.

7. We asked the teacher if us C-students could have some extra help.

8. It was just a little secret among the five of we girls.

9. I could never finish my work as quickly as Beth or her.

10. Our Eddie Puss almost lost it's ear in that fight with Joe Catsa.

11. I haven't eaten since yesterday, which is the reason my stomach is rumbling.

12. I told him he liked to gossip, and that is why he's not speaking to me today.

A Hindu form of writing using an iron pen. New York Public Library Picture Collection.

Remembrances of Things Past

The longer we live the more we remember. Things that were of little significance at the time assume major importance as we begin to understand more fully the forces shaping our existence. Three of the selections that follow deal with incidents of varying importance at the time. They assume greater importance later in the writers' lives. The opening and closing poems concern themselves with the thoughts of those who feel of little importance.

Emily Dickinson, a recluse whose fame came after her death, wrote the first poem. As you read it, see if you can sense her adaptation to her isolation from the world. The first prose selection is, in a sense, a piece about formal education. Herman Melville, in the guise of his narrator, thought of his first whaling voyage as his total college experience. From a fairly frightening occurrence he generalizes a lesson he learned. The next selection is a reminiscence by a contemporary author, C. Aubrey Menen. At the age of twelve he was transported from a staid British background to his father's native India. There he visited his Indian grandmother and learned there are several ways of looking at what seem to be peculiar customs. The piece that follows takes us back to the sixteenth century to describe a hair-raising adventure. The writer is Benvenuto Cellini, a famous goldsmith and sculptor. In his ordeal he learns to use the limits of both his mental and physical endurance. The section closes with a letter from a real loner. She is a woman who, except for this piece, would have been totally forgotten.

EMILY DICKINSON (1830–1886) grew up in Amherst, Massachusetts. With the exception of a few short trips made while her father was a Congressman, she spent her whole life there. At twenty-three, for reasons that still remain mysterious, she withdrew herself from almost all social contact. She did, however, write over a thousand poems, although only a few were published during her lifetime. Five years after her death, her sister Lavinia began publishing the poems in three volumes, and Emily's fame was immediate. Today Emily Dickinson is recognized as one of the greatest of American poets. In the 1970's, her story was made into a popular drama, *The Belle of Amherst,* that ran on Broadway and was seen on television.

As you discuss the poem, think of the many kinds of Nobodies and Somebodies in the world.

I'm Nobody! Who Are You?

EMILY DICKINSON

I'm Nobody! Who are you?
Are you—Nobody—Too?
Then there's a pair of us?
Don't tell! they'd advertise—you know!

How dreary—to be—Somebody!
How public—like a Frog—
To tell one's name—the livelong June—
To an admiring Bog!

Study Questions

1. In the first stanza, by what means does the poet invite the reader to join her?

2. Who are "they" in line 4?

3. How does a frog "tell" its name? How is "public" in line 6 a probable pun?

4. What is the "Bog" in the final line? How has its connotation been prepared for?

5. What sort of opinion does the poet have of herself? Of somebodies? How isolated does she really feel?

Emily Dickinson, Bettmann Archive. Background: George Whitely, Photo Researchers.

"Ignorance is the parent of fear, and being completely nonplussed and confounded about the stranger,
I confess I was now as much afraid of him as if it was the devil himself who had thus broken into my room at the dead of night."

HERMAN MELVILLE (1819–1891) was born in New York City, left school at the age of fifteen, and after two years of sundry occupations shipped as a cabin boy on a ship bound for England. Four years later he spent eighteen months aboard the *Acushnet,* a whaling ship from which he eventually deserted in the Marquesas Islands when he found that he could no longer endure the hardships of a whaleman's life. Out of his voyages came several novels based upon his experiences. The greatest was *Moby Dick,* from which the following selection comes. Ishmael, the narrator, is about to embark upon a whaling voyage that will be, as he puts it, "my Yale College and my Harvard." He is about to dine at an inn in New Bedford, Massachusetts, and is not too eagerly awaiting the arrival of his first roommate.

FROM

Moby Dick

HERMAN MELVILLE

But avast," the landlord added, tapping his forehead, "you haint no objections to sharing a harpooneer's blanket, have ye? I s'pose you are goin' a-whalin', so you'd better get used to that sort of thing."

I told him that I never like to sleep two in a bed; that if I should ever so do, it would depend upon who the harpooneer might be, and that if he (the landlord) really had no other place for me, and the harpooneer was not decidedly objectionable, why rather than wander further about a strange town on so bitter a night, I would put up with the half of any decent man's blanket.

"I thought so. All right; take a seat. Supper?—you want supper? Supper'll be ready directly." . . .

At last some four or five of us were summoned to our meal in an adjoining room. It was cold as Iceland—no fire at all—the landlord said he couldn't afford it. Nothing but two dismal tallow candles, each in a winding sheet. We were fain to button up our monkey jackets, and hold to our lips cups of scalding tea with our half-frozen fingers. But the fare was of the most substantial kind—not only meat and potatoes, but dumplings; good heavens! dumplings for supper! One young fellow in a green box coat addressed himself to these dumplings in a most direful manner.

"My boy," said the landlord, "you'll have the nightmare to a dead sartainty."

"Landlord," I whispered, "that ain't the harpooneer, is it?"

"Oh, no," said he, looking a sort of diabolically funny, "the harpooneer is a dark-complexioned chap. He never eats dumplings, he don't—he eats nothing but steaks, and he likes 'em rare."

"The devil he does," says I. "Where is that harpooneer? Is he here?"

"He'll be here afore long," was the answer.

I could not help it, but I began to feel suspicious of this "dark-complexioned" harpooneer. At any rate, I made up my mind that if it so turned out that we should sleep together, he must undress and get into bed before I did. . . .

The more I pondered over this harpooneer, the more I abominated the thought of sleeping with him. It was fair to presume that being a harpooneer, his linen or woolen, as the case might be, would not be of the tidiest, certainly none of the finest. I began to twitch all over. Besides, it was getting late, and my decent harpooneer ought to be home and going bedward. Suppose now, he should tumble in upon me at midnight—how could I tell from what vile hole he had been coming?

"Landlord! I've changed my mind about that harpooneer.—I shan't sleep with him. I'll try the bench here."

"Just as you please; I'm sorry I can't spare ye a tablecloth for a mattress, and it's a plaguy rough board here"—feeling of the knots and notches. "But wait a bit, Skirmshander; I've got a carpenter's plane there in the bar—wait, I say, and I'll make ye snug enough." So saying he procured the plane; and with his old silk handkerchief first dusting the bench, vigorously set to planing away at my bed, the while grinning like an ape. The shavings flew right and left; till at last the plane iron came bump against an indestructible knot. The landlord was near spraining his wrist, and I told him for heaven's sake to quit—the bed was soft enough to suit me, and I did not know how all the planing in the world could make eider down of a pine plank.

So gathering up the shavings with another grin, and throwing them into the great stove in the middle of the room, he went about his business, and left me in a brown study. . . .

But though the other boarders kept coming in by ones, twos, and threes, and going to bed, yet no sign of my harpooneer.

"Landlord!" said I, "what sort of a chap is he—does he always keep such late hours?" It was now hard upon twelve o'clock.

The landlord chuckled again with his lean chuckle, and seemed to be mightily tickled at something beyond my comprehension. "No," he answered, "generally he's an early bird—airley to bed and airley to rise—yea, he's the bird what catches the worm.—But tonight he went out a-peddling, you see, and I don't see what on airth keeps him so late, unless, may be, he can't sell his head."

"Can't sell his head?—What sort of a bamboozling story is this you are telling me?" getting into a towering rage. "Do you pretend to say, landlord, that this harpooneer is actually engaged this blessed Saturday night, or rather Sunday morning, in peddling his head around this town?"

"That's precisely it," said the landlord, "and I told him he couldn't sell it here, the market's overstocked."

"With what?" shouted I.

"With heads to be sure; ain't there too many heads in the world?"

"I tell you what it is, landlord," said I, quite calmly, "you'd better stop spinning that yarn to me—I'm not green."

"Maybe not," taking out a stick and whittling a toothpick, "but I rayther guess you'll be done *brown* if that ere harpooneer hears you a-slanderin' his head."

"I'll break it for him," said I, now flying into a passion again at this unaccountable farrago of the landlord's.

"It's broke a'ready," said he.

"Broke," said I—"*broke*, do you mean?"

"Sartain, and that's the very reason he can't sell it, I guess."

"Landlord," said I, going up to him as cool as Mt. Hecla in a snow storm—"landlord, stop whittling. You and I must understand one another, and that too without delay. I come to your house and want a bed; you tell me you can only give me half a one; that the other half belongs to a certain harpooneer. And about this harpooneer, whom I have not yet seen, you persist in telling me the most mystifying and exasperating stories, tending to beget in me an uncomfortable feeling toward the man whom you design for my bedfellow—a sort of connection, landlord, which is an intimate and confidential one in the highest degree. I now demand of you to speak out and tell me who and what this harpooner is, and whether I shall be in all respects safe to spend the night with him. . . ."

Herman Melville, Culver Pictures.

"Wall," said the landlord, fetching a long breath, "that's a purty long sarmon for a chap that rips a little now and then. But be easy, be easy, this here harpooneer I have been tellin' you of has just arrived from the south seas, where he bought up a lot of 'balmed New Zealand heads (great curios, you know), and he's sold all of 'em but one, and that one he's trying to sell tonight, cause tomorrow's Sunday, and it would not do to be sellin' human heads about the streets when folks is goin' to churches. He wanted to last Sunday, but I stopped him just as he was goin' out of the door with four heads strung on a string, for all the airth like a string of inions."

This account cleared up the otherwise unaccountable mystery, and showed that the landlord, after all, had had no idea of fooling me—but at the same time what could I think of a harpooneer who stayed out of a Saturday night clean into the holy Sabbath, engaged in such a cannibal business as selling the heads of dead idolators?

"Depend upon it, landlord, that harpooneer is a dangerous man."

"He pays reg'lar," was the rejoinder. "But come, it's a nice bed: Sal and me slept in that ere bed the night we were spliced. There's plenty of room for two to kick about in that bed; it's an almighty big bed that. Why, afore we give it up, Sal used to put our Sam and little Johnny in the foot of it. But I got a dreaming and sprawling about one night, and somehow, Sam got pitched on the floor, and came near breaking his arm. Arter that, Sal said it wouldn't do. Come along here, I'll give ye a glim in a jiffy"; and so saying he lighted a candle and held it toward me, offering to lead the way. But I stood irresolute; when looking at a clock in the corner, he exclaimed "I vum it's Sunday—you won't see that harpooneer tonight; he's come to anchor somewhere—come along then; *do* come; *won't* ye come?"

I considered the matter a moment, and then upstairs we went, and I was ushered into a small room, cold as a clam, and furnished, sure enough, with a prodigious bed, almost big enough indeed for any four harpooneers to sleep abreast.

"There," said the landlord, placing the candle on a crazy old sea chest that did double duty as a wash-stand and center table; "there, make yourself comfortable now; and good night to ye." I turned round from eyeing the bed, but he had disappeared.

Folding back the counterpane, I stooped over the bed. Though none of the most elegant, it yet stood the scrutiny tolerably well. I then glanced round the room; and besides the bedstead and center table, could see no other furniture belonging to the place, but a rude shelf, the four walls, and a papered fireboard representing a man striking a whale. Of things not properly belonging to the room, there was a hammock lashed up, and thrown upon the floor in one corner;

also a large seaman's bag, containing the harpooneer's wardrobe, no doubt in lieu of a land trunk. Likewise, there was a parcel of outlandish bone fish hooks on the shelf over the fire-place, and a tall harpoon standing at the head of the bed.

But what is this on the chest? I took it up, and held it close to the light, and felt it, and smelt it, and tried every way possible to arrive at some satisfactory conclusion concerning it. I can compare it to nothing but a large door mat, ornamented at the edges with little tinkling tags something like the stained porcupine quills round an Indian moccasin. There was a hole or slit in the middle of this mat, as you see the same in South American ponchos. But could it be possible that any sober harpooneer would get into a door mat, and parade the streets of any Christian town in that sort of guise? I put it on, to try it, and it weighed me down like a hamper, being uncommonly shaggy and thick, and I thought a little damp, as though this mysterious harpooneer had been wearing it of a rainy day. I went up in it to a bit of glass stuck against the wall, and I never saw such a sight in my life. I tore myself out of it in such a hurry that I gave myself a kink in the neck.

I sat down on the side of the bed, and commenced thinking about this head-peddling harpooneer, and his door mat. After thinking some time on the bed-side, I got up and took off my monkey jacket, and then stood in the middle of the room thinking. I then took off my coat, and thought a little more in my shirt sleeves. But beginning to feel very cold now, half undressed as I was, and remembering what the landlord said about the harpooneer's not coming home at all that night, it being so very late, I made no more ado, but jumped out of my pantaloons and boots, and then blowing out the light tumbled into bed, and commended myself to the care of heaven.

Whether that mattress was stuffed with corncobs or broken crockery, there is no telling, but I rolled about a good deal, and could not sleep for a long time. At last I slid off into a light doze, and had pretty nearly made a good offing toward the land of Nod, when I heard a heavy footfall in the passage, and saw a glimmer of light come into the room from under the door.

Lord save me, thinks I, that must be the harpooneer, the infernal head-peddler. But I lay perfectly still, and resolved not to say a word till spoken to. Holding a light in one hand, and that identical New Zealand head in the other, the stranger entered the room, and without looking toward the bed, placed his candle a good way off from me on the floor in one corner, and then began working away at the knotted cords of the large bag I before spoke of as being in the room. I was all eagerness to see his face, but he kept it averted for some time while employed in unlacing the bag's mouth. This accomplished, however, he turned round—when, good heavens; what a sight! Such a face! It was of a dark, purplish, yellow color, here and there stuck over with large blackish looking squares. Yes, it's just as I thought, he's a terrible bedfellow; he's been in a fight, got dreadfully cut, and here he is, just from the surgeon. But at that moment he chanced to turn his face so toward the light, that I plainly saw they could not be sticking-plasters at all, those black squares on his cheeks. They were stains of some sort or other. At first I knew not what to make of this; but soon an inkling of the truth occurred to me. I remembered a story of a white man—a whaleman too—who, falling among the cannibals, had been tattooed by them. I concluded that this harpooneer, in the course of his distant voyages, must have met with a similar adventure. And what is it, thought I, after all! It's only his outside; a man can be honest in any sort of skin. But then, what to make of his unearthly complexion, that part of it, I mean, lying round about, and completely independent of the squares of tattooing. To be sure, it might be nothing but a good coat of tropical tanning; but I never heard of a hot sun's tanning a white man into a purplish yellow one. However, I had never been in the South Seas; and perhaps the sun there produced these extraordinary effects upon the skin. Now, while all these ideas were passing through me like lightning, this harpooneer never noticed me at all. But, after some difficulty having opened his bag, he commenced fumbling in it, and presently pulled out a sort of tomahawk, and a sealskin wallet with the hair on. Placing these on the old chest in the middle of a room, he then took the New Zealand head—a ghastly thing enough—and crammed it down into the bag. He now took off his hat—a new beaver hat—when I came nigh singing out with fresh surprise. There was no hair on his head—none to speak of at least—nothing but a small scalp-knot twisted up on his forehead. His bald purplish head now looked for all the world like a mildewed skull. Had not the stranger stood between me and the door, I would have bolted out of it quicker than ever I bolted a dinner.

Even as it was, I thought something of slipping out of the window, but it was the second floor back. I am no coward, but what to make of this head-peddling purple rascal altogether passed my comprehension. Ignorance is the parent of fear, and being completely nonplussed and confounded about the stranger, I confess I was now as much afraid of him as if it was the devil himself who had thus broken into my room at the dead of night. In fact, I was so afraid of him that I was not game enough just then to address him, and demand a satisfactory answer concerning what seemed inexplicable in him.

Meanwhile, he continued the business of undressing, and at last showed his chest and arms. As I live, these covered parts of him were checkered with the same squares as his face; his back, too, was all over the same dark squares; he seemed to have been in a Thirty Years' War, and just escaped from it with a sticking-plaster shirt. Still more, his very legs were marked, as if a parcel of dark green frogs were running up the trunks of young palms. It was now quite plain that he must be some abominable savage or other shipped aboard of a whaleman in the South Seas, and so landed in this Christian country. I quaked to think of it. A peddler of heads too—perhaps the heads of his own brothers. He might take a fancy to mine—heavens! look at that tomahawk!

But there was no time for shuddering, for now the savage went about something that completely fascinated my attention, and convinced me that he must indeed be a heathen. Going to his heavy grego, or wrapal, or dreadnaught, which he had previously hung on a chair, he fumbled in the pockets, and produced at length a curious little deformed image with a hunch on its back, and exactly the color of a three days' old Congo baby. Remembering the embalmed head, at first I almost thought that this black manikin was a real baby preserved in some similar manner. But seeing that it was not at all limber, and that it glistened a good deal like polished ebony, I concluded that it must be nothing but a wooden idol, which indeed it proved to be. For now the savage goes up to the empty fire-place, and removing the papered fire-board, sets up this little hunch-backed image, like a tenpin, between the andirons. The chimney jambs and all the bricks inside were very sooty, so that I thought this fire-place made a very appropriate little shrine or chapel for his Congo idol.

I now screwed my eyes hard toward the half-hidden image, feeling but ill at ease meantime—to see what was next to follow. First he takes about a double handful of shavings out of his grego pocket, and places them carefully before the idol; then laying a bit of ship biscuit on top and applying the flame from the lamp, he kindled the shavings into a sacrificial blaze. Presently, after many hasty snatches into the fire, and still hastier withdrawals of his fingers (whereby he seemed to be scorching them badly), he at last succeeded in drawing out the biscuit; then blowing off the heat and ashes a little, he made a polite offer of it to the little negro. But the little devil had not seem to fancy such dry sort of fare at all; he never moved his lips. All these strange antics were accompanied by still stranger guttural noises from the devotee, who seemed to be praying in a singsong or else singing some pagan psalmody or other, during which his face twitched about in the most unnatural manner. At last extinguishing the fire, he took the idol up very unceremoniously, and bagged it again in his grego pocket as carelessly as if he were a sportsman bagging a dead woodcock.

All these queer proceedings increased my uncomfortableness, and seeing him now exhibiting strong symptoms of concluding his business operations, and jumping into bed with me, I thought it was high time, now or never, before the light was put out, to break the spell in which I had so long been bound.

But the interval I spent in deliberating what to say, was a fatal one. Taking up his tomahawk from the table, he examined the head of it for an instant, and then holding it to the light, with his mouth at the handle, he puffed out great clouds of tobacco smoke. The next moment the light was extinguished, and this wild cannibal, tomahawk between his teeth, sprang into bed with me. I sang out, I could not help it now; and giving a sudden grunt of astonishment he began feeling me.

Stammering out something, I knew not what, I rolled away from him against the wall, and then conjured him, whoever or whatever he might be, to keep quiet, and let me get up and light the lamp again. But his guttural responses satisfied me at once that he but ill comprehended my meaning.

"Who-e debel you?"—he at last said—"you no speak-e, dam-me, I kill-e." And so saying the lighted tomahawk began flourishing about me in the dark.

"Landlord, for God's sake, Peter Coffin!" shouted I. "Landlord! Watch! Coffin! Angels! save me!"

"Speak-e! tell-ee me who-ee be, or dam-me, I kill-e!" again growled the cannibal, while his horrid flourishings of the tomahawk scattered the hot tobacco ashes about me till I thought my linen would get on fire. But thank heaven, at that moment the landlord came into the room light in hand, and leaping from the bed I ran up to him.

"Don't be afraid now," said he, grinning again, "Queequeg here wouldn't harm a hair of your head."

"Stop your grinning," shouted I, "and why didn't you tell me that that infernal harpooneer was a cannibal?"

"I thought ye know'd it; didn't I tell ye, he was a peddlin' heads around town?—but turn flukes again and go to sleep. Queequeg look here—you sabbee me, I sabbee you—this man sleepe you—you sabbee?"

"Me sabbee plenty"—grunted Queequeg, puffing away at his pipe and sitting up in bed.

"You gettee in," he added, motioning to me with his tomahawk, and throwing the clothes to one side. He really did this in not only a civil but really kind and charitable way. I stood looking at him a moment. For all his tattooings he was on the whole a clean, comely looking cannibal. What's all this fuss I have been making about, thought I to myself—the man's a human being just as I am: he has just as much reason to fear me, as I have to be afraid of him. Better sleep with a sober cannibal than a drunken Christian.

"Landlord," said I, "tell him to stash his tomahawk there, or pipe, or whatever you call it; tell him to stop smoking, in short, and I will turn in with him. But I don't fancy having a man smoking in bed with me. It's dangerous. Besides, I ain't insured."

This being told to Queequeg, he at once complied, and again politely motioned me to get into bed—rolling over to one side as much as to say—I won't touch a leg of ye.

"Good night, landlord," said I, "you may go."

I turned in, and never slept better in my life.

Vocabulary

"But *avast*," the landlord added, . . . "you haint no objections to sharing a harpooner's blanket . . . . (204:1); One young fellow . . . addressed himself to these dumplings in a most *direful* manner . . . . (205:9); The more I pondered over this harpooner, the more I *abominated* the thought of sleeping with him. . . . (205:23); What sort of *bamboozling* story is this . . . . (206:14); flying into a passion again at this unaccountable *farrago* of the landlord's . . . . (206:29); Come along here. . . . But I stood *irresolute* . . . (208:26); a *prodigious* bed, almost big enough indeed for any four harpooners to sleep abreast . . . . (208:31); Folding back the *counterpane*, I stooped over the bed . . . (208:37); Lord save me, thinks I, that must be the harpooner, the *infernal* head-peddler. . . . (209:36); I came *nigh* singing out with fresh surprise. . . . (210:28); what to make of this head-peddling purple rascal altogether passed my comprehension. . . . and being completely *nonplussed* and confounded about the stranger, I confess I was now as much afraid of him as if it was the devil himself . . . (210:37); I almost thought that this black *manikin* was a real baby . . . . (211:20); these strange antics were accompanied by still stranger *guttural* noises from the devotee . . . . (211:40); I rolled away from him against the wall, and then *conjured* him, whoever or whatever he might be, to keep quiet . . . (212:17); turn *flukes* again and go to sleep. . (212: 37) ; For all his tattooing he was on the whole a clean, *comely* looking cannibal . . . . (213:2); tell him to *stash* his tomahawk there . . . . (213:7); This being told to Queequeg, he at once *complied* . . . (213:11)

Study Questions and Activities

1. Who are the main characters in this incident? How would you characterize each of them? How does each serve to build suspense?

2. On a whale ship what was the function of the harpooner? Why might a novice seaman have cause to fear having a harpooner for a bedmate?

3. Melville gives the landlord the accent of a nineteenth-century New Bedford resident. What dialectal expressions does he use? Discuss those that you cannot readily understand. How might these expressions be said today in the slang talk of your area? From the landlord's conversation how do we know that he is well acquainted with seafaring?

4. The landlord's conversation is cleverly contrived to frighten his young guest. What connotations might the young guest have from listening to the following bits of his host's description of the harpooner?

> "—he eats nothing but steaks, and he likes them rare."
> ". . . maybe, he can't sell his head."
> "It's [his head's] broke a'ready."
> ". . . [went out] with four heads strung on a string . . ."

How is the reader's connotation likely to be different from that of the narrator?

5. In his rage at the landlord the young man says, "I'm not green." What does he mean? Do you agree or disagree with him? Cite evidence from the passage to support your opinion.

6. Without looking back to the description of the bedroom, discuss what you can remember of the description. List the class's various remembrances on the board. Now go back to the description on page 208. What did you overlook? Were the details you did not remember significant or insignificant to what followed in the incident? Why?

7. Using the same techniques as in the previous question, describe the harpooner by remembrance and then by checking with the passage. What did you not remember? What did you add that the author did not write about? Try to explain your deletions and additions.

8. Besides observing the body and dress of the harpooner, what actions does the narrator observe before yelping for the landlord? How have the actions confirmed the fears the young man has been entertaining? Do the harpooner's first words serve to allay or heighten these fears?

9. By the end of the incident the narrator has grown up a bit. Which of the following quotations best indicate what he has learned?

> "Better to sleep with a sober cannibal than a drunken Christian."
> "Tell him to stop smoking, . . . and I will turn in with him."
> "I never slept better in my life."

In your own words tell what the young man has learned.

10. Try your hand at description. Pretend that, like the narrator, you meet for the first time a being utterly strange to you. He or she may be from another planet, another country, or even from another town —or section of your town. In groups or separately, write three paragraphs. In the first, describe the being. In the second, have the being do something to frighten you or please you. In the third, bring the action to a climax that will be startlingly funny, terrifying, or ironic. Choose good incidents and have them read to the class.

A Roman stylus. New York Public Library Picture Collection.

"The singing marked a stage in my life.
Shortly afterwards I lost my innocence.
My grandmother took me in hand and I never
thought the English were perfect again."

C. AUBREY MENEN (1912–) frequently writes autobiographical fiction and brings to it an unusual family. His father was an Indian of high caste; his mother, an Irishwoman living in England. Educated in England, where he made his reputation as a writer, Menen has also worked extensively in India. In the following piece he writes of his first visit to Malabar at age twelve. What he learned he writes about as an adult capable of forming logical judgments from an experience that influenced him deeply.

My Grandmother and the Dirty English

C. AUBREY MENEN

My grandmother, like Michelangelo, had *terribilita*. She had a driving will; she would not be balked and whatever she did was designed to strike the spectator with awe. She was also something of a stick. She rarely spoke to anyone who was not of her own social station and she received them formally. . . .

When I was twelve she demanded that I be brought and shown to her. I was incontinently taken half across the earth, from London to South beyond the town of Calicut. My mother came with me.

The last part of the journey was made by dugout canoe (there being no railways and no good roads near our family estate) and in this we were poled on a moonlit night up the Ponnani River. The river was lined with palm trees and crocodiles.

My mother taking fright at these beasts, I sang to keep them away from the boat. I sang a song I had been taught at school called "Drake's Drum." This had been written in the reign of Queen Victoria and told how, if the Spaniards should embark on the unlikely project of attacking nineteenth century England, Drake would come back to life and drum them up the Channel "as he drummed them long ago." I had been taught many songs of similar sentiments but this was the noisiest. I sang it with a will because my young heart (especially in such very foreign parts) glowed with the sentiment. The crocodiles yawned and, like the Spaniards in the Victorian age, showed no signs of attacking.

This singing marked a stage in my life. Shortly afterwards I lost my innocence. My grandmother took me in hand and I never thought the English were perfect again.

When our boat journey was done, servants with flaming torches led us along narrow paths between tall trees, and finally conducted us to a house. This house was large and smelt of paint. It was (my father said) not my ancestral roof.

When my grandmother had heard that my mother intended to make the visit as well as myself, she had given orders for a special house to be put in repair for my mother's accommodation. It was on the furthest confines of the family property. This was her solution of a difficult problem. My mother was ritually unclean, and therefore whenever she entered my family house, she would defile it. The house would have to be purified and so would every caste Hindu in it. It followed logically that if my mother stayed in the house, it would be permanently in a state of defilement and permanently in a state of being ritually cleaned. Since this ceremony involved drums and conch shells, my mother's visit fore-shadowed a prolonged uproar. All this was avoided by my grandmother's decision to put her up in a separate building.

I cannot say that my grandmother was ever rude to my mother. She never referred to her by name but always as "the Englishwoman." This was not necessarily an insulting expression, but my mother had Irish blood and what with this, and the house, and some other pinpricks, her temper rose. She ordered a quantity of medical stores from Calicut, and when they arrived she set up a free dispensary on the verandah, to which the peasants flocked. It was an admirably devised answer. My grandmother had shut the door in my mother's face: she now had the galling experience of seeing my mother industriously cleaning up the doorstep. As my mother well knew, each drop of iodine that she dispensed stung not only the grateful patient, but also my grandmother's conscience.

My grandmother brooded on this for a while and then sent my mother a bag of golden sovereigns. My mother, taking this to be a bribe at the worst, or at the best, a tip, sent it back. But she was wrong. It was a peace offering. It was sent again next day, accompanied by the family goldsmith who sat, slept and ate on the verandah for a week while he made the sovereigns (with tweezers and a charcoal fire) into a great gold collar which my mother still, on occasions, wears.

When, fourteen years before my trip, my father had written from England to say that he was getting married to a white woman, my grandmother had been far from giving the union her blessing. But it would be wrong to say that she had objected to it. If an American boy of twenty-two wrote home from foreign parts to say that he had taken to cannibalism, his parents would not object. They would be so revolted that a mere objection would never meet the case. So with my grandmother.

She had never met the English but she knew all about them. She knew they were tall, fair, given to strong drink, good soldiers and that they had conquered her native country. She also knew that they were incurably dirty in their personal habits. She respected them but wished they would keep their distance. It was very much the way that a Roman matron looked upon the Goths.

My eldest uncle had been to England for two years and he spoke up for the English. He said that while the Hindus were undoubtedly the most civilised race on earth and had been civilised a thousand years before the English, nevertheless, the English were now the masters of the Hindus. My grandmother's reply to this was that the English were masters of the Hindus only because "nobody would listen to *us*." By this she meant that our family along with others of the same caste had strongly objected to Vasco da Gama being allowed to land in Calicut. They had, in fact, done their best to get him and his sailors massacred. But the country was not behind them and he escaped. Everything, my grandmother argued (and not without some reason), had started with that.

But her chief complaint was that the English were so dirty, and this was rather a poser for my uncle. When my grandmother asked if, like decent people, they took a minimum of two baths a day, my uncle, who could not lie to his mother without committing a disgraceful sin, said that, well, no: but a few took one bath and the habit was spreading. He could go no further than that. But he added that my grandmother should remember that England had a cold climate. This she loyally did, and when she discussed the matter with me, she was able to treat the matter lightly, as one does the disgusting but rational liking of the Eskimos for eating blubber.

As for the question of eating, she did not have the expected prejudices. She did not think it strange that the English ate ham and beef.

The outcaste hill-tribes (called *Todas*) who made the family straw mats and cleaned the latrines, ate anything. She was not disturbed either, about their religion, because my uncle assured her that they had practically none. Their manners, however, she abominated. If she did not mind them eating meat, she considered their way of eating it beyond the pale of decent society. In my family home, each person eats his meal separately, preferably in a secluded corner. The thought that English people could sit opposite each other and watch each other thrust food into their mouths, masticate, and swallow it, made her wonder if there was anything that human beings would not do, when left to their own devices.

She was not surprised to hear, after this, that in England a woman could have more than one husband, particularly (and this was the crowning paradox) if she had been a widow. To the day of her death my grandmother could never understand how people could call themselves civilised and yet allow widows to marry again. For her the very foundation-stone of society was that a child should have one father, and obey him. Nobody ever dared her wrath sufficiently to explain the position of women in English society. She was intensely proud of the standards of her house and she permitted no lewd talk to defile them—certainly never in her presence.

With this background, then, my grandmother's peace offering of a bag of sovereigns was a considerable victory for my mother, particularly since the gold collar which the goldsmith had been told to make from them was the characteristic jewellery of a Malabar bride.

The way was now open for me. I could go and see her. I had waited about three weeks.

I had many meetings with her. I used to visit her in considerable state. The distance from our home—the isolation wing, so to speak—to the main family mansion was too far for walking in the Malabar sun. I used to go by palanquin. It was a hammock of red cloth with rather worn embroidery of gold thread, and it was swung on a black pole which had silver ornaments at either end. Four virtually naked men, two in front and two behind, caried the palanquin at a swift trot. There was considerable art in this. If the four men trotted just as they pleased, the hammock would swing in a growing arc until it tipped the passenger out on to the road. To prevent this, the men trotted in a complicated system that I never really understood: watching them and trying to trace it out was as difficult as trying to determine the order in which a horse puts its hoofs down. They kept their rhythm by chanting. I used to fall asleep on the way, listening to them. It must have presented an interesting spectacle—a red palanquin, the sweating men, and a sleeping schoolboy wearing an English blazer with its pocket sewn with a badge gained by infantile prowess at some sport that I do not now remember.

The family house was vast and cool and in my view, unfurnished. But to my grandmother's eye it was very elegant. There was nothing but the floor to sit on. She disliked chairs and thought them vulgar. What use were they, except for ostentation? She approved of beds but insisted that the mattress be made of taut string—nothing else was considered clean. She also had a taste for handsome brass-bound boxes. So beds, boxes, and oil-lamps were the sole furniture of the innumerable rooms of the house. There were no tables and no table-cloths. In my grandmother's house, if anybody dared eat in any fashion but off a fresh plantain-leaf, his next meal would have been served in the kitchen, where the servants were allowed to eat without ceremony.

My grandmother usually received me sitting by her favourite box in her boudoir. She made an unforgettable picture. She had great black eyes, a shock of white hair and lips as lush and curved as a girl of eighteen. . . . I used to sit on the floor in front of her in my school blazer and since my father had never taught me Malayalam (wishing me to be brought up like any other English schoolboy), we talked through one of my uncles.

The things my grandmother told me were a puzzle at the time. But I have come to understand them better. Much as she looked down on the English, I think that had she met some of them, had she overcome her well-bred fastidiousness and actually mixed with them, she would have found she and they had much in common. Her riding passion, like theirs, was racial pride. She believed—and this made her character—that she belonged to the cleverest family of the cleverest people on earth. According to Lord Russell, this was also the firm faith of Mrs. Beatrice Webb, who used to repeat it to herself in moments when, otherwise, she might have felt inferior, such as when she made her entry into a distinguished party. Though my grandmother never went to parties I'm sure that she, too, repeated the formula as a stiffener of her already formidable morale.

She felt that she was born of a superior race and she had all the marks of it. For instance, she deplored the plumbing of every other nation but her own. She would often say to me, through my uncle:

"Never take a bath in one of those contraptions in which you sit in dirty water like a buffalo. Always bathe in running water. If you have servants to pour it over you, that's best. But otherwise you must stand under a tap or pour water over yourself. A really nice person does not even glance at his own bath water much less sit in it." Here she would laugh to herself, while my uncle translated; not an unkind

C. Aubrey Menen. Graham Hall, courtesy E. P. Dutton Publishers.
Background: Lynn McLaren, Photo Researchers.

laugh, but a pitying one, as she thought of the backwardness of the white man's bathroom.

Another mark—and I have met it in many nations—was that she believed that English sexual morals permitted and encouraged all sorts of abominations from which a civilised person shrank. . . . I could not always follow the drift of her remarks, but I did gather that she felt strongly on one point. Why, if the English wanted their offspring to grow up decently and not lewdly, did they omit to marry them off when they were children? There was something sinister in the neglect. A child should grow up knowing quite well that all that side of his life was settled according to the best available advice and in the best possible manner for his welfare. . . .

History, I have discovered, is on my grandmother's side. The great majority of civilised peoples have always agreed with her. Romance and love and such things were, in antiquity, things for slaves. Respectable families arranged their marriages as my grandmother arranged those of her offspring. To take a single example, my grandmother and Brutus would fully have understood each other. She felt hurt that she had not been consulted over my father's marriage: while among the many sidelights that we have on that honourable man who assassinated Julius Caesar is a letter in which he complains at being left out of the bargaining that went on during the betrothal of "my dear little Attica," who was nine years old.

But a grandson was a grandson, even though her permission had not been sought to bring him into the world, and she set about being a mother as well as a grandmother to me. She knew that soon I would go back among the heathen to finish my education and she wanted me to go back knowing who and what I was. On one of my visits she gave me a small book in which were written all my duties and privileges as a member of my class. The book was written on dried palm-leaves, strung together with a cord between two covers of wood. It began with a prayer to God thanking Him for creating us—our caste, that is—so much superior in every respect to the great majority of other human beings.

My grandmother explained what followed several times and with much emphasis, for she wanted to imprint it on my memory. Our family belongs to the caste—or class—called Nayars. The Nayars of Malabar are as old as Indian history and therefore, it can be assumed, a good deal older. My grandmother told me that traditionally we had two obligations to society. We were warriors when there was fighting to do: and when there was not, we had the duty, on certain holy days, of carrying flowers to the temple.

I remember that I thought this very romantic at the time and could not understand why my grandmother took it so prosaically: to me, warriors, flowers and temples conjured up a picture of some Oriental Round Table. But my grandmother was right. Our caste is a commonplace: it exists everywhere. In England it is scattered all over the countryside. The men are what is called "Army" and the women take not only flowers, but fruit to the temple on the occasion of the Harvest Festival. It is curious, and inexplicable, that the combination of these two activities, whether in the Shires or in the coconut groves of Malabar, produces the most ferocious snobs.

My grandmother explained to me that as a Nayar, I should always be very careful to keep my dignity when dealing with Brahmins:

Brahmins are priests. The priests who have the care of souls of my family are treated as domestic chaplains. Since their temples are on our property my grandmother had several "living," so to speak at her disposal, this side of religious affairs always being left in the hands of the older women. Priests were therefore expected to make themselves agreeable, in return for which they were regularly fed. They were expected to mind their own business, which was to perform the weekly ceremonies and to direct their preaching at the lower orders, particularly the servants. The Anglican Settlement in England was much more elaborate but reduced to what it meant to the average priest-in-the-vestry, it came much to the same thing, and provides one more reason why I wish my grandmother had visited the country of my birth.

But my grandmother was quite ignorant of these striking resemblances and begged me when moving among the English to remember myself. "They will look up to you, as a Nayar, to set an example," she used to say. "They know that you have two thousand years of advantage over them and they will be willing to learn. Show them this book. They will be very interested. It was written when they still went about naked. And I will give you some trinkets which you can hand out as gifts: some amulets which we use and some things made of sandalwood, which is very rare in England so I am told, and much sought after. They will help you make friends. But remember, it is your *example* which will count more than anything."

She gave me all the things she promised and as she had foretold, they were much admired. Some of them, I believe, are still in my school museum. She also gave me her blessing, which was what I had been brought across the world to get.

I thought over her advice but I was in some confusion. My headmaster, wishing me good by and good-luck when I had set out on my trip had said much the same thing. "Let them see," he had said, "by your example that you have been trained in an *English* school. Wherever you go, it is for *you* to set the tone." He did not give me any sandalwood, but I was very impressed. I was also very greatly impressed with what my grandmother had said.

In my dilemma I remembered that I had another grandmother. She had been born, as I have said, in Killarney, but had come to England to live—briefly enough, for she had died before I was born. I asked my mother about her. She told me many things but one stood out in my mind above all others.

"My mother," she said, "was never really happy among the English. She longed to go back to Killarney. Sometimes when things had become unbearably tiresome, she would heave a long, deep sigh, shake her head and gently close her eyes."

Vocabulary

My mother was ritually unclean, and therefore whenever she entered my family house, she would *defile* it . . . . (216:20); My grandmother had shut the door in my mother's face: she now had the *galling* experience of seeing my mother industriously cleaning up the doorstep. . (216:35); Their manners, however, she *abominated* . . . . . (218:4); She was intensely proud of the standards of her house and she permitted no *lewd* talk to defile them . . . . (218:20); had she overcome her well-bred *fastidiousness* and actually mixed with them, she would have found she and they had much in common . . . . (219:24); She believed . . . that she belonged to the cleverest family of the cleverest people on earth. . . . she . . . repeated the formula as a stiffener of her already formidable *morale* . . . . (219:33); I thought this very romantic at the time and could not understand why my grandmother took it so *prosaically* . . . . (221:33); It is curious, and *inexplicable,* that the combination of these two activities . . . produces the most ferocious snobs . . . . (221:39); I will give you some trinket which you can hand out as gifts: some *amulets* which we use and some things made of sandalwood . . . . (222:20); In my *dilemma* I remembered that I had another grandmother . . . (222:35)

Study Questions and Activities

1. Why did the Indian grandmother build a special house for the boy and his mother? How do you suppose it differed from her own?

2. Why did the grandmother send gold sovereigns to the boy's mother? How did the mother misinterpret the gift? How did the grandmother clarify the purpose of the gift?

3. Why did the boy not walk from his separate domicile to visit his grandmother? Why did his mother not accompany him?

4. We hear much about the grandmother in the selection and enough about the mother to make some judgments. Using the text as evidence, characterize the mother.

5. List the prejudices that the grandmother had against the English. Compare lists and make what you consider a complete list. Which prejudices do you find rational? Why do some of them make you smile?

6. List the customs the grandmother prides herself on. Make what you consider a complete list. Which customs do you find rational? Why do some seem ludicrous?

7. Early in the story the narrator writes that, because of his visit, he lost his innocence. Define what he means by innocence. How did his grandmother help to cause that loss?

8. In the same paragraph the narrator says he "never thought the English were perfect again." Why had he felt they were perfect? How perfect does he feel his grandmother and her ways are?

9. Two separate experiences often can add up to a totally new discovery. What discovery does the narrator make by the end of the story? How does the knowledge about his maternal grandmother aid in his discovery?

10. Find Malabar on the map. You may have trouble. If you do, look for the port the grandmother mentions, Calicut. (But don't confuse it with Calcutta; each is a separate city.) If you do have trouble finding Malabar, ask yourself what point made by Mr. Menen is illustrated by the difficulty you had.

11. The selection refers to Vasco da Gama. Look up the name and explain the allusion. How did this person affect the history of India?

12. The title uses the expression "dirty English." List as many definitions for "dirty" as you can. How many of them fit the adjective in the title? What customs have you observed—in reading or during actual visits to different lands—that you were inclined, by using Grandmother's definition, to call "dirty"? If you have changed your mind about these customs, tell the reason for the change.

"I told him before all his servants:
'Lock me well up, and keep good watch on me;
for I shall certainly contrive to escape!' "

BENVENUTO CELLINI (1500–1571), a contemporary of Michelangelo and Leonardo da Vinci, won his fame as goldsmith, sculptor, soldier, and critic. Unlike his contemporaries, he left a complete autobiography; we are fairly sure that it was not always truthful, but it always affords exciting reading. In this passage he describes his allegedly unjust imprisonment and his escape, at the same time throwing light on the complex politics of Renaissance Rome.

I Escape from Prison

BENVENUTO CELLINI

After I had sent my letter, that traitor, the Perugian workman, devised a piece of malice against me which succeeded at once, owing to the avarice of Pope Paolo de Farnese. . . .

The fellow in question informed one of Signor Pier Luigi's secretaries that, having been with me as workingman several years, he was acquainted with all my affairs, on the strength of which he gave his word to Signor Pier Luigi that I was worth more than eighty thousand ducats, and that the greater part of this property consisted in jewels, which jewels belonged to the Church, and that I had stolen them in Castel Sant' Angelo during the sack of Rome, and that all they had to do was to catch me on the spot.

One morning, while my shop was being swept out, I put my cape on to take the air. I turned into Chiavica, and at this corner Crespino, the Bargello, with all his constables, made up to me, and said: "You are the Pope's prisoner." I answered: "Crespino, you have mistaken your man." "No," said Crespino, "you are the artist Benvenuto, and I have to take you to the Castle of Sant' Angelo, where lords go, and men of accomplishments, your peers." Upon that four of his under-officers rushed on me, and would have seized a dagger I wore, and some rings I carried on my finger; but Crespino rebuked them: "Not a man of you shall touch him: it is quite enough if you perform your duty, and see that he does not escape me." Then he begged me with words of courtesy to surrender my arms. While I was doing this, it crossed my mind that exactly on that very spot I had assassinated Pompeo. They took me straightway to the castle, and locked me in an upper chamber in the keep. This was the first time that I ever smelt a prison up to the age I had of thirty-seven years.

Signor Pier Luigi . . . had well considered the large sum for which I stood accused; so he begged the reversion of it . . . and asked that he might have the money made out to himself. The Pope granted this willingly, adding that he would assist in its recovery. Consequently, after having kept me eight whole days in prison, they sent me up for examination, in order to put an end if possible to the affair. I was summoned into one of the great halls of the papal castle. My examiners were, first the Governor of Rome, called Messer Benedetto Conversini of Pistoja, who afterwards became Bishop of Jesi; secondly, the Procurator-Fiscal, whose name I have forgotten; and, thirdly, the judge in criminal cases, Messer Benedetto da Cagli. These three men began to question me in gentle terms, which afterwards they changed to words of considerable harshness and menace. . . .

When I heard their charges, I could not hold from bursting into a great roar of laughter; then I said: . . . Was it not your business, before you took me up, to find out what I had done with those eighty thousand ducats? Was it not your duty to inspect the record of the jewels? If you had discovered anything missing on that record, then you ought to have seized all my books together with myself. I tell you for a certainty that the registers, on which are written all the jewels of the Pope and the regalia, must be perfectly in order; you will not find there missing a single article of value which belonged to Pope Clement that has not been minutely noted . . .

While I was delivering this speech, they listened in astonishment. Then exchanging glances one with the other, all three went together to report what I had spoken to the Pope. The Pope felt some shame, and gave orders that all the records of the jewels should be diligently searched. When they had ascertained that none were missing, they left me in the castle without saying a word more about it. Signor Pier

Luigi felt also that he had acted ill; and to end the affair, they set about to contrive my death.

During the agitations which I have just related, King Francis received news of how the Pope was keeping me in prison, and with what injustice. He had sent a certain gentleman of his, named Monsignor di Morluc, as his ambassador to Rome; to him therefore he now wrote, claiming me from the Pope as the man of his Majesty. . . . Such a demand was certainly one of the most honourable marks of favour which a man of my sort could desire; yet it proved the source of infinite annoyance and hurt to me. The Pope was roused to such fury by the jealous fear he had lest I should go and tell the whole world how infamously I had been treated, that he kept revolving ways in which I might be put to death without injury to his own credit.

The castellan of Sant' Angelo was one of our Florentines, called Messer Giorgio, a knight of the Ugolini family. This worthy man showed me the greatest courtesy, and let me go free about the castle on parole. He was well aware how greatly I had been wronged; and he granted me conveniences for working at my trade. Ascanio came to the castle and brought me things to work at. I could not indeed do much, feeling myself imprisoned so unjustly; yet I made a virtue of necessity, and bore my adverse fortune with as light a heart as I was able.

I had secured the attachment of all the guards and many soldiers of the castle. Often those soldiers told me I ought to escape, and that they would aid me, knowing how greatly I had been wronged. I answered that I had given my parole to the castellan. One brave and clever soldier used to say to me: "My Benvenuto, you must know that a prisoner is not obliged to keep faith. Escape from that rascal of a Pope . . . bent on having your life by villainy." I had, however, made my mind up rather to lose my life than to break the promise I had given that good castellan. So I bore the extreme discomforts of my situation, and had for companion of misery a friar of the Pallavicini house, who was a very famous preacher.

This man had been arrested as a Lutheran. He was an excellent companion; but, from the point of view of his religion, I found him the biggest scoundrel in the world. His fine intellectual qualities won my admiration; but I hated his dirty vices, and frankly taxed him with them. This friar kept reminding me that I was in no wise bound to observe faith with the castellan, since I had become a prisoner. . . . Cautiously he began to ask what means I should have taken, supposing my jailors had locked me up, in order to set the dungeon doors open

Benvenuto Cellini and Castel Sant'Angelo, New York Public Library Picture Collection.

and effect my flight. I then, who wanted to display the sharpness of my own wits to so ingenious a man, replied that I was able to open the most baffling locks and bars, far more those of our prison, to do which would be the same to me as eating a bit of new cheese. In order then to gain my secret, the friar made light of these assertions, averring that persons who have gained some credit by their abilities are wont to talk big of things which, if they had to put their boasts in action, would speedily discredit them. Feeling myself stung to the quick by that devil of a friar, I responded that I always promised in words less than I could perform in deeds; what I had said about the keys was the merest trifle; then, all too heedlessly, I demonstrated the facility with which my assertions could be carried into act. He affected to pay little attention; but all the same he learned my lesson well by heart.

As I have said, the worthy castellan let me roam at pleasure over the whole fortress. Not even at night did he lock me in, as was the custom with the other prisoners. Moreover, he allowed me to employ myself with gold or silver or with wax according to my whim. I laboured several weeks at the basin ordered by Cardinal Ferrara, but the irksomeness of my imprisonment bred in me a disgust for such employment, and I took to modelling in wax some little figures of my fancy, for mere recreation. Of the wax which I used, the friar stole a piece; and with this he proceeded to get false keys made, upon the method I had heedlessly revealed to him. He had chosen for his accomplice a registrar, who was in the castellan's service. When the keys were ordered, the locksmith revealed their plot; and the castellan, noticing the wax which I was using, recognised it at once and exclaimed: "It is true that this poor fellow Benvenuto has suffered a most grievous wrong; yet he ought not to have dealt thus with me, for I have ever strained my sense of right to show him kindness. Now I shall keep him straitly under lock and key." Accordingly, he had me shut up with disagreeable circumstances, among the worst of which were the words flung at me by some of his devoted servants, who called me ungrateful, light, and disloyal. One of them used those terms more insolently than was decent; whereupon I, being convinced of my innocence, retorted hotly that I had never broken faith. The man rushed to the castellan's room, and brought me the wax with the model of the keys. No sooner had I seen the wax than I told him that both he and I were in the right; but I begged him to procure for me an audience with the castellan, for I meant to explain frankly how the matter stood. The castellan sent for me at once, and I told him the whole course of events. This made him arrest the friar, who betrayed the registrar, and the latter ran a risk of being hanged. However, the castellan saved his registrar from the gallows, and gave me the same freedom as I had before.

When I saw how rigorously this affair was prosecuted, I began to think of my own concerns, and said: "Supposing another of these storms should rise and the man should lose confidence in me, I should then be under no obligation to him, and might wish to use my wits a little, which would certainly work their end better than those of that rascally friar." So I began to have new sheets of a coarse fabric brought me, and did not send the dirty ones away. When my servants asked for them, I bade them hold their tongues, saying I had given the sheets to some of those poor soldiers; and if the matter came to knowledge, the wretched fellows ran risk of the galleys. This made my young men and attendants, especially Felice, keep the secret in all loyalty. I meanwhile set myself to emptying a straw mattress, the stuffing of which I burned, having a chimney in my prison. Out of the sheets I cut strips, the third of a cubit in breadth; and when I had made enough in my opinion to clear the great height of the central keep of Sant' Angelo, I told my servants that I had given away what I wanted; they must now bring me others of a finer fabric, and I would send back the dirty ones. This affair was presently forgotten. . . .

The castellan was subject to a certain sickness, which came upon him every year and deprived him of his wits. The sign of its approach was that he kept continually talking, or rather jabbering, to no purpose. These humours took a different shape each year; one time he thought he was an oil-jar; another time he thought he was a frog, and hopped about as frogs do; another time he thought he was dead, and then they had to bury him. At this season he imagined that he was a bat, and he used to scream like bats in a high thin tone; and then he would flap his hands and body as though he were about to fly. The doctors, when they saw the fit was coming on him, gave him all the distractions they could think of; and since they had noticed that he derived much pleasure from my conversation, they were always fetching me to keep him company. At times the poor man detained me for four or five stricken hours without ever letting me cease talking. At last he wore me out; and sometimes when I looked at him, I noticed that his eyeballs were rolling in a frightful manner, one looking one way and the other in another.

He took it into his head to ask me whether I had ever had a fancy to fly. I answered that it had always been my ambition to do those things which offer the greatest difficulties to men, and that I had done them; as to flying, the God of Nature had gifted me with a body well suited for running and leaping far beyond the common average, and that with the talents I possessed for manual art I felt sure I had the courage to try flying. He then inquired what methods I should use; to which I answered that, taking into consideration all flying creatures, and wishing to imitate by art what they derived from nature, none was so apt a model as the bat. No sooner had the poor man heard the name bat, which recalled the humour he was suffering under, than he cried out at the top of his voice: "He says true; the bat's the thing!" Then he said: "Benvenuto, if one gave you the opportunity, should you have the heart to fly? I said that if he would set me at liberty, I felt quite up to flying down to Prati, after making myself a pair of wings out of waxed linen. Thereupon he replied: "Since the Pope was bidden me guard you as though you were his own eyes, and I know you a clever devil who would certainly escape, I shall have you locked up with a hundred keys in order to prevent you slipping through my fingers." I began to remind him that I might have fled, but that on account of the word I had given him I would never have betrayed his trust: therefore I begged him for the love of God not to add greater evils to the misery of my present situation. While I was pouring out these entreaties, he gave orders to have me bound and taken and locked up in prison. On seeing that it could not be helped, I told him before all his servants: "Lock me well up, and keep good watch on me; for I shall certainly contrive to escape."

No sooner had I been locked in, than I went about exploring my prison; and when I thought I had discovered how to get out of it, I pondered the means of descending from the lofty keep, for so the great round central tower is called. I took those new sheets of mine, which, as I have said, I had cut in strips and sewn together; then I reckoned up the quantity which would be sufficient for my purpose. Having made this estimate. I looked out a pair of pincers which I had abstracted from a guard of the castle and had hidden in my straw mattress. I began to try the nails which kept the hinges of my door in place. The door was double, and the clinching of the nails could not be seen; so that when I attempted to draw one out, I met with the greatest trouble. When I had drawn the first nail, I bethought me how to prevent its being noticed. For this purpose I mixed some rust, which I had scraped from old iron, with a little wax, obtaining exactly the same colour as the heads of the long nails which I had extracted. Then I set myself to counterfeit these heads and place them on the holdfasts; for each nail I extracted I made a counterfeit in wax. I left the hinges attached to their door posts at top and bottom by means of some of the same nails that I had drawn; but I took care to cut these and replace them lightly, so that they only just supported the irons of the hinges. . . .

It happened on the evening of a certain feast-day that the castellan was seriously indisposed; he kept repeating that he was a bat, and if they heard that Benvenuto had flown away, they must let him go to catch me up, since he could fly by night most certainly as well or better than myself; for it was thus he argued: "Benvenuto is a counterfeit bat, but I am a real one; and I shall be sure to catch him."

On the evening of that feast-day then, I made my mind up to escape, come what might; and first I prayed most devoutly to God, imploring His Divine Majesty to protect and succour me in that so perilous a venture. Afterwards I set to work and laboured the whole of the night. It was two hour before daybreak when at last I removed those hinges with the greatest toil; but the wooden panel itself and the bolt too offered such resistance that I could not open the door; so I had to cut into the wood; yet in the end I got it open, and shouldering the strips of linen which I had rolled up like bundles of flax upon two sticks, I directed my steps toward the latrines of the keep. Spying from within two tiles upon the roof, I was able to clamber up with ease. I wore a white doublet with a pair of white hose and a pair of half boots, into which I had stuck [a] poniard. . . .

After scaling the roof, I took one end of my linen roll and attached it to a piece of antique tile which was built into the fortress wall; it happened to jut out scarcely four fingers. In order to fix the band, I gave it the form of a stirrup. When I had attached it to that piece of tile, I turned to God and said: "Lord God, give aid to my good cause; you know that it is good; you see that I am aiding myself." Then I let myself go gently by degrees, supporting myself with the sinews of my arms, until I touched the ground. There was no moonshine, but the light of a fair open heaven. When I stood upon solid earth, I looked up at the vast height which I had descended with such spirit, and went gladly away, thinking I was free. But this was not the case; for the castellan on that side of the fortress had built two lofty walls, the space between which he used for stable and henyard; the place was barred with thick iron bolts outside. I was terribly disgusted to find there was no exit from this trap; but I stumbled on a long pole which was covered up with straw. Not without great trouble I succeeded in placing it against the wall, and then swarmed up it by the force of my arms until I reached the top. But since the wall ended in a sharp ridge, I had not strength enough to drag the pole up after me. Accordingly I made my mind up to use a portion of the second roll of linen which I had, the other was left hanging from the keep of the castle. So I cut a piece off, tied it to the pole, and clambered down the wall, enduring the utmost toil and fatigue. I was quite exhausted, and had, moreover, flayed the inside of my hands, which bled freely. This compelled me to rest awhile. . . . .

When I thought that my strength was recovered, I advanced quickly toward the last rampart, which faces toward Prati. There I put my bundle of linen lines down upon the ground, meaning to fasten them round a battlement, and descend the lesser as I had the greater height. But no sooner had I placed the linen, than I became aware behind me of a sentinel, who was going the rounds. Seeing my designs interrupted and my life in peril, I resolved to face the guard. This fellow, when he noticed my bold front, and that I was marching on him with weapon in hand, quickened his pace and gave me a wide berth. I had left my lines some little way behind; so I turned with hasty steps to regain them; and though I came within sight of another sentinel, he did not choose to take notice of me. Having found my lines and attached them to the battlement, I let myself go. On the descent, whether it was that I thought I had really come to earth and relaxed my grasp to jump, or whether my hands were so tired that they could not keep their hold, at any rate I fell, struck my head in falling, and lay stunned for more than an hour and a half, so far as I could judge.

It was just upon daybreak, when the fresh breeze which blows an hour before the sun revived me; yet I did not immediately recover my senses, for I thought my head had been cut off and fancied I was in purgatory. With time, my faculties returned, and I perceived I was outside the castle. I was aware of the wound in my head before I knew my leg was broken; for I put my hands up, and withdrew them covered with blood. Then I searched the spot well, and ascertained that I had sustained no injury of consequence; but when I wanted to stand up, I discovered that my right leg was broken three inches above the heel. Not even this dismayed me: I drew my poniard with its scabbard; the latter had a metal point ending in a large ball, which had caused the fracture of my leg; for the bone, coming into violent contact with the ball, and not being able to bend, had snapped at that point. With the poniard I cut a piece of the linen which I had left. Then I bound my leg up as well as I could, and crawled on all fours with the poniard in my hand toward the city gate. When I reached it, I found it shut; but I noticed a stone beneath the door which did not appear to be very firmly fixed. Setting my hands to it, and feeling it move, it easily gave way, and I drew it out. Through the gap thus made I crept into the town.

I had crawled more than five hundred paces from the place where

I fell, to the gate by which I entered. No sooner had I got inside than some mastiff dogs set upon me and bit me badly. When they returned to the attack and worried me, I drew my poniard and wounded one of them so sharply that he howled aloud, and all the dogs, according to their nature, ran after him. I meanwhile made the best way I could on all four toward the church of the Trespontina.

Now the dawn had risen over me, and I felt myself in danger. When therefore I met a water-carrier driving his donkey I begged the fellow to carry me upon his back to San Piero, adding: "I am an unfortunate young man, who, while escaping from a window in a love-adventure, have fallen and broken my leg. If I am discovered, I run risk of being cut to pieces; so for heaven's sake lift me quickly, and I will give you a crown of gold." He hitched me on his back, and carried me to the raised terrace by the steps to San Piero. There I bade him leave me.

I resumed my march, crawling always on all fours, and making for the palace of the Duchess, wife of Duke Ottavio and daughter of the Emperor. . . .

I should have been quite safe from recapture by the Pope if I could have stayed there, but my exploits up to this point had been too marvellous for a human being, and God was unwilling to encourage my vainglory; accordingly, for my own good, He chastised me a second time worse even than the first. The cause of this was that while I was crawling on all fours up those steps, a servant of Cardinal Cornaro recognised me. His master was then lodging in the palace; so the servant ran up to his room and woke him, crying: "Most reverend Monsignor, your friend Benvenuto is down there; he has escaped from the castle, and is crawling on all fours, streaming with blood; to all appearances he has broken a leg." The Cardinal exclaimed at once: "Run and carry him upon your back into my room here." When I arrived, he told me to be under no apprehension, and sent for the first physicians of Rome to take my case in hand. Among them was Maestro Jacomo of Perugia, a most excellent and able surgeon. He set the bone with dexterity, then bound the limb up, and bled me with his own hand. The Cardinal had me placed in a secret chamber, and went immediately to beg me from the Pope.

Vocabulary

I have to take you to the Castle of Sant' Angelo, where lords go, and men of accomplishments, your *peers* . . . . (225:1); Signor Pier Luigi . . . had well considered the large sum for which I stood accused; so he begged the *reversion* of it . (225: 12); the registers, on which are written all the jewels of the Pope and the *regalia,* must be perfectly in order . . . (225:31);

you will not find a single article of value which belonged to Pope Clement that has not been *minutely* noted . . . . (225:33); they set about to *contrive* my death. (226: 2) ; it proved the source of *infinite* annoyance and hurt to me . . . . (226:10); The Pope was roused . . . lest I should go and tell the whole world how *infamously* I had been treated . . . (226:12); yet I made a virtue of necessity, and bore my *adverse* fortune with as light a heart as I was able . . . (226:21); the friar made light of these assertions, *averring* . . . . (228:5) that persons who have gained some credit by their abilities are *wont* to talk big of things which . . . would speedily discredit them . . . . (228:7); He had chosen for his *accomplice* a registrar. . . . (228:25); Now I shall keep him *straitly* under lock and key . . . (228:31); These *humours* took a different shape each year; one time he thought he was an oil-jar . . . . (229:24); When I was pouring out these *entreaties* . . . (230:20); first I prayed most devoutly to God, imploring His Divine Majesty to protect and *succour* me in that so perilous a venture. . . . (231:11); supporting myself with the *sinews* of my arms . . . . (231:29); I thought my head had been cut off. . . . With time, my *faculties* returned. . (232: 25); I drew my poinard with its *scabbard* . . . (232:31); a most excellent and able surgeon . . . set the bone with *dexterity* . . . (233: 34)

Study Questions and Activities

1. On what charge was Cellini arrested?

2. How did he effectively disprove the charge?

3. How did the proof of his innocence contribute to his further danger?

4. Find an instance in which Cellini's bragging worked against him. Find evidence that he did not really profit from the experience.

5. What evidence is there in this passage that Cellini is an honorable man? Cite specific evidence.

6. What other traits, both good and bad, would you grant Cellini after reading this passage? Don't neglect the evidence.

7. What characteristics of Cellini come out most strongly in his escape from the castle? If you were a director filming this episode, how would you set, light, and color these scenes: his scheming to escape, the castellan's befuddlement, Cellini's break through the door, his scaling the roof and descent, his scaling the first outer wall, his encounter with the guards, his escape from the final wall, his further adventures on the way to the palace of the duchess?

8. Team yourself with a classmate and write a credible dialogue between the castellan and Cellini. In the dialogue have "the fit" come upon the castellan. Be sure to give the dialogue a plausible conclusion. Have a committee read the assorted dialogues and choose one or two to be acted out in class.

9. Although Cellini seems safe within the Cardinal's palace at the end of the excerpt, he really is not. How do we know? If you want to find out what happens next, finish reading the adventure and report it to the class.

10. Cellini lived in an age about which it has been written: "It was a time when man's disbelief in the men of God in no way lessened his faith in God Himself." How does Cellini's account of his imprisonment and escape support the above statement?

11. With a group of classmates prepare a report on the interrelated roles of the nobility and papacy during the first half of the sixteenth century. Coordinate your research activities to include the artistic, political, and religious concerns of the popes and nobles between the accession of Pope Julius II in 1503 and the death in 1549 of Paul III, the pope who imprisoned Benvenuto Cellini.

12. Find out as much as you can about Castel Sant' Angelo, in which Benvenuto Cellini was held captive. What was the building's original function? What does it house today?

What follows is an actual letter written to the United States Bureau of the Census. It was discovered and published in its present poetic form in 1957.

Compare this piece with the poem that opened this section of readings. In what ways are the writers alike? How are they different? Which piece presents the more specific reasons for the writer's loneliness? What effect do these facts have upon you, the reader? Which of the two writers would you call a non-conformist? Why?

To the Bureau of the Census

LOU ETTA WHITE

I was born in 1895. the onliest
child of Jace White and Lue
Etta Johnson. Fort
Necessity, Franklin
County, Louisiana, baptised
in the Morning side
Baptist church that has a
creek run through the grave
yard. My folks
died when I was small I knows
their names because I read them in the
Bible. I moved in with some
other folks they worked for Mr.
Bonner on his farm wasn't no
address. They was so many
children at that house,
I didn't think a soul
knew I was there and now they tell
me that you came and counted
me. Enclosed six dollars can I have
two copies, one for the
Retirements, and one for me
to show that I was there.

VOCABULARY: SENTENCE COMPLETION

Try answering the following questions. Each sentence has one or two words left blank. The choices that follow the sentence contain a word or pair of words to complete the blank or blanks. On your paper write the word or pair that makes the best fit.

1. In the armed forces, enlisted personnel are discouraged from _______ with officers.
(**a**) entreating (**b**) fraternizing (**c**) collaborating (**d**) jeopardizing

2. Only a small _______ of malcontents was responsible for the _______ display of discourtesy at Saturday's game.
(**a**) faculty—adverse (**b**) rancor—precarious (**c**) hassle—preliminary (**d**) clique—infamous

3. The artist is unfortunately _______ to include too many of his own compositions in his _______.
(**a**) averred—forte (**b**) condescended—concerto (**c**) wont—repertoire (**d**) deigned—fatuousness

4. After donning his _______ the newly elected grand master strode pompously to the podium.
(**a**) armor (**b**) scabbard (**c**) regalia (**d**) equipage

5. Despite the _______ conditions the explorers _______ endured their lot for a fortnight.
(**a**) adverse—stoically (**b**) precarious—expediently (**c**) malignant—patently (**d**) tumultous—comradely

6. Though Ms. Collins had _______ that the recipe was foolproof, the class _______ to make fools of themselves.
(**a**) averred—contrived (**b**) allowed—forbore (**c**) suggested—veered (**d**) deposed—warranted

An Egyptian scribe using a pen case with places for making red and black ink. His pens are over his ear. New York Public Library Picture Collection.

7. "There is no _______," the physician said. "The tumor is _______."
(**a**) correlation—uncanny (**b**) contrivance—forthright (**c**) precariousness—deposed (**d**) malignancy—benign

8. _______ experience allows the enjoyment of dangers that one actually would hesitate to encounter.
(**a**) Infinite (**b**) Vicarious (**c**) Cosmopolitan (**d**) Straitened

9. Because of the unseasonable snow, the thief and his _______ were easily apprehended.
(**a**) alter ego (**b**) accomplice (**c**) regalia (**d**) clique

10. The charlatan offered a _______ that would cure an _______ number of diseases.
(**a**) hiatus—alarming (**b**) reversion—incredible (**c**) sinew—enormous (**d**) panacea—infinite

9

Self-Appraisal—Who Am I?

The time has finally come to end your autobiography. Because it is an ending, this chapter is especially important. Like your first paragraph, it will be important for the effect it has upon the reader, who often rapidly looks at a piece of work. Spend some time, therefore, considering ways of ending the autobiography so that the reader will not expect more to come—at least until, years later, you are writing for profit about the famous adult you have become.

The purpose of the chapter is to estimate your achievements. You can approach this either seriously or humorously, though many will try to combine both tones; for it is well known that there are no boors so bad as those who take themselves too seriously. You might begin appraising yourself by asking yourself the kinds of people you know, the kinds of work you can do, the subjects you have mastered, the most valuable things you have learned, the worst mistakes you have made, and the ways in which you have made improvement. Think about what you hope the future holds in store for you and the ways you plan to make that future come true. Then organize your thoughts into a composition that will pleasingly conclude your journey into yourself.

Getting Started

A fairly long list of questions follows. Consider their pertinence to you—either by yourself or with a group of classmates. From your answers to these, or to related questions they call to your mind, you should be able to organize your final chapter.

PERSONAL ASSESSMENT:

1. Do you prefer indoor to outdoor life? Are you skillful with your hands? With machinery?
2. Do you handle people tactfully, make and keep many friends, get on pleasantly with those much older or younger? With what sort of people do you get along best? With what types are you usually at ease? What is the real basis for your liking someone you know? Or for your dislike?
3. Do you prefer solo or group work? Do you naturally prefer to take the lead and try new methods, or do you prefer to have a leader and obey expert instructions? Do you enjoy helping to swing a big project by teamwork?
4. Do you crave or dread travel, new acquaintances, new studies, new jobs, change in general? Are you self-sufficient? Have you lost a former feeling of self-sufficiency?
5. Is your interest impulsive or sustained? Do you find it hard to stick to a long enterprise and complete a complicated plan, or does your purpose strengthen and your interest grow as you go on studying and working?
6. Does practical business stimulate you? Do you enjoy planning budgets, keeping accounts, handling money? Is it easy for you to sell tickets or get signers or members? Do you notice the methods of the salesmen who serve you?
7. What is your best character trait? Your worst one? The one that will contribute most to your real happiness? To your material success? To the happiness of others?

VALUES:

1. What is your idea of honesty? Not the conventional platitudes from your training, but the views you have wrested from living? What is your general code of personal conduct? Are you an individualist or a conformist, or do you take a position between the two attitudes?

2. In a crisis what principles would you really act on spontaneously? After thinking? How do these principles differ from those you used to act on, those of your friends, your family, your community?

3. Do these principles concern your relationship with your father and mother? Your brothers and sisters? Your community? Your choice of friends? Your attitude toward women if you are a young man, toward men if you are a young woman? Toward marriage? Do these principles concern your reasons for pursuing an education? Your aims in your education? Your attitude toward work? Toward money? Toward honesty? Toward amusement and recreation? Toward reading? Toward writing? Toward religion? Toward morals in general?

4. Do you differ with your parents on any important questions? With your brothers and sisters? With relatives? With your friends? With other associates? Do you disagree on any important questions with the leaders in your community? With the majority opinion in your community?

PHILOSOPHY:

1. What is your attitude toward yourself? Other individuals? Inanimate and animate nature? Social institutions? Good and evil (or God and the devil if you prefer those concrete terms)?
2. What is your attitude toward work, play, love, and worship?
3. What do you say at times that you believe without really believing it? Does this area include political ideas, love of country, religion, personal morals, attitudes toward minority groups or toward other groups or individuals?
4. Where did you get your opinions on some of the important questions mentioned above? Who is chiefly responsible? Are many people responsible—parents, brothers and sisters, other relatives, teachers, ministers, organizations to which you have belonged, your whole community? What do these opinions lead you to do? Wholeheartedly? Reluctantly?

Truman Capote, self-portrait.

5. What is your philosophy of a good family life? Do you wish to repeat the pattern of your own childhood? If you would change it, in what ways? What is your theory about your responsibility to your father, mother, brothers, sisters? Their relationship or responsibility to you? Is there any difference between your theory and your practice in these relationships? What kind of relationship do you hope to have between you and the person you marry? Do you wish your children to share decisions and take responsibilities, or to be given orders, to be sheltered, and to have life made easy for them?
6. What are your beliefs about religion? About death? Immortality? Have these beliefs changed?
7. Do you have a philosophy about your place in your community, your state, your nation, your world?
8. Do you believe that human beings have some freedom to shape themselves and their own futures? Or do you believe that they have little or no freedom to shape their own destinies?
9. What forces may limit people's freedom to shape themselves and their future? What forces may we use as individuals to shape ourselves and our futures? What forces may we use in social groups to help others shape desirable futures?

THE WORLD TODAY AND TOMORROW:

1. What do you find good in today's world? What faults? Are your present goals set to enhance what you find good? To aid in correcting what you see as flaws?
2. What do you see in your personal crystal ball ten years from now? Twenty? Even more?
3. What does your crystal ball reveal to you about the world of the future? Does it agree with your hopes for the future?

Activity

Think of a single word, a phrase, or a short sentence that seems to express the essentials of you. Take a circular piece of cardboard or stiff paper and decorate it, using the slogan you coined. Wear it as a badge to class. Try to explain to classmates its peripheral meanings to you. Comments that you and others make may give you some clues to your final chapter.

A First and Last Paragraph from a Well-Organized **"Mission Successful"**

Have you ever noticed a centipede? Its many legs all work systematically; and, if he loses one leg, the loss doesn't particularly affect him. He still carries on. My idea of a perfect character is one like a simple centipede. A person with a good character has so many good qualities that, if one of them is lost, it would not be a detriment to him. But I am like a daddy-longlegs and have only a few good qualities. Like that arachnid, if I lose one leg I'm lost.

I have been brought up to follow the Golden Rule and try hard to do unto others as I would have them do unto me. I also like to be with people and am tolerant of those of all races and creeds. It is easy to be kind to those who like you, but I want to be just and kind to those who don't like me. I try to follow all my ideals and be a loyal citizen. Some day I hope to achieve a more nearly perfect character and grow to survive like the centipede.

A Summation in Third Person from "**Editorial**"

The name Maurice Stein means little to the general public now. However, with the benefits of the American way of life, the school systems, and the freedoms and heritages that Maury has enjoyed and learned to appreciate, the day may come when his name may mean something. We may hope that he will distinguish himself, whether it be in advertising, politics, or law; and at that time his name may take on a new meaning and significance. But if it should not, it will be enough if he lives so that he may proudly be called a good American.

A More Humorous Final Paragraph from "**Real Swell Guy**"

That is all I shall say about my moods. Some of my faults are being improved, and others are diminishing. To expect them all to disappear would be overly optimistic; but, as an example of their swift decrease, I can say that I used to be a braggart but now I'm a real swell guy.

A Concluding Paragraph from "**The Gypsy Tells My Fortune**"

"I must end this," the gypsy said, "for there are many people waiting to hear me." I sat there realizing that everything she said was true. Then she said, looking into the ball, "You will have a hard life ahead, but remember always to learn by the mistakes you have made. You have many assets. Use them to your best ability." I leaned closer and heard her say, "I am looking into the blank future, into the horizon of opportunity. Sixteen years of your life are gone, but you have the best years to come. Go on into your future, and may you have a successful and happy one."

A Paragraph of Reminiscences in Summary from "**On My Own**"

When I look back over my life, it seems awfully long. I remember, way back when I was in seventh grade, the mystifying secret passages of the new school; they now seem like just some more of the same halls which are to be found in the rest of the building. I remember, when I first arrived in Switzerland, how afraid I was that someone would speak to me in French; now I am pleased when they speak to me that way. I remember, when I first started stamp collecting, what a long job it seemed to be. Now I like stamp collecting not as a long, tedious task, but as an amusing pastime. All of this goes to show that what seems difficult today we will laugh at tomorrow. We often look back at the past with a sneer, thinking, "What a funny person I was, way back then." The present is always the hard part of life to take; it is the part which we can't pass off as "something we did when we weren't feeling too well."

About the Good Things in Life from **"Pause for Reflection"**

I think that one of the most valuable things I have learned in life is the appreciation of the little things which make our life so enjoyable; a glass of cold milk waiting for you when you come home from school; sandwiches made of white bread; the ability to stop in the middle of homework and take a breather. All of these are small things which are taken for granted by most people. Only when one spends some time some place where these things cannot be found does one appreciate them.

An Academic Self-Analysis from **"The Super-Ego"**

Despite my views of the way some teachers perform their task of getting a little knowledge into the heads of so many of us stubborn kids, I do quite well for myself. I have remained on the high honor roll throughout my years in the high school, and I enjoy all of my studies with the exception of math. Math has been particularly difficult for me because accuracy is of basic importance, as my teacher points out; and carelessness is another one of my bad habits. Consequently I have developed a phobia against taking math tests, and I usually panic during a test. I start problem one, let's say a square root problem. I must multiply two and three. "That's a cinch," I say to myself. "That equals nine." When I finally finish the problem I wonder why it does not come out right, and I waste a long time trying to figure it out. I succeed finally and proceed to problem two. I look up to see how much time is left. "Gosh," say I, and I work like mad on problem two, only to find that I am somehow working part of problem three and part of problem four. Problem two is by this time all bungled, and I start on problem three and complete it. It then occurs to me that I've already done that problem and I begin to go over my whole paper. I see that I have done the same problem twice, yet I have two different answers. By this time I grow very hot and feel like crying, but I don't. I manage somehow to revise my paper in the few remaining seconds before the bell rings. I scribble my last few answers as everyone else calmly leaves the room, and I hand in my paper just as the bell for my next class rings. I dash into the class and sit through that period half dead from exhaustion, hoping that the next day will never come. The next day in algebra I sit trying to be cool and collected. I get my paper and cautiously take a peek. I let out a scream, "I passed. I got a ninety." I spend that period worrying about next week's test when I might not be so lucky, and I say to myself, "Boy! what you don't have to go through for one little test."

Ceiling Unlimited

All day long I take on food to try to keep from feeling two-piece. Yet on the whole, I feel rather pleased with my achievements on the physical level. I have learned to play better than average basketball, and, although Mother says I am powerfully slow on the domestic front, I'm faster than average on the cinder path. Just naturally I wasn't good at anything manual, but I have developed a rather good badminton and Ping-Pong game—and the ability to type. Apparently I need to build myself up; all I have to do is lose a little sleep and I have a cold.

The schedule is heavy. Friday night I have Scouts and then we like to hack around. Saturday I get up early for basketball and stay down at school all day playing. Saturday night I go out with the boys, or to a party, or something. Sunday we leave for church at 8:15 A.M. and get back at 11:00 A.M. Sundays I usually work on extra things like these themes. Between basketball, track, and dramatics I hardly ever get home before 5:30 or 6:00 P.M. Unfortunately most of my activities are indoor. I spend from 7 to 9:30 or 10:00 on school work every night except Tuesday; that is my duty time on Hot Line.

Often there just isn't time enough to act as if every class is my only one, the way all teachers would like you to. I usually do my English first; then I do Latin translation but there never is time enough to brush up on declensions, conjugations, and rules. I do as little outside reading as possible; that's the doctor's order. What I need is a clear idea of what is most important, a good course in what to neglect; it always has to be something.

Right at this second I am praying for the strength to hang on till spring vacation. Every spare second I bury my head in a shiny fishing catalogue—the only thing that eases the pressure and the pain. Mother has to hide it. Good Old Sage Hill. It will take two months just to give me ambition and bounce again.

We have about a half acre so that there is plenty to do outdoors as well as indoors, winter and summer. Mother sees to it that the whole family helps to keep the house and yard attractive. I have reached the point of being able to do almost anything whether it is pleasant or not, and it usually isn't. Mother says it builds character, but all I know is that it is a good way to get blisters.

I can't say I'm looking for work of any kind this near spring vacation; but if I were, I would rather it would be outside. I certainly don't expect to be a naturalist when I grow up, but I'm going to work hard to have enough leisure to cast from a little boat into a little pond for a big fish.

An early type of pen. New York Public Library Picture Collection.

CHECK SHEET FOR CHAPTER 9

Analysis of Samples

1. Sample 1 uses what we call an analogy. Think of an analogy suitable to you.

2. Look carefully at the first sentence in sample 4. Why is there no capital on the word "for"?

3. Sample 6 reflects on the things in life we take for granted. What little things add a great deal of pleasure to your life?

4. Which of the samples makes its point mainly by use of anecdote? By use of detail?

5. What figurative language can you discover in the samples? How does it add to the interest of the writing?

6. What examples of long, sophisticated sentences can you find? Is your own writing developing as that of these writers did? If you can answer that question positively, you've accomplished a lot from writing your autobiography.

Spelling

1. adieu
2. aisle (What is its homonym?)
3. analyze (Write the three other parts of this verb and its noun form)
4. candidate
5. consensus (What common verbose phrase is often used with this word?)
6. eventual (Write its adverb form)
7. fiction (Learn also to spell *fictitious*)
8. occasion (Write its adjective and adverb forms. What other words does it resemble in its spelling changes?)
9. particular
10. possess (Write the three other verb forms, a noun, an adjective, and an adverb form)
11. probably
12. recommend (What is its noun form?)
13. summary (Learn also to spell *summation, summarize*)
14. women (Is this a singular or a plural?)

More About Punctuation: Direct and Indirect Address

When we report what someone else has said or written, we have two choices. We may quote directly, in which method we are using **direct address.** The punctuation of quotations is fairly simple, but needs some study. Take, for example, these two sentences, spoken by your teacher: Does anyone have any questions? If not, get to work.

1. Begin with the speaker, thus: The teacher said, "Does anyone have any questions? If not, get to work." (In this method we have made no changes except to put quotation marks around what was actually said and set it off by a comma. Be sure to notice that we kept all the capitals.)

2. End with the speaker, thus: "Does anyone have any questions? If not, get to work," the teacher said. (Again we have done little more than add quotations and a comma. Do notice, though, that *the* before *teacher* does not begin with a capital.)

3. Put the speaker in the middle, thus: "Does anyone have any questions?" the teacher asked. "If not, get to work." (Here the question mark at the end of the first sentence replaced the comma, and a period after *asked* signified that a new sentence was beginning.)

4. A variation on the above method is to put the speaker in the middle of a sentence, thus: "Does anyone have any questions? If not," the teacher said, "get to work." (Here *the teacher said* is separated by commas, and *get* begins with a small letter because it continues an incompleted sentence.)

Try your hand at punctuating and capitalizing the following examples of direct address:

a. My father glared at her and said the solution to the problem is simple.

b. But what am I to do if nobody asks me to dance my sister wailed.

c. Don't be a goose my mother said somebody is sure to ask you.

d. But what my sister repeated if nobody does?

e. My father snorted. Either ask someone yourself or put on your coat and come home. It's that simple. Then it was my mother's turn to glare at him. Sister kept on sniffling.

Two further things you should remember about direct address:

1. Make your characters, when they speak directly, portray themselves. If they do not speak in Standard Written English, write exactly what they do say. It is by their use of what characters actually say that good authors help effect characterization.

2. When a different character speaks, we generally begin a new paragraph, even though the first person may have said only one word.

Indirect address makes changes in person and tense and omits quotation marks. We could put our first example into indirect address by writing *The teacher told us that, if no one had further questions, we should get to work.* Or we could write *The teacher told us we should get to work if no one had further questions.* (Notice that, in the first change, the *if*-clause interrupted the whole sentence and was set off by commas. In the second, it was not set off because it no longer interrupted.)

Go back now to the sentences you punctuated for direct address and put them in indirect address, following directions.

a. My father glared and told her. . . .
b. My sister wondered. . . .
c. My mother told her. . . .
d. Again my sister wondered. . . .
e. My father snorted and advised her. . . .

Toward Better Sentence Construction

1. Maintain parallel construction of sentences. This means that, in a series of items, writers must stick to the usage they start with. If they start using gerunds, they keep on using them; if they start with phrases, they don't switch to clauses.

wrong: Bobby likes roughhousing, running, and to chase little girls.
right: Bobby likes roughhousing, running, and chasing little girls.
(All objects are now gerunds.)

wrong: We played in the attic, on the roof, and slid down the steps.
right: We played in the attic, ran on the roof, and slid down the steps.
(Each phrase now has a verb.)

wrong: I love to keep house, to manage accounts, to save money, and buying things.
right: I love to keep house, to manage accounts, to save money, and to buy things.
(All objects are now infinitive phrases.)

2. In making comparisons, be careful to compare similar things. If you don't, your meaning can be obscure and often downright funny.

wrong: I am a kid whose world is very different from most people.
right: I am a kid whose world is very different from that of most people.

wrong: It pays well if you work hard and well like any other job.
right: It pays well if you work hard and well as you would on any other job.

wrong: I don't really care to try out my ideas because they are nearly always the same as the general group.
right: I don't really care to try out my ideas because they are nearly always the same as those of the general group.

wrong: Brand B is better than any toothpaste on the market today.
right: Brand B is better than any other toothpaste on the market today.

Problems in Usage

1. Avoid the use of the double negative, constructions in which two negative words are used in place of one. Be especially careful of these negative words: *but, hardly, no, none, nothing, only, scarcely.* And avoid completely the common cliché, *can't help but.* Correct each of the following uses of the double negative.

a. I haven't had hardly enough time to finish the first paragraph.
b. You can't help but like this novel.
c. He hasn't eaten scarcely a mouthful.

2. Do not add an extra "s" to the following: somewhere, anywhere, nowhere, everywhere.

wrong: The sun is always shining somewheres.
right: The sun is always shining somewhere.

3. Do not use the expressions *so as* or *being as*. Generally the writer means to say *inasmuch as* or just plain *as*.

wrong: Being as I was planning to go, I wasn't surprised.
right: As I was planning to go, I wasn't surprised.
wrong: I set the fire so as I could get the dinner on the stove.
right: I set the fire so that I could get the dinner on the stove.
wrong: It isn't much of a fault, being as I'm still young.
right: It isn't much of a fault inasmuch as I'm still young.

4. Learn the distinction between the following often confused pairs of words: except/accept, effect/affect, beside/besides, principle/principal.

a. except—a preposition meaning *excluding;* a verb meaning *to leave out*
   accept—always a verb, meaning *to take, to receive*
b. effect—a noun, *the result of a cause;* a verb, *to bring about*
   affect—always a verb, often meaning *to have influence upon*
c. beside—always a preposition meaning *next to, aside of*
   besides—a preposition or adverb meaning *in addition to*
d. principle—always a noun meaning *a rule of some sort, a tenet*
   principal—All other uses of this homonym are *pals,* including the princi*pal* of your school, the princi*pal* parts of verbs, and the princi*pal* interest in your life and the princi*pal* that brings in interest.

What are the correct choices in each of the following sentences?

1. The (effect, affect) of the medicine was worse than the disease.

2. I had been taught never to (except, accept) a ride from strangers.

3. Who (beside, besides) Harriet is wearing a long dress to the party?

4. I have worked hard this year to perfect three (principals, principles) of conduct.

5. Shall I sit (beside, besides) you or (she, her)?

6. The (principal, principle) idea of the paragraph was not clear to either Sammy or (I, me).

7. Everyone (except, accept) Mary and (we, us) three will be on time.

ASSIGNMENT 9

Write Chapter 8, a conclusion, to your autobiography. In it you will want to assess your present self and to speculate about your future. Be mindful of your immediate and future audiences: for your teacher, make your writing as free of errors as you can; for your children and grandchildren, leave them a portrait of the special individual that is you.

Japanese woodblock showing a group writing. New York Public Library Picture Collection.

PRACTICE TEST IX

Review all the Check Sheets and then, without looking back, do the test. The teacher may want to check your work OR to give you another test of the same sort. Each error will count as two points, if anybody's counting.

I. Spelling. Have your teacher choose ten words from the Check Sheets and dictate them to you. Spell them correctly.

II. Choose the correct usage from the choices in the parentheses and write it on your paper.

1. (Somewhere, Somewheres) around the house I had laid down the pen, but I couldn't find it.

2. We had (already, all ready) started before the hurricane began.

3. Next week we shall read ("Heidi," <u>Heidi</u>, HEIDI, Heidi) and nursery rhymes.

4. We dug on the shore for juicy, succulent (muscles, mussels).

5. Ishmael gets a note from the nurse (everyday, every day) he wants to miss his class.

6. Mortimer has (lain, laid, layed) in the sun all afternoon.

7. Huck's aunt told him he (can't, couldn't) go out after dark.

8. For two weeks I (lay, laid, lied) unconscious with a high fever.

9. If a vacation in any one of these cities (interests, interest) you, call your travel agent.

10. (There, Their, They're) two of the finest people I know.

11. When the bride came down the (aisle, isle), my mother began to cry.

12. Mr. Fogg (balled, bawled, bauled) us three boys out and sent us to detention.

13. I was taught never to (accept, except) rides with strangers.

14. He was hired to teach my cousin and (I, me, myself) some Hebrew.

15. (Being as, As) he is not yet eighteen, he cannot drive to Connecticut from New York.

III. On your paper correct each of the following sentences, rewriting them completely if necessary.

1. My tastes are just like my father; we agree in everything.

2. I'm only a ninth grader, I'm not expected to know everything.

3. Nevertheless, I couldn't help but remember the times John had tried to beat me up.

4. September 11, 1942, was when I started to school.

5. It is my mother which I rely on to show me my faults.

6. My mother and father don't believe that I ever will fulfill my ambitions, which is rather discouraging.

7. The people I go around with are fairly smart, so they should help me become smarter, so I can make something of myself in life.

8. Like many people I prefer the outside in preference to the inside however that doesn't mean that I would never care to live inside.

9. It is definitely certain that I am not naturally talkative and seem to get along with persons that are about my age or older.

10. To me my achievements are great, but others think it was nothing.

11. "If you have finished the work by 2:00," Mrs. Romano said, "We'll have a short activity period."

12. I had laid in bed only ten minutes when I heard a terrific pounding in the attic.

13. My car will go faster than any car on the road.

14. How can I have any ambitions my parents say I'm a born lazy bum.

15. I like to watch the waves, hear the surf, and I can watch the girls along the shore.

IV. Shorten and improve each of the following sentences by cutting out extra words.

A. In these five merely delete unnecessary words and record them on your paper.

1. The reason why Ethan could not leave with Mattie was because he did not have a large enough sum of money.
2. It seems to me that the love affair between Winston and Julie ended at the time when the State controlled and channeled their minds and emotions.
3. Much of the information which I found in this book contradicts that which is contained in the bibliography.
4. My sister, who is a sorority member, would be unhappy in a dormitory.
5. Lieutenant Henry decided that it would be necessary for him to make a separate peace.

B. In rewriting these five, find a single word which, when inserted somewhere in your new sentence, can replace the underlined group.

6. The resident who lives in New York does not appreciate his opportunities.
7. His project, which is very ambitious, may take him the rest of the semester.
8. They had slaves who were almost too many in number to be counted.
9. The dog chased the cat up the tree.
10. Russia now has a society which has been highly industrialized.

AFTERWORD

The writing of your book is now complete. What you have completed may not have been easy, and you may feel like Huck Finn at the end of his novel: ". . . and so there ain't nothing more to write about, and I am rotten glad of it, because if I'd 'a' knowed what a trouble it was to make a book I wouldn't 'a' tackled it, and ain't a-going to no more." However, you should also experience the feeling of elation that comes from completing a task that once was beyond your powers.

There is more to the text, however, to occupy you while you put the finishing touches on your project. Immediately following is a test, based upon the suggestions made throughout the text on the use of Standard Written English. You may wish to do this for practice and then take a similar one prepared by your teacher. Chapter 10, which follows, completes the text. It consists of suggestions for preparing the various forms that will soon confront you as you move on toward college and the job market.

PRACTICE TEST ON CHAPTERS 1–9

Your teacher may want to check this work after you have completed it or to give you another test of the same sort. Each section tells how much to take off for each error. Subtract the total of your errors from 105.

Part I—Spelling [25 pts.] Number your paper from 1 to 25. If the word is spelled correctly, write OK beside the number on your paper. If it is not, respell it correctly.

1. ancestery
2. genealogy
3. destruction
4. occured
5. kindergarden
6. separate
7. nieghbors
8. aquaintance
9. dispite
10. definate
11. undoubtly
12. pastime
13. immeadiately
14. nurcery
15. permanent
16. twelth
17. teriffic
18. fullfill
19. basketball
20. accidently
21. horrable
22. aisle
23. embarassing
24. noticably
25. incidently

Part II—Punctuation [20 pts.] All but one of the following sentences need at least one additional punctuation mark. Rewrite the sentences on your paper putting in the proper marks in the proper places. Remember that some sentences need more than one mark and that one sentence will need no mark whatsoever.

1. Although I am somewhat older now I manage however to get into as much mischief as ever.

2. I sat down and read *The Good Earth* in one night and the next morning my eyes were so bad that I couldn't go to school.

3. Digging in the garden one day I was surprised to find an arrowhead which was still in good condition.

4. It was in Boston that I had my first fight and won it. I have liked fighting ever since I won that first battle.

5. I have had many terrifying experi-periences in fact most experience is terrifying to me.

6. My hobbies follow photography chemistry botany birds and pestering my relatives and friends.

7. In January we went to Philadelphia where I enrolled in the Friends' School.

8. The officers of the club included me president my brother vice president my sister secretary and Father treasurer.

9. Well now you know my life story and can see how I grew up.

10. On June 21 the longest day of the year I was expecting a call from my uncle instead he surprised me and came in person.

11. Aunt Lottie who has always been my favorite relative, would always give me a cookie when I went to see her.

12. Variety is the spice of life my father tells me but sometimes I think I've known too much variety in my life.

13. The gym teacher promised us that, if we had fewer than ten cuts for the quarter she would let us have a party.

14. Having previously decided to meet that deadline I surprised everyone by handing my paper in on time.

15. Goldenrod a noxious weed to those suffering from hay fever, is actually a beautiful flower and is cultivated in England.

16. "What do you think, my father asked me, of the Tigers' chances this season?"

17. By reading Steinbeck's book about the depression *The Grapes of Wrath,* I managed to learn a great deal about the Thirties.

18. That year the Williamses moved into the house next to ours and from the first day I was either at Joanies or she at my house.

19. "Why does it always rain on week-ends I wailed.

20. The committee, their work finshed adjourned feeling they had accomplished what they had set out to do.

Part III—Usage [20 pts.] Each of the following sentences has one mistake, EXCLUDING punctuation or spelling. Correct the mistake by writing it and placing the correct usage after it.

1. I came to Oakland in nineteen forty-five.

2. We moved here from Philadelphia, Penna.

3. Mother is a high-strung person which I love dearly.

4. My Father had often told me to be careful of rattlesnakes.

5. After we had walked a little ways, we came to a cove.

6. Because of me missing the bus, I had to serve detention.

7. I entered the Elementary school when I was four.

8. I had leaped right off of the wharf into Father's scow.

9. That sure startled me.

10. When he won the race, Jack felt as if he really hit the jackpot.

11. My first fear was climbing the stairs to bed.

12. There was hardly any people left on the pier.

13. He raised his hand and asked, "May I go to the girls room?" Boy, was he embarrassed!

14. Over 30 of us were in the crowded bus.

15. We sent the huge box of use clothing to the war refugees.

16. I don't see how he could of made such a silly mistake.

17. If Shakespeare had seen last night's performance of *Julius Caesar,* he'd be whirling in his grave.

18. Why don't us boys have the right to form a Men's Liberation group?

19. For the rest of the week Bob spent his time just laying around the house.

20. Anyone who is sane and in his right mind could see that only one of the choices offered to Ethan was proper.

Part IV—Transformation [10 points]: Rewrite each of the following sentences in a different form. Do not change the idea of the sentence. Follow the directions for each sentence.

1. *Begin with "Losing his temper. . . .":* Mr. Boggs lost his temper. He shouted at me, "You have made the same mistake again."
2. *Begin with "My mother told. . . .":* "You may go out for an hour, but not until you have finished the dishes," my mother said.
3. *Begin with "The fastest plane in the world. . . .":* My ZC-192 will be the fastest plane in the world. It should approximate the speed of light.
4. *Begin with "Beth. . . .":* Her name was Beth. She was my best friend for two whole years. Then she moved away.
5. *Begin with "The miners did. . . .":* The nature of the miners' work in those times was very dangerous.
6. *Begin with "Often obscure. . . .":* The writer's syntax is often obscure, and it frequently hides his meaning.
7. *Begin with "I. . . .":* There is not a sport that I do not enjoy.
8. *Begin with "Having. . . .":* I mowed the lawn, weeded the garden, and I was hungry, but Mother fortunately had dinner on the table.
9. *Begin with "The scoutmaster told us. . . .":* "If you want stronger muscles," the scoutmaster told us, "these exercises will be just the thing to develop them."
10. *Begin with "The Western powers. . . .":* Strong Soviet protests and new threats of rearmament are expected today by the Western powers.

Part V—Word Choice [15 pts.] From the choices given in parentheses, pick the one which is correct in Standard Written English and write it beside the corresponding number on your paper.

1. Having walked but a little (way, ways) into the cemetery, I was already frightened and eager to leave.

2. After shooting the rapids, we were all so tired we just (laid, lay) down for an hour on the sand bar.

3. May I borrow a quarter (off of, off, from) you?

4. What (is, are) the right answers to questions 2 and 4?

5. One thing I remember is the day that Harry and (I, me) thought the world was going to end.

6. He had walked three miles through the downpour and (must, had to) change his clothes.

7. When Edith and (me, I) were ready to recite,

8. there (was, were) only three minutes left.

9. (Most, Almost) all of our group

10. (was, were) ready to turn back toward home.

11. We had clambered (in, into) the cave without assessing the possible dangers.

12. Where will he be (standing, standing at)?

13. When we were eight, Jim was neither so tall nor so strong as (I, me).

14. Once more the cat had caught (it's, its) tail in the screen door.

15. He had carefully listed the (principal, principle) points of the lecture in his notebook.

Part VI—The Circus [15 pts.] Each of the following sentences has ONE error. However, it may be spelling, capitalization, wording, grammar, anything. Find it and correct it. Whenever possible, write only the error and its correction. Sometimes you will need to rewrite an entire group of words—or even an entire sentence. As this is informal writing, do not consider slang an error.

1. I have always loved such stories as those written by Faulkner, Hesse, Conrad, etc.

2. There was really nowheres else to go after that trip, or so I thought.

3. Having walked into the house unannounced; I was not surprised at my chilly reception.

4. Since I really knew what to do, I was throughly disgusted by my error.

5. Lightning has always terrified me. So I was scared stiff on the night of the storm.

6. Most everyone expects eventually to grow up, but I don't want to; I just want to be a little boy and have fun.

7. My book report was so different from Harriet that no one knew I had copied hers.

8. Running around with only his booties on, the neighbor, naturally, quickly called Mother to bring my baby brother in.

9. We worked and worked on our play, and a success was made of it.

10. In junior high a guy often feels unsure of yourself, and you want to overcome that feeling.

11. My first date was when I was in fifth grade.

12. The picture I am enclosing is my baby sister.

13. The teacher which I liked least was Miss Tabatha Katt.

14. Mother had been waiting a long time, which had made her angry with me.

15. I expect to take both Geometry and Latin in my sophomore year.

An inkwell which belonged to Marie-Antoinette. New York Public Library Picture Collection.

10

Coming Events- Lessons for Later Reference

When you have finished your autobiography, you will have something more useful than a mere memento of an English class in which, it is hoped, you had a good time writing your first book and learned a great deal about the use of Standard Written English. You will have, in addition, a record of facts that should come in handy later on when you are asked to write about yourself as you apply for college or employment. Such applications frequently ask you to submit a brief biography in addition to filling out a fairly complex and time-consuming form. You will almost certainly find that looking back on what you have just written will give you ideas for the biography as well as facts needed to complete the form.

Inasmuch as part of searching for either a college or job often calls for you to write letters, your first task in this chapter will be to review the proper forms for business correspondence. First impressions are important, and applicants for college or work will not want to make this impression by revealing the extent of their ignorance. Rather, they should be able to demonstrate that their education in English has prepared them to write in good business form as well as in good English.

Before going any further, take the following test to see how much you remember of previous training in good business form. Your teacher will review the results with you.

A Diagnostic Test on Business Form

DIRECTIONS: Roger Olson, a senior at Hibbing (Minnesota) High School, hopes to attend a College of Mining in some university after he is graduated in the spring of 1978. One of the schools which interests him is the University of Idaho, of which his father is an alumnus.

Following is the passage from the catalog of the University of Idaho which Roger used to write his letter to the Admissions Office. On page 255 is the letter which he wrote. Study them both and then, on your paper, answer as *true* or *false* these statements:

1. The outside address (1) is in correct form. (If not, correct it.)
2. The inside address (2) is in correct form. (If not, correct it.)
3. The salutation (3) is in correct form. (If not, correct it.)
4. The complimentary close (4) is in correct form. (If not, correct it.)
5. The signature (5) is in correct form. (If not, correct it.)
6. The style of the letter is the formal style required of a good business letter. (If not, why not?)
7. The letter contains few, if any, errors in grammar, spelling, and punctuation. (Cite any errors.)
8. The letter is written in time to meet the deadlines set by the college.
9. The first paragraph contains information that the catalog page requested.
10. The requests of the second paragraph are reasonable ones to make after one has read the catalog page carefully. (If not, why not?)
11. The third paragraph shows that Roger has read the catalog page carefully.
12. To follow instructions accurately, Roger should have included a transcript of his grades.
13. To follow the instructions accurately, the letter should have been accompanied by Roger's picture.
14. If Roger had read the instructions carefully, he would have realized that he had little chance for admission to the university.

ATTENTION PROSPECTIVE NEW STUDENTS

FINAL DATES FOR MAKING APPLICATIONS—All applications for admission to the University of Idaho for the first semester must be received by the Admissions Office on or before August 1st.

Applications received after the above date will be held and the students will be accepted in order of receipt of their applications only if the University can accommodate them.

The final date for making application for admission for the second semester is January 15

ENROLLMENT PROCEDURE—Prospective students, both Idaho residents and those in other states, should write to the Admissions Office, University of Idaho, Moscow, for blanks upon which to apply for admission. Enrolling in the University is neither difficult nor complex if the steps outlined in this folder are taken in the proper order.

OUT-OF-STATE STUDENTS—Within its capacity, after accommodating Idaho students, the University admits out-of-state students on a selective basis. Special consideration is given to sons and daughters of out-of-state alumni. Other factors considered in selecting out-of-state candidates are scholarship, scores received on nationally administered tests associated with college entrance, special abilities, and the need of Idaho industries for graduates in certain fields such as forestry, mining, and agriculture.

Out-of-state students should write the Admissions Office, giving the reasons for their interest in the University of Idaho, stating what they desire to study, and indicating their scholastic achievements in high school and any colleges attended.

A $25 application fee is required for all out-of-state undergraduate students. This fee must accompany the application.

LIVING QUARTERS—For complete information on "Living Accommodations and How to Get Them" see page 35.

Roger Olson
108 Winnipeg Avenue
Hibbing, Minn. 55746 1
October 12, 1977

Admissions Office
2 University of Idaho
Moscow, Idaho

3 Dear Admissions Office:

I hope that you will be glad to read that my father graduated from your university twenty-five years ago and that now I am interested in applying for admission. Dad is very interested in my going to his old alma mater, and I certainly like what he has told me about it.

I am now a senior at Hibbing High School, and my grades are good; so far I have not received a mark below a B. I am also captain and halfback of the school football team and an Eagle Scout. Last year I was president of the junior class. I want to enter college next fall, preferably the College of Mining of your fine institution.

I am wondering if you would be kind enough to send me application blanks. I would greatly appreciate having them and can hardly thank you enough for the trouble I am causing you. Could you also, without too much trouble, send me some information about living accommodations for college freshmen?

4 Thanking you again in advance, I am

Very Truly Yours,

(Rog.) 5

Roger Olson

Exercises

1. If you are thinking of applying to a special college, write that institution for a catalog. If you do not know the address of the college, ask the librarian where to find it.

2. *The New York Times*, let us say, has run the following classified advertisement. Answer it in correct business form.

AIRLINE RECEPTIONISTS NEEDED

July-August Only

$95 — $115

High School Graduates or Older
Some Writing Needed
Work in LaGuardia, Kennedy, or Newark
Include 1 reference, phone number.

Box AL212, NYT, NYC 10036

256

3. Imagine that the following advertisement has appeared in your local paper. Answer it.

SUMMER ONLY

Need two high school graduates to work in research service division of large PR Co. No experience necessary. $85 week, July and August. Write John Fried, Box Z6078.

4. Suppose that you have saved money toward a gift for your married sister, for whom you can make up a name and address—or use a real one. You know she has a rose garden and have

CHRISTMAS GIFT ORDER BLANK
OLD-TIME ROSE GARDENS

Horticulture Lane
Domino, Ohio 45012

Send following to ____________

Street ____________

City ____________

State ________ Zip ________

Quantity	Gift Suggestion Group Numbers	Price
	Shipping & Handling Charge	.75
	Sub Total	
Sales Tax 6% (Ohio Residents Only)		

Name ____________

Street ____________

City ____________

State ________ Zip ________

$ ________ ☐ Check ☐ Money Order

decided to send her a gift certificate for rosebushes to be delivered in the spring. Using the following information, recopy and fill out the order blank properly so that she will receive seven or eight rosebushes at the correct planting season. Will you need an additional letter?

GIFT SUGGESTIONS

GROUP NO. 1696
JUNIOR MISS
GINFER
WOBURN ABBEY
GOLDEN GARNETTE
Value: $10.75
Save: 1.35
Only: 9.40

GROUP NO. 1706
THE FARMER'S WIFE
LAVENDER PRINCESS
SPARTAN
GAY PRINCESS
Value: $10.75
Save: 1.35
Only: 9.40

GROUP NO. 1736
GOLDEN GARNETTE
WOBURN ABBEY
APRICOT NECTAR
SARATOGA
Value: $11.00
Save: 1.40
Only: 9.60

GROUP NO. 1735
PEACH GLOW
IVORY FASHION
CROWN JEWEL
APRICOT NECTAR
Value: $10.50
Save: 1.30
Only: 9.20

GROUP NO. 1616
BLAZE
GOLDEN SHOWERS
CORAL DAWN
Value: $ 7.75
Save: 1.00
Only: 6.75

GROUP NO. 1615
DON JUAN
CLIMBING CRIMSON GLORY
ALOHA
Value: $ 8.75
Save: 1.10
Only: 7.65

The College Application

Those planning to go to college will spend some of the first semester of their senior year filling out applications for colleges, one of which they hope to enter the next fall. The first step is to write for application blanks. When these arrive, the next step is to get to work on them. Procrastination at this point will result in panic a week or so before the blanks are due.

While applications vary with different institutions, most of them ask enough similar questions so that students can prepare ahead of time for the ones they have to write by filling out a rough information form to have on hand as they tackle the final job. A guide for such a rough form follows.

Name in Full ____________________

Permanent Address ____________________

Home Telephone Number: Area Code ( ) Number ____________________

Present Address ____________________

Date of Birth: Month________ Day________ Year ____________________

Social Security Number____________________

Indicate the dates of the tests you plan to submit:

ACT______ CEEB-SAT______Achievements______ Others ____________________

Do you plan to seek scholarship aid?_____ If so, where?____________________

I. Background Information

A. Family Data — including unusual changes in family — for example: divorce, death, remarriage.

____

Age of student when it occurred:____________________

1. How many members are there in your family group including yourself?

____

2. Fill in spaces below according to information requested.

Siblings: (Begin with oldest): Name the school.

a. ____________ _____ ____________ ____________________

(first name) Age Relationship (Education to date) Education, preschool, school, completed. College, married, etc.

b. ____________ _____ ____________ ____________________

c. ____________ _____ ____________ ____________________

d. ____________ _____ ____________ ____________________

3. Education of father ____________________ Mother ____________________

(school, college attended, degree) (school, college, degree)

Occupation of father ____________________

Occupation of mother ____________________

4. Describe your own previous part-time work or job if you have earned money for services rendered.

a. ______________________________

(Job description — be specific) (What hours of day/week do you work?)

b. ______________________________

(Name of employer or establishment) (Total hours per week)

II. **Hobbies and Personal Experiences**

A. What is your primary hobby? It may be school or nonschool related. Describe in about 150 words.

B. Write a paragraph of approximately 150 words describing an exciting, unusual incident or experience in which you were involved or that you observed. What did you learn from this experience?

III. **Extracurricular and Community Activities**

List your principal extracurricular and community activities. List these activities in order of importance to you.

Activity	Approx. No. of Hours per week	Positions held Indicate Grades 9, 10, 11, 12
IN SCHOOL (e.g. Sports, Student Govt., Publications, Music, Dramatics etc.)		
OUT OF SCHOOL (e.g. Scouting, Church Work, Music, Hobbies, etc.)		
EMPLOYMENT During School Yr.		
EMPLOYMENT During Summers		

IV. Summer Experiences

Describe briefly how you spent the last three summers. (Travel, work, camp, etc.)

Three summers ago:

Two summers ago:

Last summer:

Tentative plans for this coming summer:

If you have done any traveling in addition to what is listed above, list places you have visited:

V. Reasons for Applying for College of Your Choice

A. Why do you prefer the size of the college you chose?
Why do you prefer a coed or non-coed college?
If you choce a specialized school, what are your reasons?
Do you have any reasons for choosing a special geographical area?

Who has recommended the college to you?
Do you have relatives or good friends who have attended this college?

What do you know about the preparation this college offers?

B. What ideas do you have about a possible career or careers?

VI. Autobiography

On the back of this sheet and on additional sheets write an autobiography. This should include what you have done (lessons, travels, experiences) and what you are doing now, how the members of your family have influenced you, what events (births, deaths, family moves) have influenced your life, who your friends are and how they have influenced you, your sense of values (what you want out of life) and anything else you think important.
Be specific.

Planning for Answering Questions V and VI

Reasons for Choosing College: Most application blanks will ask, in one form or another, why you chose to apply to a specific college. Answering this question deserves some thought. Be direct in your answers. If you have not previously done so, spend some time researching the college. Your library contains many handbooks that will give you information about it. Ask your librarian to show you these books, if you are not already aware of their location, and study them. If you have relatives and friends who have attended the college, get from them specific information favorable to your choice and list that information.

Do not pad your answers. Admissions officers have thousands of application blanks to peruse each fall and are not interested in the quantity of words you write. Experience has trained them to scent an evasion within the first clause of your answer. Use such sentences as: "My uncle John Jones, Class of '62, was graduated from your School of Engineering, has held a good job with X Corporation since his graduation, and claims you have the best engineering school in the country." "I am undecided as to my future but know that it lies in liberal arts. I have chosen Excello University not only because of its reputation in this field but because its location also offers easy access to theaters, museums, and concerts." "My choice is limited partly because our family income demands I stay close to home. Within this area Unico College, according to my counselor, offers a fine course in business education." "My favorite teacher in high school has been Miss Y, an alumna of your school. She credits Dr. Blank there for much of her success, and I hope to take courses with him also."

Questions Requiring Autobiographical Data: Like the ones requiring reasons for choice, autobiographical questions vary widely in form. As you would in answering a test question, study the question carefully so that your writing will hit the target of the question. Again, do not write more than is required. The short, direct answer of 150 words is likely to be far more impressive than the thousand-word recapitulation of your life and times. If the question has asked you to list what you feel are your achievements so far, do so frankly; but resist the impulse to recall your achievements if they have been asked for in another question.

If you feel insecure with your answer, don't hesitate to submit it, along with the question you are answering, to your English teacher, counselor, or any other qualified adult. Do, however, come to them with your answer written. Your erstwhile friends may suddenly seem less friendly if you appear with puzzled look and a blank page, but they will usually be happy to tinker with something you have already prepared.

Exercises

Five autobiographical questions follow. Either with a small group or in class, discuss the organization each question calls for: the number of paragraphs necessary, the probable number of words needed, the kind of style most likely to persuade.

1. Write an autobiographical sketch in which you discuss the people, occurrences, and reading that have contributed to your decision to go to college.
2. What has caused you to choose, at least tentatively, the profession you hope to enter? You might think of such experiences as travel, reading, people you have met, actual work experience, your studies, observations of others, incidents that have impressed you.
3. Briefly tell about those experiences in your life which you feel have made you the person you now are.
4. In a brief autobiography discuss the most significant occurrences in your life so far. Have they helped you to choose a future? Have they changed your way of life? Have you profited from unpleasant as well as pleasant experiences? In what way have those occurrences been significant?

5. Write a sketch in which you talk about the most or least interesting person you have ever met. What happened to cause you to make the judgment? In what ways have you been influenced by this person?
6. As clearly and concisely as possible, tell about a person you consider important in your life and describe why he or she has had this impact upon you.

Further Advice on Answering Questions Requiring a Sentence or More

1. Unless your handwriting is impressively neat and legible, type your answers. You are not going to please the overworked admissions committee if they have to torture their eyes to gain your meaning. Besides, they know that typing is a necessary tool for college students. If you must hand-write your application, use black ink.
2. Make a rough draft of your work and check it carefully so that it follows the rules of Standard Written English. The multi-sentence question serves two purposes: it shows the committee something about your life and philosophy, but it also shows them whether or not you appear to be qualified to handle the written assignments of the college courses.
3. In your revision, carefully edit out anything that is superfluous, unnecessarily repetitive, overly general. The real secret of good writing is that it have clarity and economy. The use of facts in well-ordered sentences gives clarity. You gain economy by shortening wherever possible; be especially careful to weed out, unless absolutely necessary, such intensifiers as *quite, rather, very, definitely, awfully, terribly*. Avoid also the use of clichés.

Using the Telephone to Arrange for an Interview

The telephone enables us to shortcut both the hazards of the present postal system and the work of writing a neat, well-planned letter. It also, however, obliges us to create our best first impression by speaking carefully, clearly, and correctly. Your use of the phone in speaking to a prospective interviewer may differ greatly from the use you have put it to in speaking to friends. With them there has been no need to consider either your manner or style of speaking. Nor have you had to overcome the shyness that may seize you when talking to an important stranger.

In preparing to call for an appointment, many will find it helpful to prepare a written speech to refer to while the call is being made. As an example, let's say you are going to answer the following advertisement in your local newspaper.

> CHECKERS NEEDED for local A & P. Some experience helpful. High school students accepted for 5–9 and weekends. Call 743–0257.

Be aware, as you plan, that a secretary may answer you. The following conversation might then ensue.

YOU: I read your advertisement this afternoon asking for checkers at the store. Could you connect me with the right person to speak to?

ANSWER: Just a moment and I'll switch you to Ms. Abrams.

MS. A: Good morning. Ms. Abrams speaking.

YOU: Good morning, Ms. Abrams. I am Cynthia Dean and a junior at Hawthorne High. I saw your ad in today's paper and would like to apply for the job. I worked last summer checking groceries on the Cape and have time this year to earn money toward going to college. (Or: I've never worked as a checker, but I think I could learn quickly. And I have spare time I'd like to put to use.)

MS. A: When can you see me?

YOU: I'm free any time from 3:30 in the afternoon, or I could come in at your convenience on Saturday.

MS. A: Could you make it at four this afternoon?

YOU: Fine, thank you. I'll look forward to talking with you. Goodbye.

An analysis of the above conversation will show that you identified yourself and your desires by answering those questions considered necessary in the first paragraph of a good news story: 1, WHO, your name; 2, WHAT, the ad you answered; 3, WHERE, your high school and grade; 4, WHEN, your availability for the interview; and 5, WHY, your spare time and/or your need for college money. Hold in mind these five w's as essential to any preliminary identification.

If you write down answers to questions you expect to hear, you may save yourself the possible embarrassment of stammering or and-ughing your way through a conversation. Practice also with your family, friends, or a tape recorder. Ask them, or yourself if listening to a playback, the following questions and try to correct the difficulties you discover.

1. Do I speak slowly enough to be understood easily?
2. Do I carefully enunciate each word, or did my speech sound something like "I'm Cynth Dean anuhjuner at Hawther High"?
3. Do I need to lower my tone somewhat? Or to make my voice in a somewhat different register?
4. Did I pepper my conversation with needless sounds such as "and uh," "yeah," or "you know"?
5. Did I speak loudly enough?
6. Did I hesitate too long between words, between sentences, in answering questions?

Exercises

Have your group consider one of the following problems. Assign one person to be the applicant; another, the secretary; a third, the person in charge. The group can then listen to the three do a simulated phone conversation and discuss what they found good, indifferent, and fairly bad. Or, better yet, each trio can record the conversation on tape and play it back for group consideration.

1. You would like to have a college interview on Columbus Day weekend at a college which your group can choose. Phone for an appointment.
2. A local department store has advertised for part-time stock personnel and salesclerks. Phone for an interview.
3. You are out of school with a broken leg and cannot possibly keep the college interview you had scheduled for October 23. Phone with the appropriate excuse and a request for a new date.
4. A resort hotel near where your family spends the summer has advertised for waiters and waitresses for the summer before you enter college. Phone for an interview.
5. A family two miles from your home needs a sitter, boy or girl, from 6-10 on Friday and Saturday nights. Answer the ad by phone.

Preparing for the Interview

Be at the exact place a little ahead of time. Don't rely on your memory; it befuddles easily at the most inappropriate times. Write down the time and place and, if you are not familiar with the locality, arrive early enough to find the place and be there.

Know something about the position. If you are going for a college interview, do some research on the college's strong points, its achievements, its program. Be prepared to ask a question to show your knowledge: "Just where is the library with the Dickinson collection? I'd like to see it while I'm here." If going for a job interview, research the position by watching it if you can or by talking to someone who has had a similar job. Think of what personal attributes you can suggest as useful for that position: "I'm on the varsity football team and I'd like to keep in shape. I ought to be able to move a lot of stock."

Dress for the position. If applying for college, don't dress for a party—or for a happening. Be sure you are newly washed and combed, that your clothes—whatever their type—are clean. Don't try to be a person that you essentially are not. If applying for a job, the same ideas apply. Wear the clothes customarily worn by others in that position. But be sure that they are clean and that you are, too.

The Interview

Advising students how to behave during an interview puts the counselor in something of the position of Polonius saying farewell to Laertes: the counsel is likely to seem both self-contradictory and propitiatory. A few general tips may be of some use. Above all, try to relax. The interviewer knows you are undergoing a fairly new experience and is likely to be tolerant.

If you have brought a friend or a parent to help you through the ordeal, now is the time to bid him or her goodbye. Walk into the interview room by yourself. As you enter, greet the interviewer by name if you are sure of its pronunciation. Shake hands only if the interviewer makes the initial gesture. Wait to sit until the offer is made, and don't smoke unless you are invited to. Leave your chewing gum at home or in the motel.

Let the interviewer ask the first question but be prepared for what may seem an all too obvious question: "What can I do for you?" "Well, what brings you here today?" "Well, young lady, what is your name?" "Have you ever applied for a job before?" If you think these questions are easy, just try answering them before you appear. Many interviews begin with small talk to put the person on either side of the desk at ease. When the small talk is completed, you will be asked more important questions. Pay close attention to these questions so that you will be able to speak to their point. The college interviewer is interested in seeing how able you are to think and express yourself orally. So is the employer if he is considering you for a position in which you will be meeting the public.

Avoid extremes. Don't just answer in monosyllables and short sentences. On the other hand, don't be unduly garrulous; the interviewer, who is interested in having questions answered as well as you can, also is a busy person. Avoid evasiveness and blame-laying. If you have a poor attendance record or a low mark in something, you will have to acknowledge it. In excusing yourself, avoid such answers as "Ms. Dodoe was a lousy teacher, and I couldn't learn a thing" or "I just never could enjoy an English class." Accept some of the responsibility yourself, for it is probably rightfully yours.

When the interview is ended, you will usually be aware that it is. The interviewer may rise and offer to shake hands, or to make some less skillful conclusion. In any event, don't prolong the ordeal. Say your thank you; and, even if the interview has seemed unsuccessful, try not to let your feelings show. Then don't ooze out; just leave.

Some Questions That Might Be Asked of You During a College Interview

The following list, compiled from talks with students who have been interviewed and from interviewers, is far from comprehensive. What they represent is the type of question to be aware of. Don't be surprised if the answer to the question is before the interviewer on the application; just answer the question once more—consistently, of course.

1. What are you especially interested in doing?
2. What subject do you intend to major in?
3. What have you liked best in the subjects you took in your previous schools?
4. Have there been any subjects you found especially distasteful or difficult?
5. What extracurricular activities have you enjoyed?
6. How much training in writing have your English classes given you?
7. What do you do in your spare time?
8. What probable professions are you considering at this time?
9. How do you explain this D in chemistry your junior year?
10. What special appeal does this college have for you?
11. What courses in the catalog do you hope to take before you graduate ?
12. Have you ever been away from home for fairly long periods of time?
13. How do you get along with your family?
14. Soandso College is coeducational (or is not). Do you strongly prefer it for that reason?
15. Can you think of five adjectives that would accurately describe yourself?
16. Have you had any serious physical or mental health problems in your life?
17. Describe your community and/or school.
18. What books have you read in the last six months that were not required for your school work?
19. What books have you read during the past four or five years that have meant a great deal to you?
20. What spectator activities do you enjoy: movies, TV, sports, theater, concerts, museums?
21. What will be the "good life" for you twenty years from now?
22. What pressures do you feel operating on you to make you conform to society? Describe ways in which you and your friends escape conformity.
23. If you could telephone anyone living, to whom would you like to talk? Why?
24. Have you ever thought of not going to college? What would you do?
25. If you were just chosen as the new principal in your high school, what would be your first change?

Some Questions That Might Be Asked of You During a Job Interview

Many of the questions listed for the college interview are also relevant to a job interview. The additional questions that follow are abstracted from a list in a handy pamphlet, *Making the Most of Your Job Interview.* Should you desire a free copy, write New York Life Insurance Company, 51 Madison Avenue, New York, New York 10010.

1. Why do you think you'd like to work for us?
2. What jobs have you held? How were they obtained and why did you leave?
3. Why did you choose this particular field of work?
4. How did you spend your vacations while in school?
5. What do you know about our company?
6. What qualifications do you have that make you feel that you will be successful in this job?
7. How much money do you hope to earn at age 30? 35?
8. What do you think determines a person's progress in a good company?
9. Do you prefer working with others or by yourself?
10. What kind of boss do you prefer?
11. Do you live with your parents? Which of them has had the most profound influence on you?
12. What have you learned from some of the jobs you have held?
13. Do you feel that you have done the best scholastic work of which you are capable?
14. Have you ever had any difficulty getting along with fellow students and faculty?
15. What is the source of your spending money?
16. Do you like routine work? Regular hours?
17. What is your major weakness?
18. Define cooperation!
19. Have you had any serious illness or injury?
20. What do you do to keep in good physical condition?
21. What types of people seem to rub you the wrong way?
22. What are the disadvantages of the type of work we offer?
23. How do you feel about working overtime?

Asking for Recommendations

If you are being seriously considered as a candidate for either a college or a job, you will almost certainly be asked to give references. The number will vary, but be sure that you furnish correctly all the information asked for. Spell the name correctly, give the exact title (Miss, Mrs., Ms., Mr., Dr., The Reverend, etc.), include the area code with the phone number and the zip code with the address. If the occupation is asked for, be as specific as you can: Cashier, United Banks; Pastor, Zion Lutheran Church; Chairman, Science Department, Whittier High.

Before you list a person as a reference, call or write for permission. In the first place, to seek such approval is only common courtesy. And you don't want to put yourself in the possible situation of having prospective employers call about you and hear in answer to their requests: "Who? I can't remember anyone of that name." Finally, don't forget to thank the man or woman for speaking or writing in your behalf. You have bought a portion of valuable time, cheaply. The least you can pay is a thank-you.

Most colleges require that you submit their special recomendation form for the reference to fill out. These require considerable time and effort to do. Before submitting the form for possible recommendation, ask those you wish to complete it if they are willing to take the time. If they consent, save them all the time you can. Print or type your own name on the proper space of the form; if you are submitting this to teachers, they may have a dozen or so to fill out and may not otherwise remember you as being the one applying for Lump Gulch Junior College. Include addressed and stamped envelopes for them. Study the questions the form asks of them and include a memo of things that might help them answer questions they may know little about: your outside interests, extracurricular activities, school offices, anything that you think they may have forgotten or never known.

At the time of your acceptance, don't forget those who helped you. Take the time to call or write a note saying you were admitted and that you are grateful for the help. If you were not accepted, thank them anyway, possibly ignoring the fact you were not among the chosen but letting them know the college you will attend. If they had enough interest in you to spend half an hour or more writing about you, they will certainly be interested in what happened.

Exercises

1. In your group, assume that you finally gained an interview in one of the five situations given on page 263. Appoint an interviewer and a candidate and have them simulate the interview either before the group or on a tape to be played back.
2. Ask your counselor—or if you have an application of your own, use it—for a sample of a form given to a teacher for student recommendation. Fill it out yourself as though you were the teacher, noting the amount of time it takes you to complete. Discuss with the class or a group of classmates your private experiences with this form.
3. Using correct formal style and tone of business correspondence, write a note requesting someone you are not on first-name-calling status with—your pastor, a family friend, a former employer—to let you use his or her name as a reference for either a college application or employment.
4. Using a less formal style, write a note thanking a teacher for a recommendation to the college at which you have been accepted.
5. Using the tape recorder or a group of classmates as critics, simulate a phone conversation in which you ask someone you know fairly well to recommend you for either a college or employment.

The Résumé

As our final step in preparing to apply for college or a job, we can take up the preparation of the résumé, which is a summary—on a single page if possible—of what you have done to this date. These résumés will grow as you add experience, and you will later make deletions and additions. If you start one now, however, you will have it at hand when you need it later. Or, if you are applying for a job, you may need it now inasmuch as many prospective employers ask for a résumé when you apply.

Whatever your need, make your résumé now, keep it, and appreciate its value later on. The forms for such summaries vary, but all should be neat and preferably typed. Make judicious use of white space and centering as you do your final copy. In putting down references, vary your selection: a teacher, a former employer, a family friend, for example. Include specific and complete information. Here you may use abbreviations because a résumé must tell as much as possible about you in the most concise form.

A sample, completed résumé follows:

PERSONAL DATA SHEET

Date: September 9, 1977
Name: Mary Susan Johnson
Address: 181 Sylvester Rd., Burlington, WV 26710
Phone: (304) 464-4915
Social Security Number: 173-28-7555

EDUCATION
Grades 9-11 - Hillview High School
Burlington, WV
Grades 5-8 - Hillview Schools
Burlington, WV
Grades K-4 - Coleman School District
Coleman, MI 48618

HIGH SCHOOL COURSES
Grade 9
English, 1
French 1, 1
Algebra, 1
Social studies, 1
Homemaking, 1
Grade 10
English, 1
French 2, 1
Geometry, 1
World history, 1
Sewing, $\frac{1}{2}$
Cooking, $\frac{1}{2}$
Grade 11
English electives, 1
French 3, 1
Int. alg., $\frac{1}{2}$
Solid geom., $\frac{1}{2}$
Amer. hist., 1
Chemistry, 1

EXTRACURRICULAR ACTIVITIES
Band, 1, 2, 3
Secretary, FTA, 3
Yearbook, 3
Sunday school teacher, 3

SPECIAL HONORS
My church chose me to represent 16-year-olds last year at a Washington, D.C., conference.

SUMMER ACTIVITIES
1977 - Counselor and crafts teacher, Camp Highview, Shortt Gap, MD 24647
1976 - Junior counselor, Camp Highview
1975 - Camper, Camp Highview

WORK EXPERIENCE
Various babysitting jobs since I was 12

REFERENCES

1. The Rev. Charles Trexler
   Church of the Good Shepherd
   Longridge Road
   Burlington, WV 26710

2. Mrs. Nancy Selinka
   Camp Highview
   Shortt Gap, MD 24647

3. Dr. Norman Bussiere
   Principal, Hillview High School
   Burlington, WV 26710

Exercise

Using the utmost care, prepare your own résumé, have it checked by your teacher, make a perfect copy, and save it for the future.

Skills Index

COMPOSITION

CRITICAL ANALYSIS

MECHANICS AND USAGE

VOCABULARY AND STUDY SKILLS

SPEAKING SKILLS

The decorative borders for *It's Your Life* were adapted from title pages popular during the sixteenth century.

The text is set in linotype Palatino and Optima, both faces designed by Hermann Zapf, a contemporary German type designer.